Computer Science in Sport

Computers are fundamentally important tools in sport science research, sports performance analysis and, increasingly, in coaching and education programmes in sport. This book defines the field of 'sport informatics', explaining how computer science can be used to solve sport-related problems, in both research and applied aspects.

Beginning with a clear explanation of the functional principles of hardware and software, the book examines the key functional areas in which computer science is employed in sport, including:

* knowledge discovery and database development
* data acquisition, including devices for measuring performance data
* motion tracking and analysis systems
* modelling and simulation
* match analysis systems
* e-learning and multimedia in sports education

Bridging the gap between theory and practice, this book is important reading for any student, researcher or practitioner working in sport science, sport performance analysis, research methods in sport, applied computer science or informatics.

Arnold Baca is Professor of Kinesiology with emphasis on Biomechanics and Computer Science in Sport at the University of Vienna, Austria. He has been President of the International Association of Computer Science in Sport (2007–2013) and is Editor of the *International Journal of Computer Science in Sport*.

Routledge Research in Sport and Exercise Science

The *Routledge Research in Sport and Exercise Science* series is a showcase for cutting-edge research from across the sport and exercise sciences, including physiology, psychology, biomechanics, motor control, physical activity and health, and every core sub-discipline. Featuring the work of established and emerging scientists and practitioners from around the world, and covering the theoretical, investigative and applied dimensions of sport and exercise, this series is an important channel for new and ground-breaking research in the human movement sciences.

Available in this series:

Psychoneuroendocrinology of Sport and Exercise
Foundations, Markers, Trends
Edited by Felix Ehrlenspiel and Katharina Strahler

Mental Toughness in Sport
Developments in Theory and Research
Edited by Daniel Gucciardi and Sandy Gordon

Complexity and Control in Team Sports
Dialectics in Contesting Human Systems
Felix Lebed and Michael Bar-Eli

Paediatric Biomechanics and Motor Control
Theory and Application
Edited by Mark De Ste Croix and Thomas Korff

Attachment in Sport, Exercise and Wellness
Sam Carr

Complex Systems in Sport
Edited by Keith Davids, Robert Hristovski, Duarte Araújo, Natalia Balague Serre, Chris Button and Pedro Passos

Mixed Methods Research in the Movement Sciences
Case Studies in Sport, Physical Education and Dance
Edited by Oleguer Camerino, Marta Castaner and Teresa M Anguera

Eccentric Exercise
Physiology and Application in Sport and Rehabilitation
Hans Hoppeler

Computer Science in Sport
Research and Practice
Edited by Arnold Baca

Life Story Research in Sport
Understanding the Experiences of Elite and Professional Athletes through Narrative
Kitrina Douglas and David Carless

Computer Science in Sport

Research and practice

Edited by Arnold Baca

LONDON AND NEW YORK

First published 2015
by Routledge
2 Park Square, Milton Park, Abingdon, Oxon OX14 4RN

and by Routledge
711 Third Avenue, New York, NY 10017

Routledge is an imprint of the Taylor & Francis Group, an informa business

British Library Cataloguing-in-Publication Data
A catalogue record for this book is available from the British Library

Library of Congress Cataloging-in-Publication Data
Computer science in sport : research and practice / edited by Arnold Baca.
      pages cm. – (Routledge research in sport and exercise science)
   1. Sports – Information services. I. Baca, Arnold.
   GV568.C64 2015
   796.0285–dc23   2014016595

ISBN: 978-0-415-71545-4 (hbk)
ISBN: 978-1-315-88178-2 (ebk)

Typeset in Times New Roman
by HWA Text and Data Management, London

Printed and bound by CPI Group (UK) Ltd, Croydon, CR0 4YY

Contents

Figures

Tables

Contributors

Arnold Baca, Department of Biomechanics, Kinesiology and Applied Computer Science, ZSU, University of Vienna, Austria

Peter Dabnichki, School of Engineering and Materials Science, Queen Mary University of London, UK

Larry Katz, Sport Technology Research Laboratory, Faculty of Kinesiology, University of Calgary, Canada

Martin Lames, Department of Sport and Health Science, Technical University of Munich, Germany

Roland Leser, Department of Biomechanics, Kinesiology and Applied Computer Science, ZSU, University of Vienna, Austria

Daniel Link, Department of Sport and Health Science, Technical University of Munich, Germany

Keith Lyons, National Institute of Sport Studies, University of Canberra, Australia

Chikara Miyaji, Japan Institute of Sport Science, Tokyo

Florian 'Floyd' Mueller, Exertion Games Lab, RMIT University Melbourne, Australia

Peter O'Donoghue, Cardiff School of Sport, Cardiff Metropolitan University, Wales, UK

Jürgen Perl, Institute of Computer Science, University of Mainz, Germany

Karen Roemer, Department of Nutrition, Exercise, and Health Sciences, Central Washington University, USA

Josef Wiemeyer, Institute of Sport Science, Technical University of Darmstadt, Germany

Foreword

Coaches need to motivate their athletes, help them to learn new skills, and teach them to make good decisions. Coaching is both an art and a science. The art is learned from intuition and experience. The science is found in the data derived from innovative technology, largely stemming from advances in computers in sport. These computer-driven systems collect relevant information about the athletes including their skill level, tactical, technical, physical, and emotional performance before, during and after practices and competitions. Properly employed, these innovative tools help coaches and athletes learn new skills and improve on decision-making. This is a powerful motivator since victory can be a matter of centimeters or hundredths of a second.

Performance analysis is an objective way of recording and interpreting sport performance using the latest technology so that key elements can be quantified in a valid and consistent manner. This knowledge is then used to enhance athlete performance and effective decision-making. Performance analysts are those who can use these tools and work with coaches and athletes to maximize performance. Some coaches like working with technology and computer science and can be their own performance analysts; however, most coaches do not have the time, inclination or comfort level. Charles Darwin said, "It is not the strongest of the species that survive, nor the most intelligent, but the ones most responsive to change." Without the use of these performance analysis tools, it is becoming increasingly more difficult to reach the podium. Therefore it is important for coaches and athletes to understand how computers are used in studying and analyzing sport performance because of the insights gained and because it enables them to maximize the opportunities provided by the tools.

Computer science in sport is about more than just performance: it is also about organizing, managing, effectively accessing, and meaningfully and creatively interpreting sport information. It is about inventing new instruments and strategies that would not be possible without technology. These technical resources allow us to simulate and understand processes, develop expert systems to predict outcomes, and analyze games in incredible detail. In addition, computer science in sport is about using technology to help us learn and understand sport and sporting techniques through multimedia and e-learning.

Deciding on which state-of-the-art tools to use and learning how to use them can be a daunting task. Should coaches be learning how to use these tools or should there be a profession of performance analysts to discern which tools are effective and how to use them? These performance analysts would work with coaches to interpret the science of sport in ways that are meaningful for the coaches and athletes. This is a reality in China and in some parts of Western Europe but not so much in North America or the rest of the world.

This book, *Computer Science in Sport: Research and Practice*, is an excellent resource for coaches, athletes, performance analysts, and students of kinesiology and physical education because it gives the reader great insights into how computers can be used effectively in the analysis of sport to improve performance and to teach about sport and physical education. The authors are all members of the International Association of Computer Science in Sport, an organization that covers a wide variety of activities all related to understanding and enhancing the field. Each author is uniquely qualified in his area of expertise and is a veteran of integrating computer technology into sport and physical education. The reader has the opportunity to explore the research and most current practices in each area and gain an understanding of both performance analysis and creative approaches to understanding sport. This book is a good survey of the field, an excellent read, and an exceptional resource for your bookshelf.

Larry Katz PhD
Professor and Director
Sport Technology Research Laboratory
University of Calgary, Calgary, Alberta, Canada

Preface

This book is about *computer science in sport* (also called *sport informatics*) and covers basic knowledge and main areas of research including various application examples. Computer science in sport focuses on the conjunction of theoretical background and practical aspects as well as methodologies of information technology and sport science. On the one hand, the combined approach is represented by the use of computing tools and methods in sport science. On the other hand, however, the integration of sport-related background in computer science is also relevant for various engineering purposes such as the understanding of the human motor control and its implementation for the design of robots.

The book is generally aimed at students of kinesiology and physical education, performance analysts, and coaches and athletes interested in the use of computers and the application of informatics in sport-related fields. In particular, it is targeted at those taking computer science in sport studies or modules at universities, those undertaking undergraduate or masters dissertations, laboratory reports etc. in computer science in sport and those undertaking postgraduate research or personal research in computer science in sport. It also may assist in academic teaching and scientific research in related fields such as mathematics in sports.

The main objectives of the book are to (a) provide an understanding of the subject area of sport informatics, (b) serve as a reference book for students and scientists and (c) advise students and researchers applying computer science for solving sport-related problems.

The book is primarily designed as an educational textbook, but is also meant as a reference book for students and scientists. Today, the field of computer science in sport includes intellectual and practical skills that many sport and exercise students need to develop during their programme of study.

The chapters within this book give a good overview of fundamentals and main areas of research in computer science in sport and provide numerous applications.

Link and Lames introduce *sport informatics* as a well-established research and development field. They define this growing discipline as a set of multi- and interdisciplinary research programmes including components of sport science and informatics. According to their definition, the subject of sport informatics is (a) the application of tools, methods and paradigms from informatics to questions of sport science as well as the integration of knowledge from sport science in informatics and (b) meta-level research on these applications, i.e. creating knowledge above the level of single projects.

Within the chapter of Dabnichki and Miyaji the major developments in computers and informatics from the perspective of sport scientists, practitioners and professionals are covered. The necessary background to enable informed use of computers for the purposes of sport is provided.

Lyons discusses the use of databases and expert systems in sport. The growth in data produced by pervasive sensing is an important driver for better practice in computational intelligence in sport. The chapter explores the development of this computational intelligence with reference to the development of the athlete biological passport.

Within the first part of the chapter on data acquisition and processing, Baca introduces devices and technologies for the acquisition of sport-related data. Emphasis is put on principles of capturing analogue data such as time courses of forces. Fundamental methods for data processing (e.g. filtering techniques) are addressed. In the second part of the chapter, pervasive computing technologies are presented and illustrated by applications ranging from devices for measuring sport performance data to intelligent solutions assisting athletes during exercising.

Contemporary computer video systems are key elements of many applications in sports (e.g. motion analysis, game analysis). The chapter by Leser and Roemer outlines the functionality and capabilities of state-of-the-art computer video systems used in sports. Furthermore, some basic knowledge is given about the different types of motion analysis systems and their operating principles, including specific calibration and filter routines and available methods for the detection of kinematic parameters. Finally, applied video technologies for player tracking in game sports are illustrated and their relevance for game analysis is discussed.

Modelling and simulation are core areas of research in computer science in sport. Perl vividly outlines the potential of meaningful modelling in sport theory and practice. His chapter starts with an introduction to the basic ideas of modelling and simulation, including aspects of modelling as part of thinking and of perception of the surrounding world. This is followed by a discussion of the main tasks of modelling and simulation, namely diagnosis of a system's state and prognosis of its future development or behaviour. In this context, connection and relationship between system and model are also discussed. Dynamic systems are introduced as a key field of applications in technical as well as in behavioural modelling, completed by a comparison of discrete and continuous models. A case study dealing with examples from sport will help to deepen the understanding of this conventional part. Unconventional modelling is then addressed, with the introduction of the paradigms of fuzzy models, genetic algorithms and neural networks. Examples are then given on how net-based pattern analysis may be applied to sport – e.g. with motor processes and with game processes.

Match analysis systems have followed advances in information technology throughout the history of performance analysis; advances in input and output peripherals, data storage technology and wireless computing have been exploited by match analysis systems. Pervasive systems allow more detailed information to be captured during sport performance. Voice-over input has been used for inputting events into commercial match analysis systems. The analysis of match data has also followed advances in computer science, including artificial intelligence and virtual reality. O'Donoghue discusses the range of computer science research that has been exploited within match analysis systems.

In the final chapter, Wiemeyer and Mueller address approaches to e-learning and multimedia. They point out that the analysis of theories and evidence show that learning with computer animations (and simulations), virtual and augmented reality and Serious Games depend on numerous conditions that need to be considered to enhance human information processing and learning. Future trends for research and developments are discussed.

I would like to acknowledge the help of my colleagues and students, in particular Michaela Haßmann, Dominik Hölbling, Philipp Kornfeind, Rosmarie Sedlaczek and Karel Slijkhuis.

I hope that the techniques and applications covered will make the book an important guide for students and researchers in any discipline of sport and exercise science where computer science is used.

Arnold Baca

1 An introduction to sport informatics

Daniel Link and Martin Lames

Introduction

Over the past three decades, the discipline 'sport informatics' – also called 'computer science in sport' – has become a growing discipline. In this chapter the historical roots are reconstructed and some reflections on the nature of this new discipline between sport science and informatics are given.

The term 'sport informatics' originates from a congress in Graz (Austria), organized by the International Organisation for Sports Information (IOSI) in 1975. The related proceedings were published by Recla and Timmer (1976) with the German title 'Kreative Sportinformatik' ('Creative Sport Informatics').

Sport informatics covers all activities that include aspects of computer science and sport science, ranging from simple tools for handling data and controlling sensors up to the modelling and simulation of complex sport-related phenomena. Whereas first applications in the seventies used computers for information and documentation purposes only, current approaches deal, for example, with virtual reality in sport, computer technology for supporting top level sports, e-learning in sports training, the modelling and simulation of biomechanical phenomena, and many more.

Today, computer science in sport is a well-established research and development field. The International Association of Computer Science in Sport (IACSS) was founded in 2002 and promotes research in this area. In many countries such as Austria, Croatia, Germany, Turkey, Great Britain, China, Slovakia and India national workgroups have been established, which represent sport informatics in the national scientific community and contribute new technological innovations to sport. IACSS also maintains good relations with various other sport scientific organizations like the International Association for Sports Information (IASI), the International Council of Sport Science and Physical Education (ICSSPE) or the International Sports Engineering Association (ISEA).

The first chapter of this book reflects the development of the discipline, analyses its current situation and defines the subject area. The roots of the discipline of sport informatics lie in Germany in the early seventies and the first section in this chapter will throw a brief glance on the early developments. It aims to give readers an impression of the prevailing ideas leading to IACSS.

The second section discusses the interdisciplinary relation between computer science and sport science and identifies different types of cooperation. Based on this discussion the third section defines the subject area of sport informatics by providing a definition and a structural model of the discipline.

Historical roots

It is rewarding to start a historical view on sport informatics with a glance at the historical development of the two master disciplines involved. Computer science and sport science are dealt with in the first two subsections of this chapter with regard to their historical conceptual structure. The third subsection gives a short overview about the institutional development of sport informatics in Germany.

Computer science

In the sixties and the seventies of the last century, in Germany the term 'Informatik' was mainly associated with questions of technology. A popular German encyclopaedia described 'Informatik' as 'the science of the systematic processing of information, in particular the automatic processing using digital computers' (Engesser, 1988). In terms of this definition, the discipline includes mathematical activities, which deal with algorithmic processes for the description and transformation of information and also engineering activities, concerning aspects of the development and application of computers. This technological perspective is comparable to the common understanding of the discipline 'computer science' in the United States or Great Britain (National Research Council, 2004).

In the beginning of the eighties, the importance of computer systems increased in almost every part of modern societies. It became more and more clear that the use of computer systems leads to interactions between system processes and the processes in the real world. To study these interactions, many computer scientists adopted approaches and methods from the social and behavioural sciences. These research fields were accepted as a part of the discipline 'Informatik'. Today, many countries use the English term 'informatics' – derived from the German 'Informatik' – for the science of information. Nygaard (1986), for example, defines 'informatics' as the 'science that has as its domain information processes and related phenomena in artefacts, society and nature'. This perspective separates the mathematical/logical part from the technical one and refers to the concepts of cybernetics and systems theory.

Informatics emerges by separation from mathematics and engineering science – later approaches from human sciences were integrated. The discipline is divided into the sub-disciplines of theoretical, technical and practical informatics, which together are called 'core' informatics (Claus, 1975). The applications and questions related to the use of computers are studied by applied informatics.

Since computer science is very much appreciated for its support to other sciences, in some cases the combination of technical expertise from computer science and specific domain knowledge led to autonomous research fields like

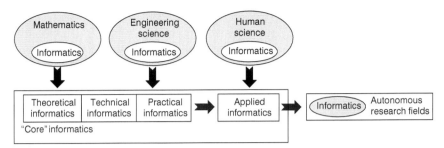

Figure 1.1 Commonly used structural model of informatics

bio-informatics, neuro-informatics and business informatics. Sport informatics could also be seen in this tradition.

In the past there was a debate about whether these research fields should be accepted as integral part of computer science. Some authors, for example, claim a strict distinction between cooperation fields and the core area of 'Informatik' (Luft, 1992). Today, the discipline in Germany (also known as 'Informatique' in France) is a kind of mixture between computer sciences and Nygaard's concept of informatics (see Figure 1.1), but nevertheless the question about its limitations is still subject to discussion.

Sport science

Sport science took, at least in Germany, a development that was in many aspects comparable to the development of Informatik. A common definition describes sport science as the set of knowledge, theories and research methods that deal with problems and phenomena related to sport (Röthig and Prohl, 2003). While this definition is evident, a widely accepted definition of the term sport is still an open problem.

Another important issue in the discussion about the nature of sport science is the relationship between the disciplines of sport science. In the late sixties, Germany saw the introduction of sport science to universities. Before, it was taught academically mostly in teacher education institutions. For this – more or less – pragmatic reason the argument was put forward that the complexity of sport could not be investigated by existing research fields. So, the necessity of one unified discipline, with a high degree of interdisciplinarity between its sub-disciplines, was a central argument for the foundation of sport science.

To support this position, Ries and Kriesi (1974) proposed a model showing three phases of the development of sport science: (1) separation from basic disciplines, (2) aggregation of sub-disciplines within a multidisciplinary science and (3) integration of sub-disciplines into a consistent and integrative science (Figure 1.2).

Scientific reality showed that – in contrast to this idealized model – sport was mostly studied through the eyes of each sub-discipline (e.g. sport sociology,

1. Separation

2. Additive aggregation

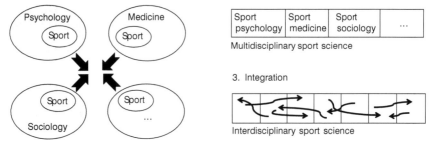

Figure 1.2 Idealized model of sport science development: separation of sport-related research fields from base sciences, aggregation into a multidisciplinary science and integration of sub-disciplines into a unified science (source: adapted from Ries and Kriesi, 1974)

sport psychology, exercise science). Due to this fact, today sport science does not describe itself as a 'unified science of sport', but as a collection of overlapping research programmes in which interdisciplinarity exists only as temporary, problem centred research projects (Höner, 2001).

Sport informatics

The idea of an interdisciplinary scientific discipline 'sport informatics' was promoted initially by Jürgen Perl, himself being a mathematician and a pioneering computer scientist in Germany. Together with Wolf Miethling he published the first monograph in the discipline (Miethling and Perl, 1981) that marked the beginning of sport informatics in the Federal Republic of Germany.

In 1985, Jürgen Perl founded the Institute for Informatics at Mainz University and established a working group in sport informatics. His idea to organize a first workshop on sport informatics in Hochheim (close to Mainz) in April 1989 gave rise to a series of workshops on this topic. The 1989 workshop was attended by many important German sport science groups and, unexpectedly, by some computer science groups in this field as well. This development starting in 1989 resulted in a series of biennial conferences.

This apparent success gave rise to a new strategic aim, which has been pursued since about 1994. The German Association of Sport Science (Deutsche Vereinigung für Sportwissenschaft, dvs) represents German academic sport science with (today) 900 members at sixty-seven universities. It is organized in subgroups (*Sektionen*) representing the disciplines of sport science and groups (*Kommissionen*) giving an organizational framework for special interdisciplinary topics. In September 1995, the general assembly of dvs established sport informatics as one of their official subgroups. This may be considered the formal birth date of the scientific discipline, because it meant the acknowledgement of sport informatics as discipline of sport science in Germany.

Figure 1.3 Scientific board of IACSS, inaugural meeting, Barcelona, 2003

Since then the biennial conferences of sport informatics in Germany have brought together the two traditions: the most recent workshop at Konstanz, Lake Constance, in 2012, was the 9th dvs Symposium of Sport Informatics as well as the 13th workshop on Informatics in Sport.

Soon after establishing a national association for sport informatics a new aim was targeted, i.e. to establish an international scientific association. Concerning globalization and the world becoming a truly global village through advances in information and communication technologies, it became clear that in different parts of this village, people were addressing the same problems.

In the area of game analysis one could, for example, mention the introduction of digital boards, efforts to enter data by natural language recognition software or the struggle for reliable computer-video couplings. These developments were brought forward independently, for example, at Mainz and Cardiff in the working groups of Jürgen Perl and Mike Hughes, respectively.

After three international meetings at Cologne (1997), Vienna (1999) and Cardiff (2001), the International Association of Computer Science in Sport (IACSS) was founded at Barcelona in 2003 and Jürgen Perl became the first president (Figure 1.3). Since then, a series of biennial international conferences has been organized (Hvar, 2005; Calgary, 2007; Canberra, 2009; Shanghai, 2011; and Istanbul, 2013) and members from different countries and almost all continents have joined the association.

The future prospects of the association are excellent. The unique combination of sport science and informatics with the large application field of sports at any level provides great perspectives. Nevertheless, the remarkable developments of the two sciences make it necessary to reflect episodically on the levels achieved in interdisciplinary cooperation between the fields and the concept of sport informatics.

Interdisciplinarity in sport informatics

First, this section outlines the mutual interests in cooperation of computer science and sport science in common projects. While the motive of sport science is quite obvious, that of computer science needs more elaborate discussion. The second part poses the questions: which quality of interdisciplinarity between sport science and computer science exists today and which quality would be desirable and realistic in future? This is done by discussing existing models of interdisciplinarity and proposing a classification for research activities in sport informatics.

Common fields of interests – why do computer science and sport science cooperate?

It is useful to differentiate between political, scientific and personal motivations for cooperation. From a political perspective one must bear in mind that interdisciplinarity is considered an important research paradigm in most countries. For example, the German Research Foundation (DFG), which is the central research funding organization in Germany, holds the view that scientific progress arises more and more at the borders and intersections of disciplines. In the same vein, the national funding agency for scientific research in sport (German Federal Institute of Sport Science) names interdisciplinarity a 'key element' of its funding policy. Announcements on funding initiatives refer to inter- and multidisciplinary approaches, integrated construction of theories, highly specialized choice of research methods and integrative presentation of results. While the precise meaning of such catchphrases is somewhat clouded in jargon, a scientist whose career depends on positive evaluation (and funding) of his research projects is ill-advised to refuse the commitment to interdisciplinarity.

Besides political considerations, sound scientific justification for cooperation does exist (see Figure 1.4). First of all – from a sport science perspective – computer science services are well appreciated in specific technological areas in which sport scientists are not necessarily experts. This applies to data handling and software development, e.g. for the purpose of training documentation, controlling sensors or visualizing data. Second, information technology is an important source of innovations for training and competition. Collaborations with computer science help sport scientists to become aware of new technologies that may lead to improvements in supporting sport activities (Stöckl and Lames, 2011). Third, sport science expects that the approaches and perspectives of computer science should be transferable to the field of sport. For example, the concept of soft computing can assist the understanding of phenomena in sport (see 'Subject area').

Seen on a broader perspective, there are also benefits of cooperation with sport science for computer science. Here we face the situation that due to the specific properties of sport science, a long-term benefit is imaginable for computer science.

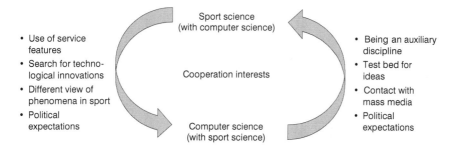

Figure 1.4 Cooperation interests of computer science and sport science

A special feature of sports that may be attractive to computer science is its degree of complexity. The existing structures in sports are neither too simple to be of interest, nor too complex to be described using mathematical models.

A test field for intention detection, a well-established field of computer science, could well be the analysis of game sports. Here, we have specific action plans that pose challenges to computational requirements (automatic recognition of players, moves and strategies) albeit with reduced complexity (limited degrees of freedom, common rules, tactical invariants) compared to similar problems. More generally speaking, sport could act as an attractive testing field for computer science, in which human behaviour can be observed and studied in simplified, yet authentic settings.

Another motive for computer scientists to engage in sport sciences might be public interest in sport and its huge role in mass media. This may give rise not only to the Basking in Reflected Glory (BIRG) phenomenon (Cialdini et al., 1976), but doing studies in football, for example, releases researchers from the sometimes tedious task of explaining the rules of the domain.

Last but not least, many computer scientists working with sport science are personally involved in sport. Even if collaboration cannot be fully justified on the basis of individual involvement, political considerations and increasing publicity seem to have importance as secondary motives.

Quality of interdisciplinarity – how do computer science and sport science work (or how should they work) together?

There are many ways in which the concept of 'interdisciplinarity' has been classified by the philosophy of science. One milestone in categorization was a congress in the year 1972, where the Organisation of Economic Co-operation and Development (OECD) proposed a classification of interactions between disciplines (OECD, 1972). In terms of this definition, multidisciplinarity is a juxtaposition of various disciplines without a connection between them. Interdisciplinarity describes any interaction between disciplines, which can range from simple communication of ideas to the integration of concepts, methodologies and epistemologies. Transdisciplinarity is the highest degree of cooperation and stands for a common set of theories and axioms for a set of disciplines (Figure 1.5).

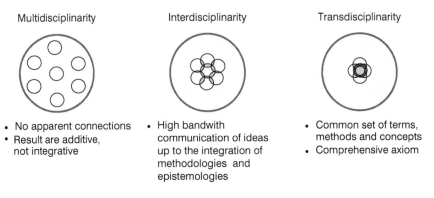

Multidisciplinarity

- No apparent connections
- Result are additive, not integrative

Interdisciplinarity

- High bandwith communication of ideas up to the integration of methodologies and epistemologies

Transdisciplinarity

- Common set of terms, methods and concepts
- Comprehensive axiom

Figure 1.5 Commonly used classification of types of interdisciplinarity (source: adapted from OECD, 1972).

On this basis, enhanced models focusing on different aspects of interaction were developed, e.g. by Heckhausen (1972), Boisot (1972) and Karlqvist (1999).

Unfortunately, a closer look at the practice of sport informatics shows that none of these models is adequate to describe the existing interaction. In this regard, we propose our own classification, using four types of cooperation (see Figure 1.6):

- Type a: Sport science applies existing approaches and tools from computer science. In this case, sport science does not take part in conceptualization and development. Computer science (or – mostly – commercial software developing companies) only acts as anonymous service provider, without contact to sport science.
- Type b: Sport science integrates knowledge from computer science. This happens when sport science needs technical solutions not existing in the market. Knowledge is assimilated either by acquiring the skills necessary or by entering into partnerships with computer science, e.g. by means of students or funded projects. One aspect of this cooperation is that computer science provides nothing but skills in software development. There is no collaboration on a scientific level.
- Type c: Computer and sport science cooperate in research programmes, which are in accordance with the research interest of both disciplines. Examples are the use of artificial neuronal networks for analysing movement patterns or application of image recognition algorithms in sport game analysis. In this case, computer science gets new insights by validating concepts and methods which have relevance for additional – perhaps more complex – problems. Sport science benefits from an improved and faster data acquisition and by getting a different perspective on the structures of sport.
- Type d: This type is comparable to type c with the small but important difference that paradigms and knowledge of sport science are used in computer science. An example would be the use of kinesiological models in controlling the motion of humanoid robots.

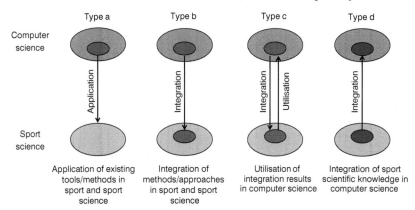

Figure 1.6 Types of cooperation in sport informatics

'Borrowing' methods of computer science (types a, b, c in Figure 1.6) matches to Heckhausen's concept of auxiliary-interdisciplinarity. The simple usage of pre-defined tools (type a) corresponds to the OECD term multidiscplinarity. The corporate development of tools/methods (type b) can be called pseudo-interdisciplinarity (Heckhausen) or restrictive interdisciplinarity (Boisot). The use of sport scientific knowledge in computer science (type d) accords with the idea of structural interdisciplinarity (Boisot).

A review of the research activities in the last twenty years reveals that many projects are of types a and b, but only very few projects of types c and d can be found. One reason why the popularity of sport informatics in the computer scientific community is not very high (there are computer scientists who never heard about it or do not show interest in any cooperation with sport science) might be that there is often no genuine interdisciplinary research. A deeper concentration on those fields where computer science can profit from sport scientific paradigms and knowledge (types c and d), could improve the situation. This would require better communication of sport scientific expertise and recognition of sport as a fruitful application field for computer scientists.

On the other hand, we must acknowledge that there is basically only low affinity between the disciplines of sport science and computer science. In contrast to other interdisciplinary linkages (like biology and chemistry, astronomy and physics or sociology and psychology), there is no common borderline with common issues and hardly any shared knowledge. Consequently, sport informatics has not yet been established as autonomous interdiscipline like astrophysics or biochemistry.

One-way transfer is also frequently found in other application fields of computer science. Basically, this results from the fact that information processing is fundamental for all sciences, whereas application fields of computer science usually cannot provide any knowledge for the core area of computer science (with exceptions like mathematics and electrical engineering). Moreover, the problems of sport science and computer science in creating real interdisciplinarity within their own sub-disciplines show that creating interdisciplinarity is far from being trivial. They are both heterogeneous sciences without a consistent level of theoretical integration, axioms, methods and terminology (see discussion in 'Interdisciplinarity in sport informatics').

What is the final conclusion of these considerations on interdisciplinarity between informatics and sport science? One might advise sport informatics to continue postulating and advancing interdisciplinarity, but also not to overemphasize the idea of integration.

Subject area

Bearing the discussion of the previous sections in mind, we suggest differentiating between sport informatics and computer science in sport. Computer science in sport stands exclusively for the use of computer technology in sport and sport science. Sport informatics also includes the application of methods and paradigms from computer/information science as well as from research programmes, which try to transfer sport scientific knowledge to computer sciences.[1] The following definition shows this enhanced self-concept:

> Sport informatics is a set of multi- and interdisciplinary research programmes which contain parts of sport science and computer science. The subject area is the application of tools, methods and paradigms from computer science on questions of sport science as well as the integration of sport scientific knowledge in computer science.

Figure 1.7 represents this standpoint: in both disciplines there is knowledge that is potentially useful for the other discipline. Conversely there is a second area, which might be an application field for the findings of the other discipline. The research programmes of sport informatics include parts of both disciplines and can be dedicated to one of the four types, identified in the last section.

The discipline can be described as a set of multi- and interdisciplinary research programmes. Most of these programmes apply the technological and methodological knowledge of computer science to study questions of sport science, but there are also some sport scientific findings, which can be useful for computer science.

Figure 1.8 shows a refinement of this rough structure by using a matrix with four areas. The upper areas give examples for research fields for computer science which are useful for sport and sport science; the lower areas give examples of how computer science can profit from sport science. The next subsections discuss the two different directions of integration.

Computer science in sport science

The table in Figure 1.8 (top left) shows topics in computer science, which may be useful for sport science. According to Perl and Lames (1995) the columns of this table are an open list of research areas of computer science important to

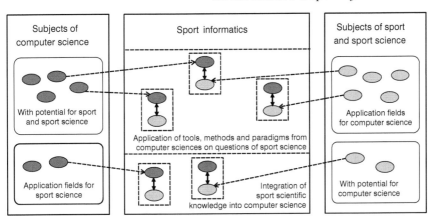

Figure 1.7 Basic structure of sport informatics

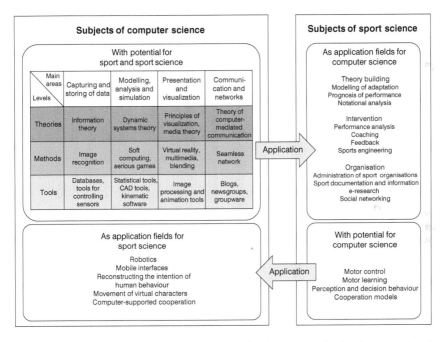

Figure 1.8 Subjects of sport informatics; the matrix shows examples for the research and application fields mentioned in Figure 1.7

sport: (1) acquiring and storing of data, (2) modelling, analysis and simulation, (3) presentation and visualization and (4) communication and networks. The rows of the table illustrate the idea that the research field sport informatics is (or should be) more than just the simple application of tools for the recording, analysis and presentation of data. In addition to the 'tool level' (which is more information technology than computer science), there are also methods, theories and paradigms, which have the potential to support sport science (see cooperation types c and d in the last section). The next paragraphs discuss some examples.

In the field of capturing and storing data, information technology provides, for example, database tools, which can be used for the storage of training and competition data (see Chapter 3 'Databases and expert systems'). This allows coaches to stay informed about the input load and the performance level of their athletes. Also, many biomechanical devices like force plates and sensors, high speed cameras or laser radars use proprietary software tools, controlling sensors and helping to manage and present measured data (Godbout and Boyd, 2012; see Chapter 4 'Data acquisition and processing'). In this context, systems for measuring the movements of players on a court based on computer vision or active sensors became more important (Gomez et al., 2012; Baca et al. 2011; see Chapter 5 'Motion tracking and analysis systems').

For the modelling, analysis and simulation, sport scientists often make use of mathematical software like Matlab, Maple, SPSS or apply software for movement analysis. Sport engineers rely on tools for computer aided design (e.g. AutoCAD or Solid Edge) to develop new sports equipment.

Tools from information technology are also important for the presentation and visualization of data. In sport games for example, the linking of video sequences and databases is useful for game observation (see Chapter 7 'Game analysis'). In athletics or gymnastics, coaches use software that enables the showing of additional information like force vectors, torsional movements or speed information on a video or superimposing pictures of two movements. Last but not least communication technology can help to organize training (Lyons, 2011): today Internet blogs and social networking websites are relevant for organizing training sessions and finding partners for game sports. Internet-based groupware tools like synchronous video, video conference and whiteboards support athletes on international championships, by enabling communication with their coach at home (Link and Lames, 2005). In this context mobile devices for coaching become increasingly important (Hummel et al., 2013).

On the method level, computer science, for example, has developed techniques for image recognition, which can be helpful to capture positional and biomechanical parameters directly from video recordings (see Chapter 5). Therefore computer science does not provide readymade tools, but rather general algorithms for colour, texture and shape comparison, which have to be adapted to the specific sport context (see cooperation types b and c in the last section). In the field of analysis and simulation of sports, the methods of soft computing have become more important (see Chapter 6): artificial neuronal networks are used to simulate the relationship between training input and performance output

(Perl and Endler, 2012), to analyse tactical or movement patterns (Perl, Grunz and Memmert, 2013; Lamb, Bartlett and Robins, 2010). Genetic algorithms help to find solutions in high dimensional configuration spaces, e.g. to optimize the design for sport equipment (Vajna et al., 2006) or to optimize throwing movements (Bächle, 2003). Last but not least, serious games can have a positive effect on perception, reaction and motor control and are potentially useful for education and intervention in sports (see Chapter 8).

At the theory level the approach of complex dynamic systems is an example that holds a lot of promise for sport science. Many processes in sport seem to rely on non-linear coupling rules, which lead to complex phenomena. The theory of complex systems helps to model and to understand, for example, interaction in sport games as well as the processes of biological adaptation due to training. Successful examples for using concepts from system theory in sport science are perturbations (Hughes, Dawkins and David, 2000), relative phase (Walter et al., 2007), chaos theory (Lames, 1999), and the paradigm of self-organization (McGarry et al., 2002).

The second part of the matrix (see Figure 1.8 top right) shows examples for application fields in sport and sport science. These fields are structured with the headlines 'theory building' (getting new theoretical insights into phenomena of sports), 'intervention' (improving training and competition) and 'organization' (managing activities related to sport). Examples for these application fields have already been mentioned in this section.

Sport science in computer science

The third and fourth parts (see Figure 1.8 bottom left and right) show examples for sport scientific knowledge fields which are potentially useful for research in computer science. We give three examples for clarification.

The first example is software for the safe and autonomous operation of robots. Traditionally the algorithms for navigation, locomotion and the grasping of objects have been based on two different concepts: planning and controlling (Latombe, 1991). Planning methods define the movements and the position of the joints at any time before the movement. This requires complete information about the entire environment and the objects to be manipulated. On the other hand, controlling methods rely on local status information during the movement, based on visual or force feedback. This allows reacting to unexpected events like obstacles, but without global information, it is not guaranteed that the algorithm finds a (the best) solution for a task.

In kinesiology it is known that human motor control does not follow the planning or controlling paradigm, but it would be better described as a self-organizing process, influenced by both aspects. For example, top level dart players show a substantial variability in velocity, joint angles and the sequential timing of body parts from trial to trial (Müller and Sternad, 2004). The presumably most important skill for elite players is to balance parameters during the movement and not to reproduce fixed motor programmes. If sport science could understand this self-organizing process in detail, these findings could also be used in the development of new paradigms for controlling robots.

The second example is cooperation in sport games. An important factor for success in soccer is the quality of interaction between the players of a team. Interaction is needed on the level of the entire team, e.g. by shifting the team formation depending on the tactics and the position of the ball, as well as on the level of subgroups, for example when a striker starts running to receive a pass before the ball was played. Some of these interactions are practiced in training; others spontaneously arise based on the situation. The conditions for successful or non-successful interaction between players (e.g. which are components of decision making in soccer, which agreements are needed for organizing the defence, which cues are used for the timing of a pass?) are of great interest for exercise science and sport psychology. If models could be developed on how cooperation in sport works in detail, these would be valuable results for computer scientific research in fields like intelligent autonomous systems.

A third example can be found in the field of mobile computing. Mobile computing – which means the use of computers during movement – is a fast growing application field for information technology. Examples are the use of handhelds in medicine (documentation of patient records), in the military (geographical information for foot soldiers) and in sport (feedback about physiological parameters). One important aspect is that mobile computers extend demands on the user's coordination and cognition (Kjeldskov and Stage, 2004). While running or walking, the user has to adjust the movements of the legs with the movements of the hand–arm system. On a cognitive level the user must pay his or her main attention to their forward locomotion and, at the same time, he or she has to look on the screen to coordinate hand movements. Up to now, our knowledge about the interrelationship between walking speed, heart rate, user input, reading performance and interface design has been quite vague. Experiences and research methods from kinesiology and biomechanics can help computer science to develop user friendly human–computer interfaces, which are usable even under physiological stress.

Conclusion

Sport informatics is a reasonable and fruitful liaison between sport science and computer science. Common projects hold a set of advantages for both disciplines, if projects are designed and performed with the objective of genuine interdisciplinary research. As scientific progress in this area is closely connected to technological progress, sport science is well advised to monitor developments and to integrate partners from computer science into its research activities. On the other hand, computer science finds an appropriate application field for testing its methods and also movement-related knowledge which might help to solve its problems. Certainly, it is an important future task for the scientific community in sport informatics to make sure that this potential will be utilized as exhaustively and successfully as possible.

Study tasks

1 What is the definition of sport informatics? Explain the ideas behind this term.
2 You want to establish studies in the field of sport informatics at your university. Which arguments could you put forward?
3 Discuss the concept of interdisciplinarity in sport informatics. Why is it so difficult to achieve high levels of interdisciplinarity?
4 Explain why we suggest differentiating between sport informatics and computer science in sport.
5 Describe and explain the structural model of sport informatics. Give examples for the two directions of collaboration.

Notes

1 The International Association of Computer Science in Sport (IACSS) decided to choose 'Computer Science in Sport' instead of 'Sport Informatics' for its name, because the term is much better known and easier to understand in most countries.

Recommended further reading

Baca, A. (2006) 'Computer science in sport: An overview of history, present fields and future applications (Part I)', *International Journal of Computer Science in Sport*, 5(special edn 2): 25–35.
Fischer, G. (1998) 'Transcending cultures – Creating a shared understanding between computer science and sport', in J. Mester and J. Perl (eds), *Sport und Informatik* V (pp. 43–52), Köln: Strauss.
Link, D. and Lames, M. (2010) 'Sport informatics – History, current structure and future perspectives', *International Journal of Computer Science in Sport,* 8(2): 68–87.

References

Baca, A., Leser, R. and Ogris, G. (2011) 'Local Positioning Systems in (game) sports', *Sensors*, 11(10): 9778–9797.
Bächle, F. (2003) 'The optimisation of throwing movements with evolutionary algorithms on the basis of multi-body systems', *International Journal of Computer Science in Sport*, 2(special edn 1): 6–11.
Boisot, M. (1972) 'Discipline and interdisciplinarity', in OECD (ed.) *Interdisciplinarity: Problems of teaching and research in universities* (pp. 89–97), Centre for Educational Research and Innovation (CERI), Paris: OECD Publications.
Claus, V. (1975) *Einführung in die Informatik* [*Introduction to 'Informatik'*], Stuttgart: Teubner.
Cialdini, R.B., Borden, R.J., Thorne, A., Walker, M.R., Freeman, S. and Sloan, L.R. (1976) 'Basking in reflected glory: Three (football) field studies', *Journal of Personality and Social Psychology*, 34(3): 366–375.
Engesser, H. (ed.) (1988) *Duden 'Informatik': ein Sachlexikon für Studium und Praxis*, Stichwort Informatik [*Encyclopedia 'Informatik'*, headword 'Informatik'], Mannheim: Dudenverlag.

Godbout, A. and Boyd, J.E. (2012) 'Rhythmic sonic feedback for speed skating by real-time movement synchronization', *International Journal of Computer Science in Sport*, 11(3): 37–51.

Gomez, G., Linarth, A., Link, D. and Eskofier, B. (2012) 'Semi-automatic tracking of beach volleyball players', in R. Byshko, T. Dahmen, M. Gratkowski, M. Gruber, J. Quintana, D. Saupe, M. Vieten and A. Woll (eds), *9. Symposium der Sektion Sportinformatik der Deutschen Vereinigung für Sportwissenschaft, Extended Abstracts* (pp. 22–27), Konstanz: dvs.

Heckhausen, H. (1972) 'Discipline and Interdisciplinarity', in OECD (ed.), *Interdisciplinarity: Problems of teaching and research in universities* (pp. 83–89), Centre for Educational Research and Innovation (CERI), Paris: OECD Publications.

Höner, O. (2001) 'Interdisziplinäre Theorienbildung als Leitorientierung für den sportwissenschaftlichen Nachwuchs? [Is interdisciplinary a profitable research paradigm for young scientists?]', *Ze-phir*, 8(1): 16–29.

Hughes, M.D., Dawkins, N. and David, R. (2000) 'Perturbation effect in soccer', in M. Hughes and I. M. Franks (eds) *Notational Analysis of Sport III* (pp. 1–14), Cardiff, UK: UWIC CPA.

Hummel, O., Fehr, U. and Ferger, K. (2013) 'Beyond iBeer – Exploring the potential of smartphone sensors for performance diagnostics in sports', *International Journal of Computer Science in Sport*, 12(1): 46–60.

Karlqvist, A. (1999) 'Going beyond disciplines: The meanings of interdisciplinarity', *Policy Sciences*, 32(4): 379–383.

Kjeldskov, J. and Stage, J. (2004) 'New techniques for usability evaluation of mobile systems', *International Journal of Human-Computer Studies*, 60(5–6): 599–620.

Lamb, P., Bartlett, R. and Robins, A. (2010) 'Self-organising maps: An objective method for clustering complex human movement', *International Journal of Computer Science in Sport*, 9(1): 20–29.

Lames, M. (1999) 'Football: A chaos game? Applying elements of chaos theory to the genesis of goals in football', in P. Parisi, F. Pigozzi and G. Prinzi (eds), *Sport Science '99 in Europe* (p. 543), Rome: Rome University.

Latombe, J.C. (1991) 'Chapter 1', *Robot Motion Planning*, Boston, MA: Kluwer Academic Publishers.

Link, D. and Lames, M. (2005) 'Effects of computer mediated communication on the quality of beach volleyball coaching sessions', in F. Seifriz, J. Mester, J. Perl, O. Spaniol and J. Wiemeyer (eds), *First International Working Conference IT and Sport and 5th Conference dvs-Section Computer Science in Sport, Book of Abstracts* (pp. 172–176), Cologne: Cologne Sports University.

Luft, A.L. (1992) 'Grundlagen einer Theorie der Informatik – "Wissen" und "Information" bei einer Sichtweise der Informatik als Wissenstechnik [Basics of a theory of "Informatik"]', in W. Coy, F. Nake, J.-M. Pflüger, A. Rolf, J. Seetzen and R. Stransfeld (eds), *Sichtweisen der Informatik* (pp. 49–70), Braunschweig/Wiesbaden: Vieweg-Verlag.

Lyons, K. (2011) 'Sport coaches use of cloud computing: From here to ubiquity', *International Journal of Computer Science in Sport*, 10(1): 26–35.

McGarry, T., Anderson, D.I., Wallace, S.A., Hughes, M.D. and Franks, I.M. (2002) 'Sport competition as a dynamical self-organizing system', *Journal of Sports Sciences*, 20(10): 771–781.

Miethling, W.-D. and Perl, J. (1981) *Computerunterstützte Sportspielanalyse [Computer Supported Notational Analysis]*, Ahrensburg: Czwalina.

Müller, H. and Sternad, D. (2004) 'Decomposition of variability in the execution of goal-oriented tasks: Three components of skill improvement', *Journal of Experimental Psychology: Human Perception and Performance*, 30(1): 212–233.

National Research Council (2004) *Computer Science: Reflections on the field, reflections from the field*, Washington, DC: The National Academies Press.

Nygaard, K. (1986) 'Program development as a social activity', in *Proceedings of 10th IFIP World Computer Congress* (pp. 189–198), Dublin. Amsterdam: North-Holland

OECD (ed.) (1972) *Interdisciplinarity: Problems of teaching and research in universities*, Centre for Educational Research and Innovation (CERI), Paris: OECD Publications.

Perl, J. and Endler, S. (2012) 'PerPot individual anaerobe threshold marathon scheduling', *International Journal of Computer Science in Sport*, 11(2): 52–60.

Perl, J., Grunz, A. and Memmert, D. (2013) 'Tactics analysis in soccer – An advanced approach', *International Journal of Computer Science in Sport*, 12(1): 33–44.

Perl, J. and Lames, M. (1995) 'Sportinformatik: Gegenstandsbereich und Perspektiven einer sportwissenschaftlichen Teildisziplin [Sport Informatics Subject Matters and Perspectives of a Sport Scientific Sub Discipline]', *Leistungssport*, 25(3): 26–30.

Recla, J. and Timmer, R. (eds) (1976) 'Kreative Sportinformatik [Creative Sport Informatics], Der Internationale Jubiläums-Kongreß 1975 in Graz', Schorndorf: Hoffmann.

Ries, H. and Kriesi, H. (1974) 'Scientific model for a theory of physical education and sport sciences', in U. Simri (ed.) *Concepts of Physical Education and Sport Sciences* (pp. 175–198), Netanya: Wingare Publishing.

Röthig, P. and Prohl, R. (eds) (2003) *Sportwissenschaftliches Lexikon, Stichwort Sport* [*Encyclopaedia of Sport Science*, keyword sport], Schorndorf: Hofmann.

Stöckl, M. and Lames, M. (2011) 'Modeling constraints in putting: The ISOPAR method', *International Journal of Computer Science in Sport*, 10(1): 74–81.

Vajna, S., Edelmann-Nusser, J., Kittel, K. and Jordan, A. (2006) 'Optimisation of a bow riser using the Autogenetic Design Theory', in I. Horváth and J. Duhovnik (eds), *Tools and Methods of Competitive Engineering Vol. 1* (pp. 593–602), Ljubljana: University of Ljubljana.

Walter, F., Lames, M. and McGarry, T. (2007) 'Analysis of sports performance as a dynamical system by means of the Relative Phase', *International Journal of Computer Science in Sports*, 6(2): 35–41.

2   Computers, informatics and sport

Peter Dabnichki and Chikara Miyaji

Introduction

Computers and the associated science *informatics* are the two fastest developing areas of technology that have delivered a sea change in the everyday lives of billions of people. It is impossible to imagine our very existence – and possibly our world – without computers. 'Computer' has become a very familiar – even overused – word, and it seems that we have lost the meaning of it. It all started more than a century ago with the need to design a faster and more sophisticated calculator that could also perform logical operations. The reality nowadays could not be further away as computers have penetrated every aspect of modern life. Critical operations such as electrical production and distribution, transport systems, house and industrial water supplies, intensive care in hospitals down to our everyday shopping are not feasible without computers. As they affected all walks of life and society as a whole, they inevitably affected all aspects of sport as well, from training practices and preparation of athletes for competitions to big events organization and broadcasting. Sport could only become an integral part of society with mass participation and acceptance as a cultural phenomenon, both athletes' achievements and popularity were only possible due to the speedy and accurate information transfer, making sport an integral part of society with mass participation and acceptance as a cultural phenomenon.

This chapter covers the major developments in computers and informatics through the prism of the end user in the field of sport and sport science. It introduces both the computer as a device and the related scientific field of informatics, providing the necessary background to enable informed use of computers for the purposes of sport:

- First, we show the basic structure and working principles of computers.
- Next, we discuss how computers process and store data.
- Finally, we look into the practical implications for using computers in a sport-related context.

This chapter is aimed at readers with little or no background in computer science/informatics; readers with stronger interests and a desire to gain deep insight into computer software are referred to more specialized in-depth sources in the further reading section.

Computer fundamentals

Let us look at a computer when it is switched off, when we only see a tower, a blank screen and a keyboard that does not respond to our touch. What do these components have inside and how are they put into operation? How do they interact and respond to our instructions? *Hardware* is the generic term for all internal and external physical parts of the computer we can physically touch.

Computer hardware – as advanced as it may be – is of no use to the ordinary person without the special built-in programs that run the computer. The collective term for these programs (pre-installed and/or added later by user/service provider) is *software*.

Hardware

The physical parts of a computer can be divided into *core* (i.e. the primary components essential for operation) and *peripherals* (additional devices connected to, but not an integral part of, the computer).

According to the most stringent definition, the only pieces of a computer considered to be parts of the core are: central processing unit (CPU), power supply, motherboard and computer case. Though it is located inside the case and sometimes even incorporated into the same circuit as the CPU, random access memory (RAM) is considered a peripheral. However, we do not agree with this definition as RAM is required for every major function of a computer and, if removed, will effectively disable its function.

Core components

The main part of the computer is hidden in the tower and it is a giant circuit called a motherboard (see Figure 2.1). As the name suggests, all important parts forming the heart of the computer and crucial for its functioning are embedded in the motherboard.

The electronics in the motherboard may vary depending on the intended use and the manufacturer. However, microprocessor design fundamentally reflects a logical structure called *Von Neumann architecture* (as shown in Figure 2.2) that has not changed substantially in the last 60 years.

Every reader would have seen at least once a sticker on a computer station stating proudly 'Intel inside'. Why is it so important for the computer manufacturers to advertise this feature? The microprocessor is the brain of the computer, and Intel is the world's biggest microprocessor manufacturer, although many others (AMD and Motorola amongst them) are prominent. The main parts of microprocessor structure are briefly explained in the following, including function and specifications:

Figure 2.1 Motherboard – the giant circuit that contains all the core hardware of a computer

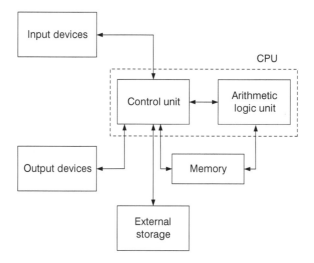

Figure 2.2 Logical structure of a microprocessor

THE CENTRAL PROCESSING UNIT (CPU)

The CPU consists of two interacting systems: the arithmetic logic unit (ALU), which performs both arithmetic (addition, subtraction, multiplication, division) and logical operations (comparison, data relocation, decision making to jump or follow an instruction), and the control unit (CU), which has the instruction register and decoder, computer clock and program counter for coordinating and timing all ALU operations.

The speed at which operations are executed by the ALU is determined by the crystal-controlled clock. Clock rate is measured in Hertz (named after the famous 19th century German physicist Heinrich Hertz), where 1 Hz means one crystal oscillation per second and 1 MHz is equal to 1 million cycles in a single second. The clock rate is the maximum speed of the processor.

By increasing the internal clock rate, more instructions are processed per unit of time. This key performance metric is called program execution time, defined as:

Program execution time = Number of instructions in program
    × Clock cycles per instruction × Time per clock cycle

It is not a straightforward task to estimate the running time as the numbers of instructions in programs vary depending on the performed task. Furthermore, external factors such as speed of data access and speed of data flow in and out of the program may affect its performance.

Current computers reach a clock rate of a few GHz and it is constantly rising. Multi-core processors enhance the computing power due to parallelization of tasks. From a user standpoint, the key performance metric is how quickly a program runs as no one enjoys an image being rendered slowly line by line on a computer screen. When selecting a computer model one needs to carefully assess the requirements of the tasks likely to be performed and select the appropriate speed and number of processor(s) as their increase has definite cost implications.

RANDOM ACCESS MEMORY (RAM)

RAM is used to temporarily store data for quick and easy access. At program start, the program – or parts of it – get loaded from the hard drive, where it is permanently stored, into the RAM, where it is temporarily available. Running programs from the RAM allows them to function without any lag time, because reading data from the RAM is much faster than reading data from the hard drive. If you imagine that you need some information in the library and to answer any question you need to climb the shelf (corresponding to the hard drive), check your facts and then return the book on the spot; RAM is in effect keeping the book open in front of you.

The more RAM a computer has, the more data can be loaded from the hard drive into it, which can effectively speed up program execution. RAM consists of small memory chips inserted in special slots on the motherboard. Most computers provide you with the option of speeding up by expanding RAM, but this is limited by the type and number of slots. Under Windows, for example, the amount of RAM installed can be checked by opening the 'System Control Panel', normally done by right-clicking 'My Computer' and then selecting 'Properties'.

Some fields of sport science such as biomechanics and performance assessment involve the use of images and require powerful computers with large RAM of 16 GB upwards.

EXTERNAL (MASS) STORAGE, AND INPUT AND OUTPUT DEVICES

These are addressed in the 'Peripherals' section.

We should mention that microprocessors nowadays are used everywhere – from microwave ovens to televisions and sophisticated medical devices. In particular, they have revolutionized photography and filming with direct benefit to sport applications. However, in the forefront of microprocessor development have always been the game consoles manufacturers who – as in the case of Nintendo and Microsoft – adopted some techniques developed in sport biomechanics to promote exercise among their young users.

Peripherals

Besides the parts commonly called peripherals (mouse, keyboard or printer), *peripherals* are defined as auxiliary devices external to the computer core. Generally, there are three main types to be distinguished:

• *Input peripherals* (mouse, keyboard, touchscreen, webcam, microphone, etc.) are used to interact with or send data (image scanner, digital cameras, etc.) to the computer.
• *Output peripherals* provide output to the user, mostly graphic (screen, printer) but also acoustic (headphone, loudspeaker) or tactile (braille display).
• *Storage peripherals or data carriers* store data processed by the computer, realized either as drives (hard drives, flash drives, CD/DVD drives, etc.) or as temporary interfaces which can be removed any time (USB stick, Internet socket, Bluetooth adapter, etc.).
    A specific example for USB connectable devices used only one way is the *software protection dongle* or *hardware key* needed to unlock high-price software such as motion analysis programs used in sports biomechanics.
    All internal (inside the case) and external data drives are assigned a single letter destination, where C: is reserved for the built-in hard drive, D: could be a second disk or CD/DVD device, etc. They are made visible through 'My Computer' (the root directory that contains both files and folders) and data can be transferred from one to another.

This formerly strict distinction has been weakened as there are combined input/output devices. Smartphones and tablet computers have interfaces that allow their use as peripherals by a computer, but they have also expanded the importance and functionality of peripherals. These *smart devices* are – unlike the peripherals outlined above – not dependent on the host computer, i.e. they possess a high degree of autonomy (see 'Computers and smart devices as part of the network'). For information on technologies connecting peripherals to a computer (e.g. USB, Bluetooth, etc.) refer to Chapter 4.

Software

Software can be classified into three different levels, ranging from essential to extra features:

- A vital part of the pre-installed software is the basic input/output system (BIOS) responsible for booting up (starting) the computer. When you turn on your computer and while the screen is black, this program checks the functionality of all hardware components and initiates loading of the
- Operating system, i.e. the core programs that ensure the basic functionality of the computer (Windows, OS, Linux and UNIX being the most commonly used). Once the process of booting up is completed, the operating system takes control. This is the stage ordinary users are familiar with and when they start controlling their own computer.
- Further to these essential core routines, there is a myriad of software products to perform a variety of tasks such as text processing, spreadsheet or image processing software, web browsers and virus protection programs, games and other applications. Examples for sport science specific software are given in Chapters 5–8.

Informatics

Claude Elwood Shannon is widely credited as the 'father of information theory' (James, 2009). Since his pioneering work on representation and transformation of information (Shannon, 1948), this new *informatics* as a field of science has emerged from a solely theoretical discipline to an application-oriented discipline. Initially responding to the needs of advancing computers, informatics has become the science of searching, accessing, processing, presenting, sorting, transmitting and storing data. As a multidisciplinary field of science, however, it is also devoted to study of structure, behaviour and interactions of natural and man-made systems (Avery, 2012).

Data coding and information formats

Many routines are based on and inspired by related natural world phenomena such as cognition, communication, evolution and co-existence. Natural systems carry information at hierarchical levels, from biological molecules, through nervous systems and organisms into societies at large. Information characteristics are hierarchical structure (information carried at higher levels is represented by informational processes at lower levels), data coding (common agreement on a character set representing the information) and data packaging (data is divided into packages that each higher level is able to process at once).

Numeral systems

Among all numeral systems, the positional systems using base 10 (decimal), 8 (octal), 16 (hexadecimal) and 2 (binary) are the most used. In everyday life we are used to a decimal system, which employs 10 digits (as we have 10 fingers) and each digit position represents a power of 10 (100, 1,000, etc.).

Data presentation in computers is based on a binary numeral system in which there are only two possible states: off (0) and on (1), often visualized by a light bulb (light or dark), a switch (open or closed) or any other two-state device. In the binary system, each digit position represents a power of 2 (4, 8, 16, etc.). The binary system has proved to be best for computers and is now the dominant one in digital computing, besides the octal (using digits 0 to 7) and hexadecimal (using digits 0 to 9 plus letters A to F) numeral systems.

The unit of information is called *1 bit* (derived from binary digit) and represents one light bulb, switch or the like. Imagine two switches: the first could be on, the second off or vice versa, or both could be on or both off. For 2 bits there are already $2^2 = 4$ possible states: 00, 01, 10, and 11. The number of possible states is always a power of 2, and the next largest unit is $2^8 = 256$ bits and is called *1 byte*. For the modern computer even the unit byte is a negligible amount of information, so multiples of bytes (not powers of 10) are used: $2^{10} = 1,024$ bytes (not 1,000 bytes) are called 1 kilobyte (KB). The more widely used multiples of bytes are megabyte (MB), gigabyte (GB), terabyte (TB) and petabyte (PB), all defined as 1,024 times the preceding one as listed below:

- 1 bit × 8 = 1 byte
- 1 byte × 1024 = 1 KB

and so on.

Character coding

A sequence of bits is called a bit stream or data, as it represents numbers, characters or operations to be performed. With just 7 bits, $2^7 = 128$ numerals, alphabetic characters and some symbols can be represented in the American Standard Code for Information Interchange (ASCII). These characters and the corresponding binary encoding are associated in a look-up table. For example, when one types 'A', the computer stores '1000001'. The ASCII code is the standard way of coding Latin and similar alphabets, but it cannot be used to code more complex languages such as Chinese and Japanese that use thousands of characters. For this purpose, Unicode (using 16 or more bits) or UTF-16 (encoding used in web applications) have been developed.

File formats

Text is a complex formation of words (assembled characters) that is normally linked through grammatical rules and semantics. If not specifically formatted, it is called 'plain text'. When more sophisticated formats such as font variations, character size and information layout is added, it is called 'rich text'. Apart from text, any large bit sequence is called a *file* and *file formats* are necessary to also code the structure and ordering of data within a file. The way of recognizing the file format is the so-called extension added after the file name and a dot.

The most common data file formats are (including extensions):

- *DOC, DOCX*: the format for Microsoft Word rich text documents that can be read or converted by a large number of applications. DOCX is the latest version introduced in 2007.
- *PDF*: the format representing rich text with graphics defined by Adobe. The advantage is that text formatting is preserved on different platforms and that is why many applications convert their specific formats into this Portable Document Format.
- *HTML*: Hypertext Markup Language, the format for tagging text files to achieve font, colour, graphic and hyperlink effects to represent text and graphics on browser.
- *CSV*: the Comma-Separated Values format is used to represent data in a very simple way. Originally this format was used for various spreadsheet or database applications, such as Microsoft Excel.
- *JSON*: JavaScript Object Notation is a data representation predominantly used in web applications. It uses JavaScript syntax as 'plain text' with Unicode, where objects are assigned name/value paired attributes: { "date": "2013.02.14", "subject": "Chikara Miyaji" }

2D graphics format

There are two categories of 2D graphics formats:

- *Raster graphics* are stored as pixel by pixel (the dot on the screen) information. Photos taken by camera are in effect raster graphics. One of the most popular is the Joint Photographic Experts Group (JPEG) format with lossy compression suitable for photos. Portable Network Graphics (PNG) has lossless compression suitable for raster graphics with lines or text.
- *Vector graphics* are stored as a series of commands and not pixel information, with the main advantage of scalability. Scalable Vector Graphics (SVG) is used in particular for web browsers written in Extensible Markup Language (XML). XML is a more versatile language to define formats and is used in sports applications such as 3D human modelling to define models.

Video format

Video is roughly composed of unique consecutive 2D images called frames. Important specifications of video images are (see Table 2.1):

- *Colour depth*: depending on the number of bits, finer levels of colour can be expressed in each pixel: high colour (16 bits), true colour (24 bits) or deep colour (48 bits). True colour, for example, allows for 256 shades of red, green and blue, giving a total of 16,777,216 colour variations.
- *Resolution:* basically, any number of pixels for height × width of video images can be chosen. For practical reasons, however, resolution has been fixed within various standards called
- *Aspect ratio*: this measure describes the proportional relationship between the image's width and height. The old standard video aspect 4:3 was replaced by the new 16:9 high-definition standard that better corresponds to our human field of view.
- *Frames per second (fps)*: the sampling rate or frequency rate is the number of unique images per second composing the video, determining whether or not image flicker occurs. The human eye can perceive separated images for a refreshment rate of up to 20 Hz (Read and Meyer, 2000) and beyond this threshold, consecutive images look like they are moving images.

In order to increase sampling rate while maintaining low data amounts, the *interlaced scan* method was invented. This process involves the creation of two fields (images) taken at different time points, where the first image covers odd lines and the second one (1/60 s later) covers even lines as illustrated in Figure 2.3. Images of two consecutive time points are then overlapped, forming one image at half the frame rate perceived as belonging together by human eye.

As the rapid evolution of the sensor technology made it possible to substantially increase the frame rate for video rendering, non-interlaced *progressive scan* is expected to be the future. For example, affordable cameras currently capture 120 fps, while costly high-speed cameras go up to 100,000 fps. Both are used in motion tracking, ranging from school class use to fast sport action such as golf swing analysis.

Table 2.1 Video type with corresponding pixel size and aspect ratio

Type	Number of pixels	Aspect ratio
VGA	640 × 480	4:3
SVGA	800 × 600	4:3
XGA	1024 × 768	4:3
HD 720p (HD)	1280 × 720	16:9
HD 1080p (Full-HD)	1920 × 1080	16:9

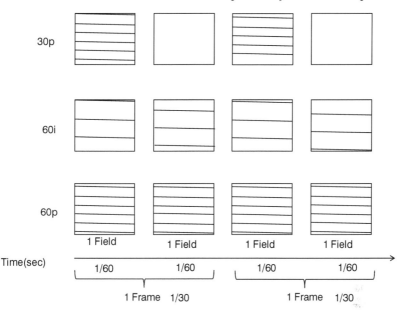

Figure 2.3 Schematic representation of interlaced and non-interlaced. 30p: scans all in a field every 1/30 s; 60i: scans half in a field every 1/60 s; 60p: scans all in a field every 1/60 s. For European standards the respective values should read 25p and 50i and 50p.

Data organization

All the data stored in computers in digital form need to be organized in a way that the user can easily search and access. An arbitrary number of files recognizable by their file names are therefore ordered in a tree-like hierarchical structure. This structure can grow as each directory or folder (as visualized in Windows) could become a sub-directory of the next higher level (folder in folder). An example of a simple directory with several files in it is shown in Figure 2.4.

Data compression

In order to efficiently process, analyse and store data it is critical to determine a preliminary estimate of the amount of data to be collected. This amount is frequently underestimated, leading to a shortage of hard disk space and slow running of the computer. Data sets can easily become too large to transfer (e-mail programs limit the size of the attachment) or even to store on a hard drive (file size is limited by the file system or the operating system).

Consequently, there is a need to decrease the amount of data and save disk space data using either lossy or lossless compression algorithms. Lossless compression allows a complete reconstruction of the entire original data set from the compressed data; hence it is used to compress text or sensor data for which every single bit of information is essential.

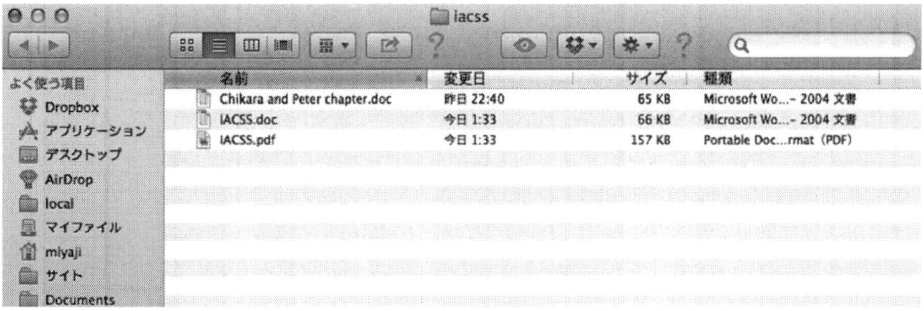

Figure 2.4 A directory (folder) with the files in it

In Figure 2.4 the size of the IACSS.doc is 66 KB, hence a total of 540,672 bits are needed to store it on a hard drive. The original file is converted to the compressed file IACSS.zip (29 KB) using one of many 'zip' compression programs available. The resulting compressed file is approximately 56 per cent smaller than the original, reducing the number of bits needed to 237,568 bits. The rate of lossless compression depends on the algorithm and the type of data. Predictable data composed of repeating bit sequences can be compressed by redundancy reduction, while random bit streams reach a lower compression rate.

Lossy compression is applied to images, music or videos, where some features of the detailed data can be neglected without obvious loss of quality. One of these lossy algorithms has already been introduced: the JPEG graphics format. Pictures are normally quite large as good quality digital images need several MB for one picture file. Figure 2.5 shows the same image file with two different JPEG compression rates. Even though file sizes vary from 12 KB to 49 KB – four times as much – the images are hardly distinguishable.

Data exchange

Up to now, we have discussed data that are stored statically, i.e. data remains in the same place although their quantity may change due to compression. Soon after the introduction of computers, it became apparent that their individual powers

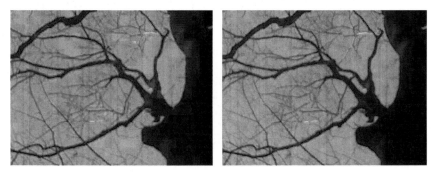

Figure 2.5 Images with different levels of JPEG compression: left: strongly compressed (12 KB); right: lower compression rate (49 KB)

exponentiate if they are combined and share data. In our highly dynamic world, data exchange via networks is of utmost importance.

Information networks

Networks appear in different sizes, some of which are illustrated below. All of them can be either – and formerly have been exclusively – wired, or wireless since the 1990s for which the letter W is added as a prefix:

- *Personal area network (PAN)* is used for communicating among computers and devices in close proximity of around a few metres within a room or laboratory.
- *Local area network (LAN)* facilitates interaction between computers and devices such as printers and scanners, usually within an office building or home.
- *Metropolitan area network (MAN)* may span a large university campus, a city or a multinational campus. It is normally operated by a single organization, but used by many individuals and organizations.
- *Internet and World Wide Web (WWW)*: the Internet originates from a military and university connection in the USA, while Hypertext Transfer Protocol (HTTP) – on which WWW is based – was invented by the European Organization for Nuclear Research (CERN) in Switzerland. The Internet, affectionately called 'the Net', is a giant network that spans the globe. There are millions of computers and other devices linked with cables that would encircle the equator many times plus a huge amount of wireless networks. This is certainly the biggest cross-border project of humankind in our entire history.

   Unknown to the vast majority of its users, the Internet is a technological environment and the World Wide Web, or simply 'the Web', is only one of many services provided. The WWW is a giant collection of HTML pages that can be viewed by special software products called web browsers. It is estimated that there are over 100 billion public pages on the Web today and over 400 billion private web pages (not freely accessible to all Internet users). This enormous amount can neither be owned by a single organization nor does any government have authority over its operations. For everyone to be able to participate on an equal footing, some technical rules against copyright infringements, and safety software known as firewalls and virus scanners is required.

Data transfer

The speed of data transfer, called bit rate, is defined as the number of data bits transferred per unit of time, hence data rate unit is bits per seconds (bps). Please note that the unit here is megabits and not megabytes. When downloading data

Table 2.2 Data transfer rate for the most common devices

Bps	Device
100 Mbps	Maximum speed of 100BASE-TX
480 Mbps	Maximum speed of USB 2.0
5 Gbps	Maximum speed of USB 3.0
10 Gbps	Maximum speed of Thunderbolt

from an external carrier the upper limit of bit rate is determined by the physical socket on the computer, the so-called 'port'. The most commonly used ports are listed in Table 2.2 (see also Chapter 4).

The following example calculates the theoretical transfer time as 0.78 seconds for a 100 MB file via a USB 3.0 port with a maximum bit rate of 1 Gbps:

100 MB × 8 bit = 800 Mbit

800 Mbit / (1 Gbps × 1024 MB) = 0.78 s

In an addition to physical data carriers plugged into physical sockets, file sharing on cloud platforms has become popular. The term *cloud* describes distributed data storage but also computing power (Zhuge, 2004). Bit rate for data transfer from external carriers such as the cloud, however, is still much slower than for data transfer from internal hard drives, as illustrated in Figure 2.6.

In the example below, bit rate for transferring from the cloud space onto a private computer is calculated for the same 100 MB file that takes 5 minutes:

100 MB × 8 bit = 800 Mbit

800 Mbit / (5 min × 60) = 2.6 Mbps

Computers and smart devices as part of the network

The advantages of networks are the large number and mobility of devices linked together. As far back as 1999, Kevin Ashton predicted that the future lay in smart devices that are capable of collecting and transmitting data without human oversight. He defined this new autonomic system as 'The Internet of Things' (Ashton, 2009). Yet we suggest the prediction of smartphones entirely replacing computers (Pitt, 2012) rather premature for a number of reasons:

- *Processing power*: computers have substantially higher processing power, as microprocessor power is limited in mobile devices mostly due to the waste heat problem.
- *Operating system*: smartphone and tablet operating systems are limited compared to fully featured desktop and laptop operating systems.
- *Storage space*: there is no base for comparison of storage space as smartphones rely purely on flash memory, which is technically limited in size.

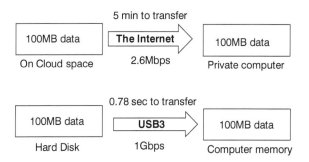

Figure 2.6 Two data transfers from different types of storage

In conclusion, computing is more and more about large and complex programs using multiple computers for parallel and grid computing. We confidently state that although mobile phones are excellent devices for pervasive computing applications (see Chapter 4), they are currently not an alternative to powerful and universal computers (Dabnichki, 2006).

Conclusions

We hope that the reader is now fully equipped to comprehend and practically use the remainder of this book. We have attempted to put the most relevant computer related knowledge in a nutshell for a sport scientist. However, we strongly recommend that readers enrich their diet with the sources we recommend at the end of this chapter.

Study tasks

1   How many ones or zeros do 8 bytes have? How many possible states could be expressed through these 8 bytes of information?
2   Can you remove the motherboard from a computer and still use it?
3   If a person trains 2 hours every day over 10 years, how much disk space is needed to capture all that training with 2 Mbps video?
4   You have Adobe Acrobat Reader and a Microsoft Word file. Could the reader open the file directly? Justify your answer and provide a method to open the file.
5   A sport scientist uses an interlaced video of 50 Hz and splits the image assuming that the time difference is 1/50 s. Is this a correct assumption and why?
6   Is the World Wide Web a computer network and if not what it is?
7   You are downloading images from your mobile phone. Do you need a network to do this? What does your mobile represent?
8   Is this statement correct in computer terms: $7 + 9 =$ '1000'?

Recommended further reading

Dabnichki, P. and Baca, A. (2008) *Computers in Sport*, Southampton: WIT Press.

Harris, D.M. and Harris, S.L. (2007) *Digital Design and Computer Architecture*, New York: Elsevier.

Rafiquzzaman, M. (2005) *Fundamentals of Digital Logic and Microcomputer Design*, New York: Wiley.

Schneidewind, N.F. (2012) *Computer, Network, Software, and Hardware Engineering with Applications*, New York: Wiley.

References

Ashton, K. (2009). 'That "Internet of Things" thing. In the real world things matter more than ideas'. Retreived from <http://www.rfidjournal.com/articles/view?4986> (accessed 3 March 2014).

Avery, J.S. (2012) *Information Theory and Evolution*, 2nd edn, Singapore: World Scientific.

Dabnichki, P. (2006) 'The future synergy of computer modelling and smart technologies in sport', in A. Baca, L. Katz, J. Perl and O. Spaniol (eds) *Computer Science in Sport. Dagstuhl Seminar Proceedings*, Germany: Schloss Dagstuhl.

James, I. (2009). 'Claude Elwood Shannon. 30 April 1916 – 24 February 2001', *Biographical Memoirs of Fellows of the Royal Society*, 55: 257–265.

Pitt, J. (2012) *This Pervasive Day*, London: Imperial College Press.

Read, P. and Meyer, M.-P. (2000). *Restoration of Motion Picture Film*, Oxford: Butterworth-Heinemann.

Shannon, C.E. (1948). 'A mathematical theory of communication', *The Bell System Technical Journal*, 27: 379–423.

Zhuge, H. (2004) *The Knowledge Grid*, Singapore: World Scientific.

3 Databases and expert systems

Keith Lyons

Introduction

Sport has been an early adopter of innovations in database development including the use of expert systems (Less, 1985; Perl, Lames and Miethling, 1997; Baca, 2007). This chapter explores some of uses that have been made of databases and expert systems to transform our understanding of performance in sport.

First of all we need to clarify the terms we are going to use. There are some important definitions to consider.

A *database* is a collection of information stored in a structured digital format. Developments in computing have made it increasingly efficient to input, store and manage data in *non-relational* and *relational* databases. There is a growing interest in the automatic extraction of knowledge from such data (Rainsford and Roddick, 1999). *Knowledge discovery in databases* refers to the overall process of discovering useful knowledge from data (Fayyad, Piatetsky-Shapiro and Smyth, 1996). *Data mining* is a step in the knowledge discovery in databases (KDD) process. Fayyad, Piatetsky-Shapiro and Smyth (1996) point out that KDD has additional features to data mining, namely 'data preparation, data selection, data cleaning, incorporation of appropriate prior knowledge, and proper interpretation of the results of mining'. An *expert system* is 'a computer program that reasons using knowledge to solve complex problems' (Feigenbaum, 1991: 1). Expert systems use artificial intelligence to improve 'by an order-of-magnitude the human professional and semi-professional work that once was thought to be beyond the help of computerized information processing' (Feigenbaum, 1992: 15). *Artificial intelligence* 'is the science and engineering of making intelligent machines, especially intelligent computer programs' (McCarthy, 2002: 2).

Databases

People who have grown up in the digital age have had increasing access to database technology and database management systems (DBMS). It has been normal to expect that data can be stored and interrogated with sophisticated tools. Those who remember a time before desktop and personal computers can recall the use of pen and paper to create spreadsheets of data that were standalone records.

The term spreadsheet has been transferred from its original use in newspapers and then in bookkeeping journals to refer to a computer application that makes it possible to compile and analyse data in tabular form. For many people, Microsoft Excel has been their introduction to spreadsheets. There are other applications available. With the advent of cloud computing a tool like Google Docs has become available to extend the use of spreadsheets.

Spreadsheets are very helpful if you wish to store independent (*non-relational*) data. Our example of spreadsheet use in sport comes from the sport of canoeing. The problem to be addressed is 'Can we have an accurate, up-to-date record of all members of the national sporting organization who have a current coaching or instruction award?'

The canoeing organization has had a high turnover of staff in its coach education department. It needs a 'record of truth' to ensure that all coaches and instructors have valid qualifications. This record has important legal as well as sport coaching implications. It forms the institutional knowledge of the organization.

This is how the organization accomplished this task. It:

- designed a form to be completed in writing by each coach or instructor that contained obligatory answers to questions about their status;
- asked candidates to submit payment for their award with their form;
- used an Excel spreadsheet to record all these answers when the form and payment was received in the office;
- allocated an automated unique identifier to each record in the spreadsheet once it had confirmed and entered all information visually.

The spreadsheet created by the organization has eight fields: *ID, Name, Membership Number, Qualification Name, Qualification Achieved, Qualification Expires, Assessor's Name, Training Provider's Name.* (ID is the first field and is generated automatically. It provides the unique identification number of the record.)

No data entry is made until each field is confirmed manually and all entries are double-checked. No data entry can be initiated unless payment is received.

An example of a record created by the organization following this process is:

ID	1
Name	John Draw
Membership Number	01234
Qualification Name	Flat-water Instructor
Qualification Achieved	2014-01-01
Qualification Expires	2017-12-31
Assessor's Name	Jane Sweep
Training Provider's Name	UCan2

The data protocol for each field is defined as:

ID	Unique number
Name	Full name
Membership Number	Number
Qualification Name	Full word title
Qualification Achieved	YYYY-MM-DD
Qualification Expires	YYYY-MM-DD
Assessor's Name	Full name
Training Provider's Name	Full word title

This spreadsheet has worked well for the organization. They have a standalone record of coaching and instruction awards that can be used by anyone in the organization.

Question: What would you do to improve this spreadsheet?

The organization is committed to continuous improvement and they are looking to enhance the functionality and usability of the spreadsheet. We wonder if your suggestions for improvement included linking this spreadsheet to other databases held by the organization.
   Do your suggestions include?

• using a primary key field;
• creating Membership, Qualification, Assessor and Provider tables.

(A primary key field provides a unique value that ensures that there are no duplicate records in the database. Creating data tables makes it possible to plan for relationships between data held in other databases.)
   Would your solution look like this?

ID	Primary key field (automatic, incremental)
Membership Number	Membership table
Qualification Name	Qualification table
Qualification Achieved	Flat data
Qualification Expires	Flat data
Assessor's Name	Assessor table
Training Provider's Name	Provider table

(Flat data in this example refers to data with no relationships or links between records and fields except with regard to the table structure. The flat data here are two entries for qualification achieved (YYYY-MM-DD) and qualification expires (YYYY-MM-DD).)

When the organization planned its original spreadsheet, a determined effort was made to limit the number of fields used. A strategic decision was made about a person's name. In the spreadsheet used by the organization a coach or instructor gives his or her full name. At present this is checked against a membership record held separately. This approach has the advantage of being able to print qualification certificates from the *Name* field and to do so correctly. At present the operational definition of a coach or instructor's name is full name (Given name, Family name).

As our discussion above has indicated, going beyond a single, standalone spreadsheet design leads you to relational database principles. A relational database is able to access information in multiple tables (Codd, 1970, 1982). For most people, a relational database management system (RDBMS), such as Microsoft Access, provides an introduction to the potential of linking data in a structured way. Vines (2011) points out that RDBMS software offers tools to:

*   design the structure of your database;
*   create data entry forms so you can get information into the database;
*   validate the data entered and check for inconsistencies;
*   sort and manipulate the data in the database;
*   query the database (that is, ask questions about the data);
*   produce flexible reports, both on screen and on paper, that make it easy to comprehend the information stored in the database.

The RDBMS literature emphasizes the importance of spending a significant amount of time planning how information will be stored and retrieved in a usable way. This involves an iterative process of planning, testing and modifying. Central to this process is the use of a primary key field (or fields) to sort and retrieve information.

Here is another example from the sport of canoeing to illustrate how a relational database is used to address an important organizational service requirement.

Each year, the organization runs competition events that are used to select the members of junior and senior teams to compete in international competitions, including continental and world championships, and, every four years, the Olympic Games. The selection events are open for every member of the organization to enter.

Until comparatively recently, all athlete entries for selection events were accepted as paper forms (either online as digital files or as paper). On receipt in the organization's office all digital files were printed off onto paper for manual entry of data. One of the new members of staff at the organization was asked to design an electronic version of this paper system to make it more manageable and efficient.

The first task the organization faced was to identify the scope of the problem. Each year the organization selects hundreds of athletes to participate in national teams when they have met the selection performance criteria. Each athlete must self-nominate for selection events but can nominate for multiple teams. Some of these nominations are chronological age defined (for example, Under 18 on 1 January 2014). All athletes can nominate for senior teams if they are over the age of 15 years. Some teams are not selected in some years. The nomination process requires payment of a nomination fee (by credit card or bank cheque) and a signed agreement by the athlete (or by a parent/guardian if the athlete is under 18 years of age) to abide by the organization's rules and code of conduct.

These operational requirements indicate that a relational database is required to use information from each athlete's nomination form and to ensure that, if the athlete nominates for more than one team, this is recorded accurately.

The member of the organization's staff with responsibility for the database design (Anna) decided to spend some time learning about existing practices in the organization's office. It was important for her to speak with all staff involved in the selection process and with athletes who used the system. After these conversations and discussions, Anna identified the fields of data and the tables that could be collected by an online, automated system. She decided to establish four tables.

Basic athlete information (full name, date of birth, correspondence address and contact information) populated fields in a 'Member' table. Fields for specific nomination information, including confirmation of the signature of the code of conduct, confirmation of payment of fees and the name of the parent/guardian (if under the age of 18) were created in a 'Nominations' table. This table had other fields for office administration purposes such as payment date, payment type and payment amount. Anna included a field for the membership identification (ID) number in this Nominations table to identify the member making the nomination.

Anna then planned the table that would record for which teams the athlete was nominating. This 'Teams' table referenced the nomination ID from the Nomination table to ensure that the organization's office could keep track of who had nominated for which team and if the nomination fee had been paid. The Teams table included the team ID (which references the team information from a 'Team Details' table) and the current status of the athlete (one of: nominated, selected or not selected).

After testing the system herself and with a group of athletes, Anna thought carefully about the kinds of user of the system. Her tests led her to think about the guidance and instruction athletes would need to complete the nomination procedure. Many of the athletes had only ever used paper nomination procedures. Anna discovered too that some athletes tried to hurry the data entry process or left important sections of the form blank and therefore incomplete.

Unless she addressed these issues of the imagined user, Anna would have created more work for a small number of the organization's staff. A decision to automate the system, ironically, could have proven more inefficient.

Anna decided that extra automated checking and mandatory fields were required in her design. For example, she used the Member table to identify whether a person nominating for selection was less than 18 years of age and then making the guardian/parent field compulsory if this was the case. Anna realized too that although the organization was developing and testing the system in a modern web browser, the users were not necessarily doing the same. It was important, therefore, to check that the online form could be completed in older versions of Internet Explorer as ultimately the organization wanted all members to be able to nominate as quickly and easily as possible. This iteration of planning, testing and modifying helped to reduce the nomination form to the absolute minimum information requirements. At present, this new system is monitored each week to ensure that the information collected is accurate and appropriate. The organization treats this as a record of truth.

These are examples from three of the four tables used in the Nomination system.

Nomination table

ID	Membership Number	Total Fee	Total Paid	Athlete Consent/Agreement Rules and Code of Conduct
1	04321	70	70	Signed

In which:

ID	Membership Number	Total Fee	Total Paid	Athlete Consent/Agreement Rules and Code of Conduct
Primary key field (automatic, incremental)	Membership Table	Flat data	Flat data	Flat data

Teams table

ID	Nomination ID	Team ID	Selection Status
1	9	12	Not Selected
2	9	15	Selected

In which:

ID	Nomination ID	Team ID	Selection Status
Primary key (automatic, incremental)	Nomination Table	Team Details Table	Flat data

Team Details table

ID	Team Name	Team Discipline	Team Year
1	Senior Team	Canoe Sprint	2014
2	Junior Team	Canoe Slalom	2013

In which:

ID	Team Name	Team Discipline	Team Year
Primary key (automatic, incremental)	Flat data	Flat data	Flat data

Anna wrote the system with PHP code and used the open source database MySQL. She liked the large amount of documentation available to support MySQL and was an active user of the support forums. She developed the Nomination system on her Mac computer and used a program called MAMP (WAMP in Windows) to test the system prior to its publication online.

Anna's brief was to develop a system that was as efficient as possible with very low and strict cost limits. The system was to be dynamic enough to make quick updates possible. In all, the system took 200 hours to plan, design, test and modify. It was delivered in an appropriate time for the organization. It is subject to ongoing monitoring and refinement at the time of writing this chapter (2014). One of the prime limitations of the approach taken is that there is very little documentation about the system for others to use. It remains subject to the availability of Anna's expertise and interest.

Expert systems

Computerized systems require human expert input. Johnson (1983), Farrington-Darby and Wilson (2006) and Moxley, Ericsson, Charness and Krampe (2012), amongst others, have noted that this expertise can be difficult to capture accurately. Three decades of experience in developing these systems have refined how this domain expertise is captured and operationalized by knowledge engineers (Hjørland and Albrechtsen, 1995; Börner, Chen and Boyack, 2003; Hjørland, 2004).

Expert systems are developed to solve problems in a specialist domain. They are typically comprised of a knowledge base, an inference engine and a user interface. When an expert system is asked to solve a problem, it uses rules in its knowledge base to infer solutions. These rules, derived by human experts, often take the form of IF ... THEN. Feigenbaum (1991) presented an early schematic of the features of an expert system.

There is growing use of expert systems in sport. Some of the examples that can be found in the literature include discussions of: injury (Alonso, Caraça-Valente,

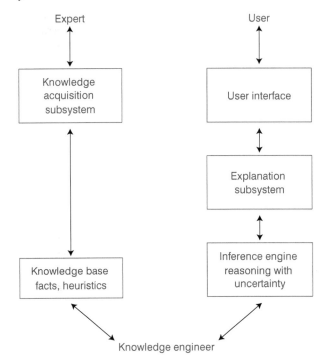

Figure 3.1 Basic structure of an expert system (source: Feigenbaum 1991)

González and Montes, 2002); sport talent detection (Rogulj, Papic and Pleština, 2006; Bottoni, Gianfelici, Tamburri and Faina, 2011; Bazmara and Jafari, 2013; Balli and Korukoğlu, 2014); team sports (Trninić, Jelaska, and Papić, 2009); weight training (Novatchkov and Baca, 2013a); strength training (Novatchkov and Baca, 2013b); cycling (Ofoghi, Zeleznikow, Dwyer and MacMahon, 2013); and goalkeeping in association football (Bazmara, Jafari and Pasand, 2012).

We present an example here to explain how expert systems work in practice. The example we have chosen is from an imagined institute of sport that builds upon the work of Zeleznikow, MacMahon and Barnett (2009) in one of Australia's state institutes of sport, the Victorian Institute of Sport (VIS).

In all institutes of sport, coaches and sport science support staff work to enhance and optimize athlete performance. There are very strong ethical and legal guidelines in place to direct and monitor performance enhancement. These include the World Anti-Doping Agency's (WADA) World Anti-Doping Code and the testing of athletes to monitor their compliance with the Code. Increasingly, institutes of sport have turned to KDD, and artificial intelligence (including expert systems) to provide decision support for short, medium and long-term athlete development. There are growing career prospects in this space for those keen to apply artificial intelligence to sport performance.

In our imagined institute of sport, coaches and sport scientists plan for and deliver training environments that improve athletes' physical, mental, technical and tactical abilities. There is growing interest in this institute in personalizing (individualizing) training protocols. In the last decade, there has been substantial growth in the use of real-time data acquisition technologies. There are now so many types and volumes of data that coaches and social scientists are having difficulty managing and using the data. There is agreement that if the institute can use KDD approaches it will be possible to improve how athletes train and compete.

The Director of our institute made a very important decision seven years ago. She appointed two KDD experts. One had 20 years' experience as a data analyst, with much of this time spent developing protocols for data capture, storage and retrieval. The other was a programmer with 30 years of experience in writing computer code. The Director's decision was bold: neither of the experts had a background in sport and she had to convince others that early adoption of KDD was a competitive advantage for the institute.

Each year, the institute collects a vast amount of data about athletes' performance in training and competition. Expert coaches and sport science support staff use their experience and knowledge to develop athletes' performance whilst they are at the institute. Like Zeleznikow, MacMahon and Barnett (2009), our two KDD experts have worked closely with coaches and support staff to elicit their expert insights in order to build a computerized knowledge base about successful performance.

They have a project to share with you as readers to illustrate their work and highlight the potential of expert systems to support informed decision making in training and competition environments. The project is focused on physiotherapy services to athletes in a daily training environment.

Our two KDD experts noticed that a number of athletes new to the institute found it difficult to manage their volume of training. Some of them became injured in training and needed to work with physiotherapists to regain their fitness. Our two KDD experts thought about how the link between training and treatment might be made much more effective. Their goal was to develop a prospective decision support system to modulate training rather than have a reactive system that reported on injuries that had occurred.

They spent some considerable time with coaches, sport scientists and physiotherapists to map the demands on athletes. They talked with the athletes to get their perspective on this too. From these conversations they were able to:

- acquire detailed training programmes (short, medium and long term);
- identify all use of micro-sensors to gather data from training and competition environments;
- elicit from coaches and sport scientists their understanding of athletes' adaptation to training;
- elicit from physiotherapists their athlete functional movement assessment rubrics, their monitoring procedures and treatment modalities;
- ensure that all data were captured and stored with an agreed, standardized protocol.

Our two KDD experts were mindful of the detailed work on gait undertaken by Lai, Begg and Palaniswami (2009) and of the potential of intelligent interpretation of isokinetic information as discussed by Alonso, Caraça-Valente, González and Montes (2002). The expert system that they produced had:

- a carefully designed, inviting user interface;
- a powerful knowledge base;
- an extensive IF–THEN rule inference engine;
- a recommendation system.

The overall aim of this expert system was to optimize athletes' availability for training and competition. The knowledge base and inference engine were designed to identify any high risks to athlete well-being by monitoring the catabolic effects of exercise. It was anticipated that this system would identify prospective risks to athletes and enable coaches, sport scientists and physiotherapists to manage any potential or actual injury.

A major outcome of their work was the recognition that potential scholarship athletes at the institute should have a pre-arrival preparation phase. The preparation programmes were planned by the institute staff and delivered locally by their coaches and schools. One sport, association football, embraced this opportunity. After two years there was a noticeable decline in the acute onset *osteitis pubis* referrals. A second sport at the institute, volleyball, worked closely with the interdisciplinary KDD team to reduce training days lost to athletes' *patellar tendinitis*.

Elsewhere, KDD teams of researchers and service providers have been extending the expert system approaches used at the imagined institute of sport. Novatchkov and Baca (2013b) have provided a detailed overview of the use of fuzzy logic in sports settings. They note that fuzzy logic 'allows the effective realization of approximate, vague, uncertain, dynamic, continuous and, at the same time, more realistic conditions, which are closer to the actual physical world and human thinking' (2013b: 8). They illustrated their review with a case study of their work in strength training.

The availability of lightweight unobtrusive sensors is making it increasingly possible to collect detailed data about weight training performance by elite and recreational athletes. These data become a rich resource for service providers and researchers keen to extend KDD with fuzzy logic approaches. Youngson (2011) has outlined the steps required to ensure that these sensors provide reliable and valid data.

In our imagined institute, the KDD team is starting to use fuzzy logic approaches to monitor neuromuscular fatigue in training environments (Taylor, 2012). They will build on the work shared by Novatchkov and Baca (2013a; 2013b) and explore the optimum time of the day to train. Taylor, Cronin, Gill, Chapman and Sheppard (2010) have added an extra dimension to work in this area by exploring when it is the best time to measure performance compared to the optimum time to train given athletes' adaptation to diurnal rhythms. The KDD team will have rich data and will use the powerful insights fuzzy logic provides to enhance adaptations to training volume, frequency and intensity. It is interesting to note that these insights have been available to researchers for over 90 years and can be traced back to Jan Łukasiewicz and Alfred Tarski.

Conclusions

This chapter has been written as an introduction to database design and expert systems. It is hoped that the use of examples from a national sporting organization and from an imagined institute of sport has located the use of databases and expert design in a very practical context.

The presence of low cost, high specification sensors and enormous computational resources has transformed the world of sport. Anyone contemplating a vocation in sport should understand how the collection of valid and reliable data is part of a journey to transform how athletes train and compete. The availability of wearable devices for leisure and recreation activity adds further opportunities to understand personal performance.

Disciplined approaches to data collection, storage, interrogation and analysis will be the foundation of this new age of performance understanding.

Study tasks

1   As you work your way through this chapter, please can you give some thought to the level of human involvement in the discovery of knowledge in databases?
2   What are the benefits of having an electronic spreadsheet rather than a paper spreadsheet?
3   What would you do to improve the spreadsheet design used by the canoeing organization?
4   How would you go about designing an Athlete Selection Relational Database for the canoeing organization?
5   Why is it important to document how to use a relational database within a small organization?
6   Does working in a large organization change the need for documentation?
7   Why is it important to personalize data collection and analysis?
8   What are the merits of developing a prospective approach to data analysis? Can you foresee any challenges to such an approach?

Recommended further reading

Bartlett, R. (2006) 'Artificial intelligence in sports biomechanics: New dawn or false hope?', *Journal of Sports Science & Medicine*, 5(4): 474–479.

Schumaker, R.P., Solieman, O.K. and Chen, H. (2010) *Sports Data Mining*, New York: Springer.

Vincent, J., Stergiou, P. and Katz, L. (2009) 'The role of databases in sport science: Current practice and future potential', *International Journal of Computer Science in Sport*, 8(2): 50–66.

References

Alonso, F., Caraça-Valente, J., González, A. and Montes, C. (2002) 'Combining expert knowledge and data mining in a medical diagnosis domain', *Expert Systems with Applications*, 23(4): 367–375.

Baca, A. (2007) 'Computer science in sport – History, research areas and fields of application', Keynote lecture, 6th International Symposium "Computer Science in Sport", Calgary, Canada, 3–6 June 2007.

Balli, S. and Korukoğlu, S. (2014) 'Development of a fuzzy decision support framework for complex multi-attribute decision problems: A case study for the selection of skilful basketball players', *Expert Systems*, 31(1): 56–69.

Bazmara, M. and Jafari, S. (2013) 'K nearest neighbor algorithm for finding soccer talent', *Journal of Basic and Applied Scientific Research*, 3(4): 981–986.

Bazmara, M., Jafari, S. and Pasand, F. (2012) 'A fuzzy expert system for goalkeeper quality recognition', *International Journal of Computer Science Issues*, 9(5): 318–322.

Börner, K., Chen, C. and Boyack, K. (2003) 'Visualizing knowledge domains', *Annual Review of Information Science and Technology*, 37(1): 179–255.

Bottoni, A., Gianfelici, A., Tamburri, R. and Faina, M. (2011) 'Talent selection criteria for Olympic distance triathlon', *Journal of Human Sport & Exercise*, 6(2): 293–304.

Codd, E. (1970), 'A relational model of data for large shared data banks', *Information Retrieval*, 13(6): 377–387.

Codd, E. (1982), 'Relational database: A practical foundation for productivity', *Communications ACM*, 25(2): 109–117.

Farrington-Darby, T. and Wilson, J. (2006) 'The nature of expertise: A review', *Applied Ergonomics*, 37(1): 17–32.

Fayyad, U., Piatetsky-Shapiro, G. and Smyth, P. (1996), 'From data mining to knowledge discovery in databases', *American Association for Artificial Intelligence*, 17(3): 37–54.

Feigenbaum, E. (1991) 'Expert systems: Principles and practice', Report No. KSL 91-97, Stanford, CA: Knowledge Systems Laboratory.

Feigenbaum, E. (1992) 'A personal view of expert systems: Looking back and looking ahead', Report No. KSL 92-41, Stanford, CA: Knowledge Systems Laboratory.

Hjørland, B. (2004) 'Domain analysis in information science', in M. A. Drake (ed.) *Encyclopedia of Library and Information Science*, New York: Marcel Dekker.

Hjørland, B. and Albrechtsen, H. (1995) 'Toward a new horizon in information science: Domain-analysis', *Journal of the American Society for Information Science and Technology*, 46(6): 400–425.

Johnson, P. (1983) 'What kind of expert should a system be?', *Journal of Medicine & Philosophy*, 8(1): 77–97.

Lai, D., Begg, R. and Palaniswami, M. (2009) 'Computational intelligence in gait research: A perspective on current applications and future challenges', *IEEE Transactions on Information Technology in Biomedicine*, 13(5): 687–702.

Less, A. (1985) 'Computers in sport', *Applied Ergonomics*, 16(1): 3–10.

McCarthy, J. (2002) 'What is artificial intelligence?'. Retrieved from <http://bcrc.bio.umass.edu/courses/fall2007/biol/biol270h/3-Discussions/13-ET_Intelligence/13f-AI/13f-1_AI-Intro.pdf> (accessed 3 March 2014).

Moxley, J., Ericsson, K., Charness, N. and Krampe, R. (2012) 'The role of intuition and deliberative thinking in experts' superior tactical decision-making', *Cognition*, 124(1): 72–78.

Novatchkov, H. and Baca, A. (2013a) 'Artificial intelligence in sports on the example of weight training', *Journal of Sports Science & Medicine*, 12(1): 27–37.

Novatchkov, H. and Baca, A. (2013b) 'Fuzzy logic in sports: A review and an illustrative case study in the field of strength training', *International Journal of Computer Applications*, 71(6): 8–14.

Ofoghi, B., Zeleznikow, J., Dwyer, D. and MacMahon, C. (2013) 'Modelling and analysing track cycling Omnium performances using statistical and machine learning techniques', *Journal of Sports Sciences*, 31(9): 954–962.

Perl, J., Lames, M. and Miethling, W. (eds) (1997) *Information technology in sport: a handbook*, Schorndorf: Hofmann.

Rainsford, C. and Roddick, J. (1999) 'Database issues in knowledge discovery and data mining', *Australian Journal of Information Systems*, 6(2): 101–108.

Rogulj, N., Papic, V. and Pleština, V. (2006) 'Development of the expert system for sport talents detection', *WSEAS Transactions on Information Science and Applications*, 3(9): 1752–1755.

Taylor, K. (2012) 'Monitoring neuromuscular fatigue in high performance athletes', doctoral thesis, Edith Cowan University, Perth. Retreived from <http://ro.ecu.edu.au/cgi/viewcontent.cgi?article=1582&context=theses> (accessed 3 March 2014).

Taylor, K., Cronin, J., Gill, N., Chapman, D. and Sheppard, J. (2010) 'Sources of variability in iso-inertial jump assessments', *International Journal of Sports Physiology and Performance*, 5(4): 546–558.

Trninić, S., Jelaska, I., and Papić, V. (2009) 'Kinesiological, anthropological, and methodological aspects of efficacy equation in team sports games', *Acta Kinesiologica*, 3(2): 7–18.

Vines, R. (2011) 'Databases from scratch 1: Introduction'. Retreived from <http://geekgirls.com/2011/09/databases-from-scratch-i-introduction/> (accessed 4 January 2014).

Youngson, J. (2011) 'Reliability and validity of the GymAware optical encoder to measure displacement data'. Retrieved from <http://powertool.gymaware.com/wp-content/uploads/2011/06/GA-Report2.pdf> (accessed 3 March 2014).

Zeleznikow, J., MacMahon, C. and Barnett, T. (2009) 'Providing automated decision support for elite athletes', in *Proceedings of the 7th International Symposium of the International Association of Computer Science in Sport* (pp. 240–248), Canberra, Australia. Bruce, ACT: National Institute of Sport Studies, University of Canberra.

4 Data acquisition and processing

Arnold Baca

Introduction

There are manifold parameters that have been identified to provide relevant information for describing or analysing sports related phenomena. Reaction forces, kinematic and electromyographic quantities play an important role in biomechanics research, position data of players (and ball) enable the assessment of the tactical behaviour in game sports, heart rate, pulmonary parameters and oxygen saturation of blood are investigated in exercise physiology, skin resistance and electroencephalographic parameters are utilized in psychophysiological research. Individual values or time histories of these parameters have therefore to be acquired and further processed.

One particular problem in sports related investigations is often the huge amount of data that has to be collected. This is not only due to a large number of different signals, but, moreover, because of the high sampling frequency, which is required in order to obtain precise and accurate results. To correctly assess maximum impact forces at the take-off for a long jump, for example, force data should be acquired every 0.0005 second (Nolan and Halvorsen, 2007). If a large amount of data is to be transmitted wirelessly, additional problems arise. This is particularly the case in real time applications. Furthermore, environmental conditions (temperature, electromagnetic radiation, mechanical vibrations of the sport equipment, etc.) may negatively affect the quality of the acquired data, making it necessary to (pre-)process them prior to further analysis.

The main principles of data acquisition (DAQ) are introduced within this chapter. Specific emphasis is put on capturing analogue data representing time functions of parameter values such as, for example, force data. Transmission technologies are discussed and compared. Fundamental methods for digital signal processing (e.g. filtering techniques) are addressed.

Definition

Within the process of DAQ, signals correlated to real world physical quantities, such as:

- force, displacement, torque, mass, etc. from the field of mechanics,

- voltage, current, charge, etc. from the field of electronics,
- time, temperature, humidity, etc. from other fields

are obtained by specific sensors, transformed – if required – into another physical dimension (in most cases a voltage) and then converted into a sequence of digital numeric values that can be processed by a computer.

The rest of the chapter is organized as follows: first, an overview of sensor technology relevant for sports specific applications is given. Then aspects of signal sampling are discussed. Wired and wireless data transmission techniques including wireless sensor networks are outlined next. A section on digital signal processing concludes the technical part.

In the practical part of the chapter, the concept of ubiquitous computing as applied to sport is introduced. It is shown how underlying technologies benefit from advances in DAQ systems and their components. Selected applications ranging from devices for just assessing sport performance up to intelligent solutions assisting athletes during exercise complete the chapter.

Sensors

In order to measure any physical quantity, such as force, temperature, light or sound intensity, a sensor is required. Sensors convert input quantities into signals, which can be interpreted by an observer or can be read by an (in most cases) electronic device. Depending on the sensor type different electronic quantities (voltage, current, charge, etc.) are provided as output that changes in time. Some sensors require additional components (e.g. electronic circuits) in order to generate signals, which may be precisely captured by a DAQ device.

Selected sensor types relevant to sports application and their principal functions are described below. For better differentiation, the categorization is related to the corresponding measured physical or physiological quantity.

Time difference

- Differences between two or more points in time can be measured using the following methods: electronic (stopwatch), optic (light barrier), mechanic (starting block).

Distance/velocity

- *Distance*: linear motion can be directly measured using slide potentiometers or magneto-resistive position sensors, both providing a position-dependent change of electric resistance. An indirect measurement option is provided by the cable pull (draw-wire) sensor that converts linear into rotary motion and uses a rotary potentiometer or encoder.
- *Velocity*: the optical rotary encoder creates a sequence of pulses, where the frequency is directly proportional to the velocity of the cable. Cable pulls can be

used underwater, but both their oscillation tendency and their retracting force are sources of measurement errors. A contactless and therefore reactionless option for velocity measurement is the radar gun using the Doppler effect. Measurement reliability decreases with larger angles between the trajectory of the moving object and the laser beam as well as with scattered light from disturbing sources, e.g. other moving objects.

- *Application examples*: cable pulls are used for the determination of the sliding seat position in a rowing boat, pulling velocity of weight training machines or horizontal velocity of racing dives. Radar guns are used for ball velocity measurement as known from the tennis serve.

Angle/angular velocity

- *Angle:* goniometers can be devised using a rotary potentiometer between two arms. The two arms are attached with straps or adhesive tape to adjacent body segments measuring uni-axial joint angles (e.g. Biometrics Ltd., Newport, UK). In addition, angle may be determined by optical or (electro-)mechanical encoders or by using gyroscopes. A gyroscope is a spinning rotor mounted on two perpendicular gimbal rings utilizing the principle of conservation of angular momentum. Magnetic inclinometers make use of the terrestrial magnetic field to measure slope or tilt of surfaces.
- *Angular velocity*: measurement may be based on an optical rotary encoder (see above) or on electric pulses induced by a magnet. Moreover, specific gyroscopes may be applied.
- *Application examples*: determination of crank position in cycling is mostly done using magnetic sensors installed in the crank axle. The bike's speed can be calculated by multiplying wheel circumference by rotary speed, again measured by a magnetic sensor, giving a pulse with each wheel revolution.

Force/pressure

Measurements are primarily performed using strain gages, piezoelectric crystals or capacitive sensors.

- *Strain gage*: fine electric wires are applied onto a foil in a zigzag pattern of parallel lines. A beam or membrane under tension, compression or bending load is deformed. The strain gage must be placed in the direction of deformation. The electric wires are stretched or compressed, increasing or decreasing the electric resistance.
- *Piezoelectric crystal*: the structure of crystal lattice changes when exposed to mechanical stress, leading to a charge separation resulting in an electric potential difference.
- *Capacitive sensor*: The principal of the plate capacitor is used to measure distance changes of plates, as the capacitance alters proportional to

the external force. The space between the two plates is filled with dielectric material, an electric insulator which is polarized by an applied electric field.

- *Application examples*: pulling force in ergometer rowing is measured integrating a strain gage based sensor between the chain and the handle. Force platforms equipped with either strain gage or piezoelectric crystals capture ground reaction forces in gait or running analysis. Pressure distribution underneath the foot can be found using (stationary) platforms or (mobile) insoles composed of a pressure sensor matrix (capacitive sensors).

Acceleration

- *Piezoelectric/semiconductor/capacitive sensors*: a damped spring-mass system is set in motion by an external force. Applying Newton's second law ('The net force acting on a body is directly proportional to, and in the same direction as, the acceleration of the body and proportional to its mass'), the acceleration may be determined. Modern accelerometers are often realized as micro-electro-mechanical systems (MEMS). MEMS are very small devices, which are made using techniques of micro-fabrication.
- *Application examples*: monitoring of daily human physical activity is normally based on multi-axial acceleration sensors with automatic movement pattern recognition and classification. Sensors attached to the subject's shoes provide indirect determination of foot strike loading in running. An application of acceleration sensors in motion analysis can be found in Chapter 5.

Orientation in space (inertial sensors, inertial measurement units)

- *Inertial sensors or inertial measurement units (IMUs)* are used to capture 3D orientation of objects and are based on combinations of accelerometers, gyroscopes and sometimes magnetometers. Rotations about all three axes in space (pitch, yaw and roll) are often calculated inside the sensor circuit using mathematical algorithms.
- *Application examples*: Xsens (Xsens Technologies B.V., Enschede, the Netherlands) offers full-body suits or strap systems with a total of 17 inertial sensors that provide wireless and camera-less 3D kinematics measurements. Such inertial sensors can be used to determine orientation of individual segments in space.

Sound intensity

- Measurements of the sound pressure are primarily performed using a microphone, which transforms pressure into an electric signal. The functional principle of microphones is based on the type of sensor used for measuring pressure. Piezoelectric and condenser microphones (measuring capacitive change; see above) are typical examples.

- *Application example:* in motion analysis, markers emitting ultrasonic sound are applied to the human body to measure the movement. Details are given in Chapter 5.

Biosignals (ECG, EMG, EEG)

- *Skin electrodes* placed at several points on the subject's thorax (electrocardiogram, ECG), at muscle bellies (electromyogram, EMG) or on the head (electroencephalogram, EEG) are used for non-invasive biosignal measurement. The original electric signals created by the sinus node of myocardium (ECG), membrane potential of skeletal muscle cells (EMG) or brain waves (EEG) have very small amplitudes, in the order of microvolts (EMG) to millivolts (ECG, EEG). These signals are derived using bipolar electrodes with integrated amplifier and transducer.

Respiratory gas concentrations

- *Spiroergometry* analyses the amount of oxygen (O_2) and carbon dioxide (CO_2) in the expirate of a subject for calculation of several parameters to determine pulmonary performance, such as maximum oxygen uptake (VO_2max) or respiratory compensation point (RCP). In addition, respiratory minute volume, respiratory frequency and breathing volume are measured. Different technologies are used in spirometers.
- *Application examples*: spiroergometry is used in exhaustion tests on a stationary bike ergometer or treadmill. Besides these tests under laboratory conditions, mobile devices for field testing are available even for swimming.

Respiratory frequency

- Respiration causes repeated expansion of the thorax where the extent and frequency of expansion change with respect to the depth and frequency of respiration. Electroconductive textiles follow the same approach as strain gages. Wires woven into the original tissue are elongated under thorax expansion leading to measurable changes of electric resistance.
- *Application examples*: a common application is the measurement of respiratory frequency in running tasks, where combined heart rate and respiratory straps are used.

Temperature

- *Thermometers* for ambient temperature measurement usually contain liquids or bimetal, while thermal imaging captures infrared radiation of any surface. Temperature sensors make use of temperature dependent material properties to convert temperature (gradient) into measurable electric quantities. Thermistors are semiconductors that have a negative (NTC)/positive temperature coefficient (PTC) and therefore a better conductivity with higher/ lower temperature. Thermocouples consist of two dissimilar metal alloys with a known relationship between junction temperature and output voltage.

- *Application examples*: ambient temperature is often monitored to ensure constant laboratory conditions or in sports with temperature dependent material selection, e.g. ski wax. Thermal imaging provides skin temperature at various positions of the human body surface, while needle thermistor probes are capable of measuring muscle temperature during activity.

Oxygen saturation

- *Pulse oximetry* is a non-invasive method for monitoring oxygen saturation of blood. Infrared light of two different wavelengths created by two light sources on one side of the pulse oximeter is passed through a fingertip or earlobe. Changes in light scattering and absorption depending on the amount of oxygenated haemoglobin are detected by a photo sensor on the other side.
- *Application examples*: pulse oximeters are used in sporting aviation or mountaineering to prevent altitude sickness (hypoxia). The Moxy Monitor (Fortiori Design LLC, Spicer, USA) emits infrared light into muscle tissue and determines local oxygen saturation in the targeted muscle (SmO_2) by detecting scattered light.

With regard to subsequent data processing, two general types of sensor devices can be defined based on their output.

- Sensor devices providing analogue output convert the physical measurement values into proportional electric signals (voltage, charge or current), which subsequently are processed in a measuring chain (amplifier, filter, analogue-to-digital converter; see 'Signal sampling').
- When digital output is provided, signals are created as above, but the whole measuring chain is already integrated in the sensor device and data is output via digital interfaces (e.g. SPI, I²C, UART... see 'Data transmission').

Signal sampling

Time continuous (analogue) signals representing sports related parameters have to be converted into sequences of digital numbers in order to be processed by a computer.

As mentioned in the previous section, analogue-to-digital (A/D) conversion takes place either within the sensor's electronic circuit, or externally. In the latter case, the output from the sensor device is either directly available as a voltage or is converted (e.g. from electric charge) into a voltage. Voltage is then converted to an integer. The signals of interest have to be connected to a DAQ system. A typical setup is shown in Figure 4.1. The central component of a DAQ system is the A/D converter (ADC), which converts a physical quantity, which is usually a voltage, into a digital number. The DAQ system is characterized by the resolution of the

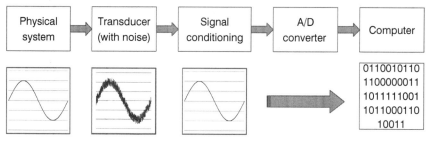

Figure 4.1 Setup for external data acquisition

ADC and the maximum sampling rate it is capable of, if periodical conversions are to be performed.

Resolution

The resolution of the ADC is normally expressed in bits. Typical values are 8, 10, 12 and 16 bits. The number of discrete values available is a power of two. In the case of a resolution of 16 bits, for example, the analogue input can be converted into $2^{16} = 65,536$ different integer values. The values either represent the range from 0 to 65,535 (i.e. unsigned integer) or from –32,768 to 32,767 (i.e. signed integer), depending on the entire measuring range.

For example:

Full measuring range			*Integer range*		
–10V	...	+10V	–32,768	...	+32,767
0V	...	+10V	0	...	+65,535
–5V	...	+5V	–32,768	...	+32,767

The resolution can also be defined electrically, and expressed in volts.

For example:
Measuring range: –10 V ... +10 V; 16 bits ADC. The smallest theoretical change to be detected is 20 V / 65,536 = 305 µV.

Sampling rate

The *sampling rate* or sampling frequency defines the rate at which the analogue signal is converted into a digital value. It should be selected in a way that, on the one hand, no relevant information from the signal gets lost between two consecutive measurements, and, on the other hand, a manageable number of values are processed or stored. Figure 4.2 illustrates the effect of the sampling rate on the reconstruction of a signal to be sampled.

In Figure 4.2 a sampling rate of 25 Hz does not allow the first peak to be reconstructed. The sampling rate 50 Hz already shows that there may be a feature

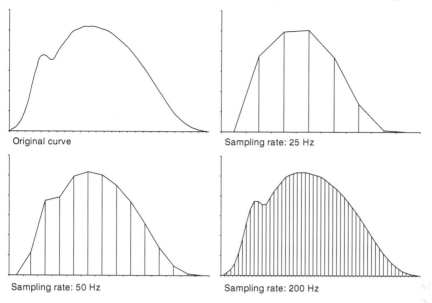

Original curve

Sampling rate: 25 Hz

Sampling rate: 50 Hz

Sampling rate: 200 Hz

Figure 4.2 Effect of sampling rate on signal reconstruction

in the ascending part of the curve. With a sampling rate 200 Hz the peak can be recognized. When applying much higher sample rates, the gain of additional information would be low. The memory space required and the processing time would, however, increase considerably.

Any analogue signal consists of components at various frequencies. In the case of the sine wave, all signal energy is concentrated at a single frequency. In practice, analogue signals usually have complex waveforms, with components at many frequencies. The difference (in Hertz) between the highest and the lowest component in a signal is called *bandwidth*. A full reproduction of the signal is only possible if the sampling rate is more than twice as high as the highest frequency of the signal. This statement summarizes the *Nyquist-Shannon sampling theorem* (Smith, 1997).

A practical example on how to select a sampling rate is illustrated in Figure 4.3: the duration from the maximum to the minimum value is about 0.02 seconds. If five measurements are performed within this time interval, the course of the curve may well be reconstructed. From this, the time interval, Δt, between two measurement can be calculated as $\Delta t = 0.02 \ / \ 5 \ \text{s} = 0.004 \ \text{s}$. This corresponds to 250 samples per second or 15,000 digital numbers per minute.

Aliasing

Aliasing is an effect that is observed when a signal is imperfectly reconstructed from the sampled data. It occurs when the sampling rate is not sufficiently high

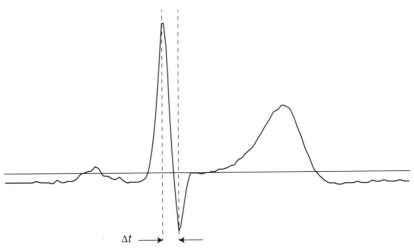

Figure 4.3 ECG (electrocardiogram) signal. $\Delta t = 0.02$ s

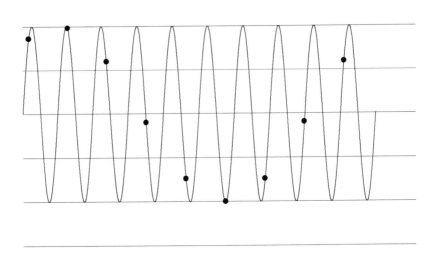

Figure 4.4 Aliasing

enough to create an accurate representation. This effect is demonstrated in the example of a sinusoidal function in Figure 4.4.

A number of techniques exist to combat the problems of aliasing in a sampled signal. Low pass filters (see 'Digital signal processing') are commonly used for this purpose.

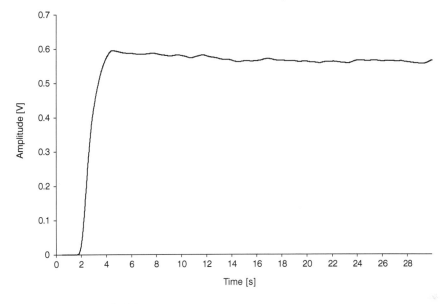

Figure 4.5 Course of a joint torque

Synchrony

In a majority of studies the courses of more than one signal are of interest. In these cases, more than one signal must be sampled. In many setups incorporating external DAQ devices, only one ADC is available, which cannot perform multiple conversions in parallel. In order to enable synchronized measurements, many ADC integrated circuits include a subsystem called the *Simultaneous Sample and Hold*. Capacitors store the analogue voltages at the input at the same instants of time. These simultaneous captured voltages are then sequentially A/D converted.

Exercise examples

Example 1

A typical course of a joint torque (in volts) is shown in Figure 4.5. A DAQ system comprising a 16 bit ADC is available for data acquisition. Three different full measuring ranges may be selected: −10 V ... +10 V; −5 V ... +5 V; 0 V ... +10 V. In addition, the signal may be amplified by a selectable factor (1, 10, 100 or 500) prior to sampling.

a. Select an appropriate full measuring range and amplification factor. Justify your choice.
b. What voltage would then produce an integer value of 2,000 after conversion?
c. Select an appropriate sampling rate. Note that the goal of the study is to reliably estimate the (approximate) maximum.

d. Discuss possible limitations if not only the torque, but, moreover, the EMG signals of two muscles are acquired synchronously.

Solution 1

a. In order to be able to minimize the differences, the amplification factor should be 10 and the full measuring range 0 V ... +10 V.
b. An input value of 10 V corresponds to an integer value of 65,535 ($2^{16} - 1$). Since the signal is amplified by a factor of 10, a measured value of 1 V corresponds to 65,535. If x is the unknown voltage, then the following condition holds: 1: 65,535 = x : 2,000. Hence, x is 2,000 divided by 65,535, i.e. 0.0305 V.
c. Assuming that there are no fluctuations in the signal, 100 Hz should be appropriate. (Note that e.g. 1,000 Hz will not result in a huge amount of data to be processed or stored either and could also be used.)
d. For analysing the EMG data, a higher sample rate might be required. In order to obtain full synchronicity, the DAQ system should, for example, support *Simultaneous Sample and Hold*.

Example 2

A typical output signal of a vibration sensor attached to a tennis raquet is shown in Figure 4.6. It may be used to investigate the vibration properties of the raquet.

A DAQ system comprising a 12 bit ADC is available for data acquisition. Three different full measuring ranges may be selected: –10 V ... +10 V; –5 V ... +5 V;

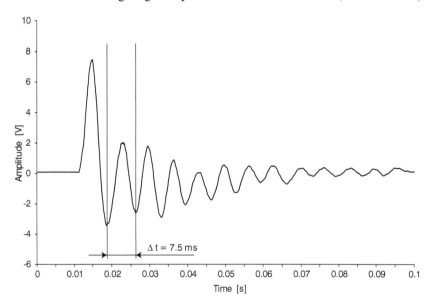

Figure 4.6 Signal from a vibration sensor attached to a tennis raquet

0 V ... +10 V. In addition, the signal may be amplified by a factor of 1, 10, 100 or 500 before being sampled.

a. Select an appropriate full measuring range and amplification factor. Justify your choice.
b. Estimate the maximum integer value when applying the selected setup for the acquisition of the depicted signal.
c. Provide the criteria for selecting the sampling rate.

Solution 2

a. The maximum absolute value of the signal is about 7.5 V. In order to best be able to identify small differences, the amplification factor should be 1 and the full measuring range –10 V ... +10 V.
b. An input value of 10 V to the ADC corresponds to an integer value of 2,047. Since the signal is amplified by a factor 1, a measured value of 1 V corresponds to the nearest integer value to 2,047 / 10, which is 205. Hence, 7 V corresponds to the nearest integer value to 7 × 2,047 / 10, which is 1,433.
c. If just the curve shape is of interest, 15 values in 7.5 ms might be appropriate. This would correspond to 1 value every 0.5 ms and a sampling rate of 2,000 Hz. If a frequency analysis is to be performed, than the sample rate should be selected considering the Nyquist-Shannon sampling theorem. In practice, this would mean that the sampling frequency would have to be at least twice the highest frequency component of the signal.

Example 3

A force plate is used to analyse the jumping power of figure skaters. Voltages proportional to the vertical ground reaction forces are thus obtained. The voltages range from 0 to 0.6 V.

A DAQ system comprising a 16 bit ADC is available for data acquisition. Three different full measuring ranges may be selected: –10 V ... +10 V; –5 V ... +5 V; 0 V ... +10 V. The signal may be amplified by a selectable factor (1, 10, 100 or 500) before being sampled.

a. Select an appropriate full measuring range and amplification factor. Justify your choice.
b. Estimate the maximum resulting voltage value when applying the selected setup.
c. Discuss possible limitations if not only the vertical force, but, moreover, the (two) horizontal forces are acquired synchronously.
d. Discuss the advantage of the DAQ system compared to one equipped with a 12 bit ADC.

Solution 3

a.   In order to best be able to make out small differences, the amplification factor should be 10 and the full measuring range 0 V ... +10 V.

b.   The measured signal is amplified by 10, resulting in an input value of 6 V to the ADC. An input voltage of 10 V corresponds to an integer value of 65,535 ($2^{16} - 1$). Hence, the correct result is the nearest integer value to 6 × 65,535 / 10, which is 39,321.

c.   In order to obtain full synchrony, the DAQ system should, for example, support *Simultaneous Sample and Hold*.

d.   Small differences in the input signal may be better detected.

Manufacturers of DAQ systems

The following companies offer a wide range of products for applications related to data acquisition, measurement, testing and control:

• National Instruments Corporation (Austin, Texas, USA): www.ni.com
• Keithley Instruments, Inc. (Cleveland, Ohio, USA): www.keithley.com
• Data Translation, Inc. (Marlboro, Massachusetts, USA): www.datx.com

Excursus: programming DAQ systems

As an example, LabVIEW® (short for Laboratory Virtual Instrument Engineering Workbench) from National Instruments (Austin, Texas, USA) is briefly introduced. LabVIEW® is a development environment for a visual programming language.

The graphical approach allows non-programmers to build programs by dragging and dropping virtual representations of lab equipment. Each program consists of front panel (user interface) and block diagram (graphical source code).

An example showing both front panel and block diagram is depicted in Figure 4.12 later in this chapter.

Data transmission

Data transmission is the process of data transfer in point-to-point or point-to-multipoint communication networks using either connection wires or wireless technologies. Data are represented as electromagnetic signals or digital bit streams, created by the host and uni-directionally received by one or more slave(s). The host and slave roles can also be re-assigned for bi-directional communication.

The communication network can be organized in different topologies, related mainly to the number of devices and number of connections between them (see Figure 4.7).

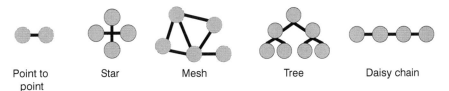

Figure 4.7 Network topologies: point to point, star, mesh, tree, daisy chain

Interfaces based on wired connections

Serial communication

This type of communication is characterized by sending and receiving data one bit at a time.

RS-232 (UART)

The RS-232 standard was developed in the 1960s and was used widely until the 1990s. Consecutive 8 bit (= 1 byte) data packets are sent asynchronously. A Universal Asynchronous Receiver Transmitter (UART) microchip is needed for parallel–serial or serial–parallel conversion when sending or receiving bytes (= parallel) as a sequence of bits (= serial). The achievable baud rate decreases with cable length (caused by line losses). As a consequence, the maximum distance for a point-to-point connection is limited to a few hundred metres. Only point-to-point connections are possible. Aside from computer modems, individual sensors and other laboratory devices were also connected via RS-232.

UNIVERSAL SERIAL BUS (USB)

The USB, an advancement of the RS-232 serial bus with further features like hot-plug functionality (meaning that units can be connected or disconnected at any time), is one of the most popular interfaces today. It enables high-speed data transfer and an enormous number of possible connections using USB hubs with one host and several slaves in a star topology. The first widely adopted revision (USB 1.1) was released in 1998 (data rates up to 12 Mbit/s) followed up by a newer version (USB 2.0) in 2000, which is still the most common release. It not only supports higher data rates (up to 480 Mbit/s) but also an increased cable length (5 m) allowing more flexibility in outdoor applications (e.g. more distance between sensor device and computer). USB 3.0 (released 2008) represents the latest and fastest modification of this serial bus and is fully backward compatible to preceding USB devices (2.0 and 1.x).

One big improvement compared to the classic serial bus (RS-232) is the use of so called 'device classes' in order to identify different types of slave devices, categorized by their functionality. For the development of sports specific sensors, the 'Personal Healthcare' device class is of particular interest. By exchanging device class information, computers and smart devices can automatically select the correct drivers after connecting a slave device into the USB port and ensure functionality without a need for human intervention. Since many electronic products are designed for 5 V power supply, USB ports may also be used for charging the batteries of such devices.

The USB interface is commonly used for DAQ devices, wired sensor devices (various measurement systems), wireless adapters (WLAN, Bluetooth®, ANT) and it can be expected that the overall number of available USB devices will increase in future.

IEEE 1394 (FIREWIRE)

Comparable to and in competition with the USB, the IEEE 1394 standard was developed by Apple Inc. (Cupertino, California, USA) in the late 1980s and called FireWire. It is also known as i.LINK (Sony Europe Ltd, Weybridge, UK), and Lynx (Texas Instruments Inc., Dallas, USA). Deep market penetration was achieved through the digital video (DV) camcorders and high-speed cameras. FireWire enables direct communication among all devices without a host (peer to peer), with a maximum of 63 devices and a maximum of 3,200 Mbit/s. Cable length is limited to 4.5 m, although up to 16 cables can be combined in a daisy chain. Its importance will decrease in the future, as USB 3.0 has already outstripped FireWire due to its higher data transmission rate.

I²C/SPI

Both the Inter-Integrated Circuit (I²C) and the Serial Peripheral Interface (SPI) are simple 'low-level' interfaces. The common principle is to manage bi-directional communication with only two (I²C) or three wires (SPI) aside from supply and ground. Both interfaces are mainly used for communication between microcontrollers and (several) sensors as a high data rate can only be achieved with a short cable length. The I²C/SPI bus is organized in tree or daisy chain topology. With the increasing use of MEMS (see 'Sensors'), it can be expected to gain importance in sensor networks.

Network communication

ETHERNET (LAN)

Ethernet is basically a Local Area Network (LAN) connection among PCs and connected devices such as printers or servers. The data rate has constantly increased up to 100 Gigabit/s (2014) and cable length is no longer limited to one building as optical fibre links allow ranges of up to 10 km. The classic point-to-point topology can be extended to star, tree or mesh topologies using additional hardware devices (routers, switches). Ethernet is today's number one standard for computer networks with an unrivalled market position. One big edge is the use of Network Attached Storage (NAS), providing high storage capacity together with easy access.

GIGE VISION (LAN)

GigE Vision is a specific open standard of Gigabit LAN for video processing devices. Video cameras with high resolution and recording frequency can be connected. Data transfer is not only as fast as 1,000 Mbit/s, but also covers 100 m in distance. Therefore, entire stadiums can be wired with widespread infrastructure to display results in near real time. Applications for such purposes are Simi Motion (Simi Reality Motion Systems GmbH, Unterschleißheim, Germany) for motion analysis or VIS.TRACK (Deltatre AG, Ismanning, Germany) for match analysis.

Interfaces based on wireless connections

Wireless LAN (WLAN, Wi-Fi)

A Wireless Local Area Network (WLAN) enables any client equipped with a wireless network interface controller (WNIC) to be connected anywhere within the range of an access point (hotspot). The term Wi-Fi refers to a specific WLAN standard, but it is often used as a synonym for wireless interfaces in general. Currently, not only desktops and workstations have WNICs, but also smart devices, microcontrollers and sensors. WLANs operate in the 2.4 GHz or 5 GHz radio frequency band, which both are divided into a multitude of channels and have country-specific regulations. Stability, data rate and – in particular – range are better outdoors (100 m) than indoors (35 m) due to signal distortion and damping when passing through walls (e.g. those made of reinforced concrete). Another disadvantage is the fairly high power consumption compared to other wireless interfaces. Wi-Fi allows ad hoc communication without an access point intermediary and is used in many consumer electronics applications and Wireless Sensor Networks (WSN, see below).

Bluetooth®

Bluetooth® is a standard for short distance communication among devices operating in the 2.4 GHz band. The latest version, 4.0, called Bluetooth® Smart or Bluetooth® Low Energy (BLE), eliminates former disadvantages concerning power consumption and data rate. Ranges are comparable to WLAN interfaces (Class 1 devices with the most powerful transmitter). Supported topologies are point to point, star or star-bus (a combination of a star topology superimposed on a backbone bus topology – only BLE). Even though Bluetooth® is restricted by patent and licence issues, it is a widespread and still emerging standard. Timekeeping, heart rate and inertial sensor measurements may be transferred via Bluetooth® communication.

ANT

The ANT protocol was developed by Dynastreams Innovations Inc. (Cochrane, Canada) and operates at 2.4 GHz radio frequency just like the standards mentioned above. ANT+ is the add-on for interoperability promoted by the ANT+ alliance with more than 300 members (2014). The ANT hardware consists of a radio frequency transceiver with a fully embedded ANT protocol and algorithms for efficient data transmission enabling ultra-low power operation. It remains in sleep mode most of the time, so it has very low overall power consumption leading to longer battery life. Compared to other short distance wireless standards, it has a rather low data rate of 1 Mbit/s. Channels are bi-directional, and in addition to point-to-point topology, star, tree and mesh communication structures are supported. Many manufacturers use ANT for collection and transfer of sensor data in fitness, healthcare and well-being applications (heart rate monitors, weight scales, pedometers …).

ZigBee

ZigBee is a low-power, low-cost technology for point-to-point, star, tree or mesh communication structures. It is more sensitive to interference from other wireless technologies using the same 2.4 GHz band as it has no frequency hopping (a technique avoiding data collision as is used by Bluetooth® and ANT). In addition, the data rate is much lower than provided by ANT and a central coordinator node is needed. Applications range from industry to sports and healthcare data collection.

Proprietary protocols

Proprietary protocols are manufacturer-specific and therefore incompatible with products by other manufacturers. Design and structure are not published. Yet there are still sports applications running on such proprietary protocols, e.g. most of the Polar® heart rate straps (Polar Electro Oy, Kempele, Finland), the Kéo pedal power measurement system (Look, Nevers, France) or the Trigno™ Wireless System (Delsys®, Natick, MA, USA) for surface EMG data transmission.

Wireless sensor networks (WSN)

Wireless Sensor Networks consist of spatially distributed autonomous sensor nodes, which cooperatively monitor various signals from the environment, (pre-) process the data and exchange them with other sensor nodes. Each sensor node in a sensor network typically consists of one or more sensors, a microcontroller, a communication unit for wireless data exchange and an internal power supply (Akyildiz, Su, Sankarasubramaniam and Cayirci, 2001).

Since sensor nodes are capable of exchanging data in an ad hoc network, sensors do not necessarily have to be in the receiving range of a fixed installed sensor node. Data can also be transmitted via intermediate nodes, so-called hops (e.g. sensor nodes attached to another athlete). In order to store and manage this incidental amount of fragmented data, complex methods, such as, for example, distributed database architectures (e.g. Roantree, Whelan, Shi and Moyna, 2009) may be required.

Systems set up from sensors (Body Sensor Units, BSU) and a central processing unit with a communication device (Body Central Unit, BCU) capturing and transmitting parameter values from the human body are commonly named (Wireless) Body Area Networks (W)(BAN) or Body Sensor Networks (BSN) (Guang-Zhong, 2006). BCU can be integrated into a WSN, BSU into sensor nodes.

The possibility of miniaturizing sensor nodes and BSU makes them perfectly suitable for acquisition of (biophysical, physiological, etc.) parameter values during regular sports activities without affecting the performance of the athlete.

Established industry standards for communication protocols that are used for WSN in sport and sport science are, amongst others, ZigBee, ANT and Bluetooth®. Recent developments – in addition to its energy efficiency – give reason to expect that ANT will become an important standard for sensor applications in sport. Kusserow, Amft and Tröster (2009, 2013), for example, use a system for the recognition of daily activities based on accelerometers having been extended to sensor nodes by means of a microprocessor and a communication unit based on the ANT protocol. Despite continuously transmitting accelerometer data (32 Hz), the operating time of these nodes is almost 5 days, when a battery is supplied.

Many commonly used devices (heart rate monitors, speed sensors, Global Positioning System (GPS) devices, etc.) use ANT protocol-based ANT+ functions and are therefore compatible with each other.

Digital signal processing

Digital signal processing (DSP) is the process of modifying a digital signal to adjust, revise or improve its fidelity.

Data acquired and/or transmitted in digital form need to be processed before being used for further interpretation. In the following section, some of the main stages in digital signal processing are described and typical application examples provided.

Signal operations

Amplitude scaling/linearization

Measured data typically need to be scaled, e.g. from volt to newton by applying a simple multiplication factor. In addition, an offset correction (addition/subtraction) may be required. This simple procedure presupposes that the sensor output is completely linear in respect to the physical values.

Depending on the sensor, output signals sometimes need, however, to be linearized (because of the non-linear behaviour of the transducer). In order to do so, several single point measurements are required. From these, a mathematical function is constructed for correcting the non-linear data.

The entire process involving all these procedures is also known as calibration. An example involving offset correction and scaling is presented in Figure 4.8.

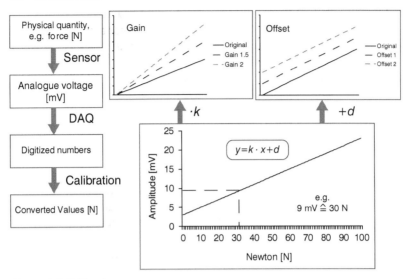

Figure 4.8 Calibration

Time shifting, up-/down-sampling

When synchronizing different measurement systems (e.g. a video camera and a force measuring system), electrical control signals are used for triggering the beginning and/or the end of a DAQ process. Alternatively, specific events may be used for synchronizing different data streams. For example, by hitting a force platform with a wooden stick and simultaneously capturing the video data, the synchronization can be realized through a time alignment of the two data sets to that event.

Such time shift operations do not modify any signal values but enable the correction of time offsets among different signals.

A more complex operation in the time domain involves the modification of the time steps, which may be necessary for the combination of signals recorded with different sampling rates (e.g. two isolated systems like an EMG device and gyroscopes in a smartphone). The easiest way to increase the sampling rate (up-sampling) is to use linear interpolation between the several instants of time in order to obtain additional data points in-between. Decreasing (down-sampling) can be achieved, for example, by interpreting only every second data point to halve the sampling rate.

Normalization (amplitude/time)

Signal values may be scaled with respect to a predefined level such as the absolute maximum. Thus, different athletes may, for example, be better compared to each other. In a running analysis, ground reaction forces are typically scaled by the individual body weight.

If reasonable, like in motion analysis of cyclic sports movements (e.g. cycling, rowing), predefined events in the time structure of the motion may be used to divide the motion capture into separate cycles. Normalization by cycle length then means to stretch or compress the acquired data sequence to a common length (e.g. 100 data points for one movement cycle). This allows a direct comparison of results by different subjects or under different conditions (speeds, intensities).

Fourier transform

Signals are often given as an amplitude function over time. Another possibility is the presentation of the corresponding signal components in the frequency domain. Signal filtering operations may then be applied on selected frequency ranges (= frequency bands). The fast Fourier transform (FFT) is a mathematical algorithm used to perform this signal transformation on finite discrete signals (= time series of data points with a finite length). For a better understanding, some examples of different signal waveforms and their corresponding frequency components are shown in Figure 4.9.

The frequency spectrum shows the frequency content of the signal waveform. It is normally composed of particular frequencies with high amplitudes (first and higher harmonics) or rather evenly distributed (signal noise). In neuromuscular studies for instance, EMG signals representing the muscle activation are often interpreted by focusing on specific changes in their frequency behaviour (e.g.

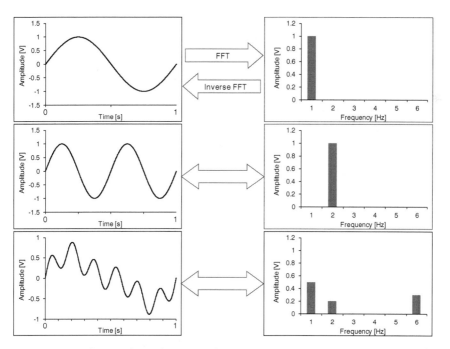

Figure 4.9 Fourier transform: time versus frequency domain (examples)

fatigue index parameter based on median frequency). The FFT analysis also enables researchers to investigate the damping behaviour and resonant frequency of specific sports equipment (e.g. tennis raquet, alpine skis) during impact scenarios.

Filtering techniques

Captured data is quite commonly interfered by artefacts, which may cause problems in the further interpretation. Different filter types (analogue and digital) are used to overcome this disturbing factor. In sports related studies, many measurement methods need to comprise such filtering for the acquired signals (e.g. EMG, kinematics, dynamics). Signal components within a frequency band, where artefacts or noise occur, have to be suppressed whilst the main signal amplitude has to remain unchanged. For the design of filters, one main characteristic is the so called cut-off frequency that defines the boundary of the beginning/ending of the attenuation. Different types are presented in Figure 4.10. In a low-pass filter, for example, lower frequency components of the signal pass, whereas components higher than the cut-off frequency are attenuated.

Analogue filters are electronic circuits, which are often integrated into signal amplifiers. These filters are applied on the electrical signals before they are digitized with ADCs. Their filter properties can be adjusted by varying the values of the used components in the electronic circuits (e.g. resistors, capacitors, inductors).

Alternatively, digital filtering of already sampled signals is used for removing artefacts or emphasizing specific features of keen interest. Digital filters may be implemented within software routines (e.g. as described in Chapter 5 for motion analysis software) using a broad range of mathematical algorithms and functions which can be easily adapted to the specific needs. Due to the enormous computational power of modern processors (e.g. single-board computers, smartphones, tablets), it is also possible to apply filtering in real time prior to data being transmitted.

It is sometimes practical to record unfiltered signals as filtering is then performed offline in order to evaluate different settings for filter parameters and hence find the optimal filter configuration.

Practical examples illustrating the application of filtering in sports related problems are given in Table 4.1.

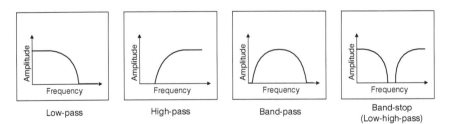

Figure 4.10 General filter types (low-pass, high-pass, band-pass, band-stop)

Table 4.1 Practical application examples of filtering

Application	Task/problem	Filter type	Low cut-off	High cut-off
Analysis of the acceleration of a bicycle frame	Detection of surface irregularities on the trail and automatic adjustment of the shock absorber	high pass	about 20Hz	–
	Overlaid motion of the pedalling movement (low frequency)			
Electromyographic measurements during running on a treadmill	Analysis of the muscle activation pattern	band pass	40Hz	5kHz
	Overlaid artefacts based on skin movements (low frequency), electromagnetic distortions from environment in the lab (high frequency)			
Pulling force measurements in team rowing (on water)	Investigation of the synchronization between team members	low pass	–	100 Hz
	Mechanical vibrations of the boat and other equipment produce interferences in the signal (high frequency)			

Ubiquitous computing

Developments in computer hardware and software have led to powerful small-sized sensors, microprocessors and wireless communication devices. Small, interconnected technological devices may be integrated in everyday life without even making people aware of their presence. The term pervasive computing or, alternatively, ubiquitous computing describes this evolution and propagation of information processing in the human environment (see Chapter 2).

Like most areas of everyday life, these pervasive or ubiquitous computing technologies also penetrate the field of sport. Here, they provide a means for developing systems to acquire, process and transmit data during various sport activities.

Without affecting athletes, various performance data are recorded during training and competition and transmitted to remote stations (the notebook of a coach, a broadcasting station, etc.) in almost real time.

Automated tracking systems are used for estimating the positions and velocities of athletes, forming the basis for calculating run distances and determining running intensities or for performing tactical analysis.

Sport and physical activity is analysed based on multiple signals, such as heart rate, heat, force (touch) or respiration. Smart textiles (also e-textiles) provide an excellent means for sensing these signals. Digital components are integrated into specific fabrics. Knitted stretch sensors being part of electroconductive textiles (see above) may, on the one hand, be used to measure respiration frequency, but on the other hand also to identify specific types of motion, such as gestures.

One particular challenge in sports related real time applications is how to communicate the relevant information to the athlete. Recent developments in head mounted displays seem to provide promising new means. SmartGoggles (Sensics, Columbia, Maryland, USA), for example, are proprietary spectacles that extend vision by displaying information or images on the inside surface of the lens. Information provided by sensors may thus be directly shown to athletes, as already done by the Airwave™ (Oakley, Orange County, California, USA) goggles for skiing and snowboarding.

Five fields of application will be distinguished below and illustrated with typical examples. Coaching and training is considered first, introducing the concept of *remote coaching*. The potential of wireless tracking methods is outlined on the example of ball tracking. Third, systems for decision making are discussed. They include systems for supervising rules and regulations in order to support judges. Applications for leisure and health promotion are considered next. Finally, applications related to social networking are discussed.

Coaching and training systems

Tools and methods from computer science may assist coaches in all stages of coaching – during preparation for a competition, during a competition and after a competition. Real time performance monitoring systems are particularly useful during training and competition because of the immediate availability of the results. It is observed that such systems are becoming ubiquitous in sports. In addition to supporting coaches and athletes they are also applied in order to produce spectacular presentations for media companies (Lames, 2008).

In order to transmit performance relevant information such as position, reaction force or heart rate data, wireless technologies are increasingly applied. The combination of miniaturized technological devices and wireless technologies ensures that athletes are not disturbed during sports activities. They are able to exercise under ecologically valid conditions.

Collins and Anderson (2004), for example, report on a system for monitoring performance data in rowing. A palmtop computer with in-built WLAN capabilities and a DAQ board within an expansion box are coupled. The mobile device captures the data from sensors mounted on the rowing boat and transmits them to the notebook of the coach, who may provide immediate feedback. Kornfeind (2006) proposed a similar system applicable in on-water (boat) and off-water (rowing machine) conditions. A mobile measurement setup collects biomechanical data (forces, acceleration, angles, boat speed) from several sensors. The measurement data are transmitted to a laptop over a WLAN connection. In a typical practical use the coach gets a live view of the forces (e.g. pulling force) produced by the rower.

Baca and Kornfeind (2007) have generalized this principle to different sports and suggest a remote coaching system, which will be described in more detail later ('Sports applications', Example 3).

Their complete system enables coaches and experts to give rapid feedback to athletes during training ('online training sessions') from any remote location having Internet access. Athletes can easily compare their performance with others or relate it to norm profiles during exercising. Information exchange between athletes is facilitated. Figure 4.11 describes an application scenario for rowing.

Tracking systems

Data characterizing individual performance are frequently obtained by observing the athletes' motion and/or that of their sports equipment. Kinematic information describing the motion of the centre of mass and the change of the body configuration of athletes in time is important for biomechanical analyses; information on the change of positions of players in time are required for individual notational analyses and tactics analyses in game sports.

Sophisticated algorithms from computer vision enable not only the capture of the kinematics of an individual athlete's motion without the use of markers (Moeslund, Hilton and Krüger, 2006), but also the capture of the patterns of a group of players in game sports simultaneously (Lames, 2008).

Alternatively, GPS receivers calculate their own position using the signals received from at least four GPS satellites applying triangulation algorithms. Higher accuracy is obtained by additional technology, such as is the case in Differential GPS (DGPS) systems (e.g. Larsson, 2003).

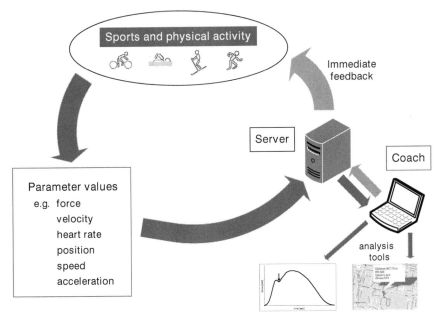

Figure 4.11 Application of a remote coaching system. During the training session, selected parameter values (force, velocity, heart rate, ...) are collected and transmitted to the server; experts analyse the curves online and their advice enables the coach to direct the rowing technique in the desired direction

Systems following a similar principle require that athletes are equipped with (small, light-weight) signal transmitting devices (tags). Their application is restricted to a local bounded three-dimensional area. The computation of the position is not done within the object to be tracked, but in a central control unit based on the measurement of the different times an electromagnetic wave emitted from the tag reaches a number of receivers. It is thereby possible to refer to any object and to estimate its specific position in real time. This procedure is done simultaneously for all tags and repeated continuously. All objects are thus tracked three-dimensionally. The environment under investigation has to be surrounded by receiver stations, which receive the signals emitted from the tags. More details on all these technologies are given in Chapter 5, in the section 'Player tracking systems'.

One particular challenge in the application of tracking systems in team sports is ball tracking. Holthouse (2012) summarizes the problems to be solved. In particular, sensor electronics have to withstand high impacts and to be light weight in order not to affect ball properties. A solution based on a small electronic beacon that mounts inside the bladder of footballs is also presented. The SmartBall technology (Catapult, Melbourne, Australia) uses tracking units attached to the athletes, which are able to detect this beacon within a specified range and send the respective information in real time to a computer on the sidelines. Thus, who has the ball and pass chains can be determined, and ball velocities in passes as well as other parameter values may be estimated.

Decision making systems

One particular aspect of technology in sports is to aid judges in their decisions. The Hawk-Eye system (Hawk-Eye Innovations Ltd., Winchester, UK), for example, is fully integrated in cricket and tennis, in order to accurately decide if the ball is inside or outside the court. Chi (2005, 2008) reports on a system used in tae kwon do competitions. Piezoelectric force sensors are inserted into the body protectors worn by the athletes. They sense the amount of force that has been exerted to a competitor's body protector. The signal is then transmitted to a computer, which indicates the points made. Judges are thus assisted in deciding whether a hit was a scoring point or not.

Leisure and health promotion systems

Systems for measuring activities in sport are not only applicable in elite sport, but also to a growing extent to sports activities in leisure time and for entertainment. Through integrating computer and communication technologies into 'smart' sports equipment, enhanced functionality can be achieved. Stevens et al. (2006) propose concepts for ubiquitous fitness support and identify three different needs for assistance to be addressed: motivation, care-taking and advice. Intelligent fitness devices, for example, could take care of the user by self-adapting to the user's needs, thereby protecting them from conducting exercises in a way that may injure their bodies.

Chi (2008) distinguishes between two variants of making use of pervasive computing technologies in sports entertainment: sports computer games and on-screen displays of performance data in the broadcasting of sports events.

Sports computer games, e.g. Nintendo®'s Wii™ (Nintendo Co., Ltd., Kyoto, Japan) or Microsoft®'s Xbox®Kinect® (Microsoft Corporation, Redmond, WA, USA) are widespread. One main intention is to motivate people to become more active with a rather entertaining background. Games controlled by the players' motion have gained wide popularity. Motion patterns are captured using sensors and (wireless) signal transmitting devices attached to the players' body segments and/or depth cameras measuring the time of flight of a light signal between the camera and the subject for each point of the image. Comparative investigations of four different types of videogames indicate that, in general, there is a significant increase in energy expenditure (Lyons et al., 2011), with fitness and dance games having the biggest impact. *Exergaming* (combining the words exercise and gaming) or serious gaming offers new options for training in sport, even though sustainability is a critical factor (Wiemeyer, 2010; Chapter 8).

Performance data collected can be used by sports broadcasts to help illustrate informative segments. Ski jumping contests are, for example, illustrated by fading in heart rate data from the jumpers, marathon races by showing the position of the runner on a map of the course, table tennis matches by visualizing the impact positions of the ball on the table (Baca and Kornfeind, 2006).

Specially adapted sensor and wireless communication networks are used in preventative and rehabilitative sports. Feedback methods in therapy are provided by solutions like the 'Therapy Top' (Kranz et al., 2011). Users perform movements on custom-built balance boards, which are visualized in order to enable the evaluation and control of the motion. Developments of that kind can be very effective and, moreover, represent a low-cost intervention alternative for health promotion and rehabilitation.

Social networking

Another upcoming field of application in the area of pervasive computing in sport refers to the emerging social networking services (SNS), usually representing a website with multiple users who can publish and share their interests, impressions, feelings, emotions, opinions etc. between each other based on video clips (Novatchkov and Baca, submitted). Sports related lifeloggers, for example, not only record their daily actions (e.g. during extreme sports like skydiving, ski mountaineering or bike dirt jumping) at any place and time but also are able to post them on the Internet, in this way sharing their extraordinary moments, events, situations and excitement online with others. One specific approach focuses on the sharing of real world data regarding the snow conditions of different routes by the development of a recommender system on the basis of trust propagation (Avesani et al., 2005).

Résumé

Sport is an extremely exciting field to apply pervasive computing technologies (Chi, 2008). These technologies do not only provide innovative and effective support to coaches and elite athletes, but are also applicable in mass sport, in health sport and to referees. Moreover, they are utilized by spectators watching broadcasts and by players practising virtual games. Information and communication technologies are to become more and more pervasive in sports. Rapid technological developments (reduction in size, increased power) will result in applications that, at present, can hardly be foreseen.

It should, however, always be kept in mind that they also have the potential to change the characteristics of sports. A soccer game with an electronic error-free referee may serve as an example.

Sports applications

Powerful DAQ components together with high resolution ADCs allowing high sampling frequencies enhance the execution of measurement tasks in sports applications. Various sensor signals may be sampled periodically and measurements of different signals may be synchronized with each other (e.g.

dynamometrically captured joint torques and electromyograms of several muscles in biomechanical analyses) or with video captures. Numerous applications can be found in literature. Biofeedback systems, for example, permit the sampling of physiological parameters like heart rate, respiratory rate and amplitude, skin temperature, electromyographic activities, electroencephalographical activity, blood pressure and skin conductance. The instantaneous presentation of the measured parameters in audio-visual form shows the subject to what extent mental influences change these parameters. Many measurement devices deliver these data already digitized and can thus be linked to the interface of a computer (e.g. heart rate monitors). Applications are, for example, given by Paul and Garg (2012) and Ekblom and Eriksson (2012).

Computer aided DAQ provides valuable support in performance and talent diagnostic surveys, as shown in publications like Witte et al. (2007) on karate and Graumnitz (2011) on competitive swimming.

Nevertheless, the possibility of trouble-free DAQ should not induce its aimless use. Even without a well-defined research design, statistically significant differences between subject groups can be easily found for several parameters, but one should not draw immediate conclusions from these results. It might be an interesting result that the time function of a measured parameter shows a statistically significant difference between beginners and advanced learners. Yet it remains practically irrelevant without further consideration of possible reasons and explanations. Caution must be exercised when deriving results, which are only an estimate based on measured values, as they can be imprecise and defective.

Three examples of applications are presented below.

Example 1: analysis of bi-legged jump performance

The subject stands on a force plate and, after hearing an acoustic signal from the computer, tries to jump as high as possible. In order to eliminate the influences of gaining momentum, arms should be kept close to the hips. Piezoelectric sensors inside the force plate generate an electric charge proportional to the applied vertical force. This charge is converted into an electric potential using a charge amplifier. The PC is equipped with a data acquisition card (National Instruments, Austin, Texas; 16 bit ADC; 32 channels, maximum sample rate 200 kHz) which samples the voltage curve with a frequency of 1,000 Hz. The voltage curve (which is proportional to the ground reaction force during the jump) provides a base for an evaluation program to determine various jump parameters, especially the jump height achieved and the jump impulse.

In addition, the curves of horizontal ground reaction force and force application point in the sagittal direction can be shown as a function of time (Figure 4.12). A LabVIEW® (National Instruments, Austin, USA) program has been developed to record the data representing the ground reaction forces and to calculate jump parameters. The reaction force curves and selected parameters are presented.

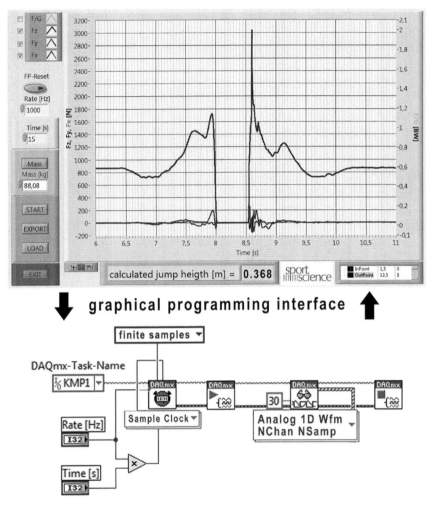

Figure 4.12 Jump performance test: top: front panel (user interface); bottom: detail from block diagram (graphical source code) of the LabVIEW® application

Example 2: feedback system for double rowing

Athletes and coaches require effective methods to support and guide the training process. As a consequence of advances in technology, systems are constructed that present relevant sports specific feedback information during and shortly after training and competition. Such feedback systems are primarily designed for the purpose of achieving better performance (Baca, 2003) but also for the avoidance of excessive fatigue and load.

Integrated and coordinated approaches from sports science (biomechanics, motor learning, exercise physiology, sports psychology), engineering and computer science may result in a high level of training economy and enable the continuous guidance and control of the training process (Broker and Crawley, 2001). An overview of properties of measurement or feedback systems used in training is given in Chapter 8.

Rowing, which again shall serve as an area of application, is a physically demanding sport that requires a well-coordinated and powerful sequence of actions. Consequently, the execution technique plays a major role in the efficiency of the performance. In boat classes with more than one athlete, timing across the rowers is an important performance factor – similar movements are considered an efficiency criterion (Hill, 2002). While the externally visible movements in competitive rowers are described as highly synchronous, rowers develop individual force–time profiles both on swivels and on footrests (Hill, 2002).

A number of feedback systems for rowing are mentioned in literature (e.g. Smith and Loschner, 2002; Zitzewitz et al., 2009; Rauter et al., 2011). Individual feedback can be derived from kinematic, kinetic and electromyographic parameters of the boat–rower system. In particular, time curves of reaction forces on feet and pulling forces enable valuable conclusions about the rowing technique.

Dynamic analyses in the boat are, however, difficult to realize and demanding in time and instrumentation. In many cases, analyses are therefore based on rowing simulators (ergometers) on land. One typical simulator is the Concept 2® ergometer (Concept2, Vermont, USA). If put onto slides, a construction allowing the ergometer to roll back and forth during the rowing stroke, the situation in the boat is better imitated. This setup may also provide the basis for offering feedback on certain aspects of the rowing technique.

A cascaded double ergometer system equipped with measuring technology has been developed (Baca and Kornfeind, 2008) to assist double pairs. Two Concept 2® rowing ergometers are connected by putting them on three slides (Figure 4.13) and sensor technology is embedded. This system was constructed in order to:

- give feedback on reaction forces and selected coordination parameters in (almost) real time
- analyse the adaptability of athletes or to identify master/slave behaviour in specific double pairs (depending on the respective position of the athletes on the cascaded ergometer)
- assist coaches in team and position selection.

The double ergometer system is equipped with devices based on load cells and strain gauges, which enable the determination of reaction forces perpendicular and in parallel to the platforms for both feet separately. Based on these two force components, the vertical and horizontal reaction forces at the feet can be calculated. For measuring the pulling forces force transducers (U9B, Kistler, Winterthur) have been integrated into both chains. A handle position sensor in the form of a rotary potentiometer on each flywheel axis is used to determine the extension length. A 16 bit data acquisition card from National Instruments (Austin, Texas) sampled all sensor signals with a rate of 200 Hz.

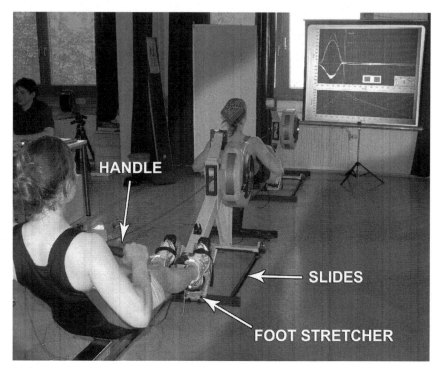

Figure 4.13 Feedback system for coordination training in double rowing

The application of the system for stroke by stroke feedback is illustrated in Figure 4.13. A screen is positioned in front of the rowers. Pulling forces of both rowers are presented simultaneously. The rowers try to alter their movement pattern in order to better match the curves.

A LabVIEW® (National Instruments, Austin, USA) program has been developed to record the data measured and to calculate characteristic parameters quantifying synchrony. The pulling force curves and a selectable set of these parameters may be presented to the rowers stroke by stroke in almost real time or as summative feedback after a series of strokes.

Example 3: mobile coaching system

Based on their remote coaching concept mentioned above, Baca et al. (2010) have developed the Mobile Motion Advisor (MMA) for the support of athletes and coaches in different sports. The MMA helps to adapt and evaluate certain performance parameters in respect to the individual performance level. Characteristic parameters of the physical activity can be continuously supervised. In this way, coaches are able to guide a number of athletes individually. Athletes get feedback on the quality of their motion, which helps to interpret the body's reactions to physical load.

For such purposes, sensors, carried by the person or mounted onto sports equipment, are used to measure different parameters like heart rate, velocity or reactive forces of an exercising person. These parameters are sent to a smartphone application via ANT. The measured data is then transmitted to an application server using wireless communication technologies.

In more detail, physical and physiological values (e.g. force, acceleration, pressure, heart rate, breathing rate) are collected from the athlete with appropriate sensors. The resulting analogue signals are then digitized using a microcontroller (Microchip PIC) with an integrated ADC. After pre-processing the signals (offset, scaling, filtering), either a Bluetooth® or an ANT module is used to establish a connection between the measurement device(s) and a mobile client (e.g. smartphone) in order to transfer the data (serial data stream). On the mobile device an embedded application program handles the Bluetooth® communication to the sensors and the data storage process. Depending on the connection status (offline/online) the captured data are buffered either temporarily locally or transmitted directly to the server database. Possible communication profiles for the Internet connection are General Packet Radio Service (GPRS), Universal Mobile Telecommunications System (UMTS), and if available also WLAN.

Basically, such a framework allows the monitoring of the physical performance parameters of athletes and, moreover, the use of the bi-directional route to positively affect the training process. It is not necessary to have a continuous Internet connection during exercising. In the case of interruptions the data are buffered locally and sent later.

Figure 4.14 shows the whole data flow from the sensors to the smartphone application (athlete–client) and from there to the server (expert–client). Based on the collected data, which are, for example, presented on a web interface via flash charts, feedback instructions can be generated by experts and sent back to the person exercising.

In addition, sub-modules (e.g. intelligent algorithms) may be integrated on the server for processing the acquired sensor information. In this way, peculiarities in the data may be detected and subsequently be considered by the expert when providing feedback. Alternatively, feedback instructions may automatically be generated.

The following goals can thereby be achieved:

- assistance during sport activities;
- improvement of training performance;
- avoidance of overload;
- increase of motivation by individual feedback (e.g. for school classes).

MMA assisting in endurance running

The implementation of the MMA for endurance running includes an intelligent feedback module for guiding further execution (Tampier et al., 2012; Baca, 2013). Load-based performance development is predicted by applying the antagonistic meta-model PerPot, which has been developed by Perl (2004, 2005). This meta-

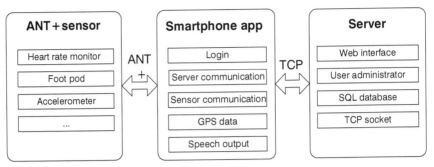

Figure 4.14 Data flow from sensors to server; transmission control protocol (TCP) is a protocol for exchanging data in computer networks

model was originally created to qualitatively analyse phenomena like delayed reaction on load or collapse effecting overload. When applying the model to data from practice, it turned out, however, that PerPot was able to provide quantitative results and to predict load-based performance development very precisely.

PerPot models physiological adaptation on an abstract level as an antagonistic process (Perl, 2008): a load input flow is identically feeding a strain potential and a response potential. The response potential increases the performance potential by a positive flow, while the strain potential reduces it by a negative flow. All flows show specific delays, thus modelling the time the components of the modelled system need to react. In particular in endurance sports, delays play an important role for the process of fatigue and recovery (Perl, 2005, 2008). A more detailed description of PerPot is given in Chapter 6.

In order to initialize the PerPot model with the individual performance parameter values (strain potential, response potential) required, a run similar to a step-test has to be performed. Based on the estimated parameters, the system is able to calculate the optimal goal time and speed for a given distance, thereby forming the basis for the generation of feedback. During the run, these parameter values are updated repeatedly.

Preliminary results of the developed application for running indicate that the MMA provides support to athletes and coaches for guidance and control of the training process, thereby having a positive influence on the motivation and performance of athletes.

Study tasks

1   Discuss the quality criteria to be considered when selecting a DAQ system.
2   Pick out three different biomechanical studies and find out the details of the sensors used.
3   Give practical examples where aliasing may occur.
4   Assume that the voltages in Example 3 in 'Signal sampling' range from 0 to 0.08 V and that a DAQ system comprising a 12 bit ADC is available. Solve questions a) and b) under these conditions.

5   What are the particular features of the wireless communication technologies Bluetooth®, ANT and ZigBee that should be considered when used for wireless sensor networks?

6   Give some practical sports related examples where filtering of captured data may be required.

7   List other additional decision making systems not mentioned in 'Ubiquitous computing'.

8   In the first example in 'Sports applications' the jumping height is determined from the vertical ground reaction force. Discuss the possible influence of the sampling rate used for measuring ground reaction force on the accuracy of the calculated jump height. Note that some basic knowledge of mechanics is required to solve this task.

Recommended further reading

Derrick, T.R. and Robertson, D.G.E. (2014) 'Signal processing', in D.G.E. Robertson, G. Caldwell, J. Hamill, G. Kamen and S.N. Whittlesey (eds), *Research Methods in Biomechanics* (pp. 279–290), 2nd edn, Champaign, IL: Human Kinetics.

Di Paolo Emilio, M. (2013) *Data Acquisition Systems: From Fundamentals to Applied Design*, New York: Springer.

Richards, J. and Thewlis, D. (2008) 'Measurement of force and pressure', in J. Richards (ed.) *Biomechanics in Clinic and Research* (pp. 89–101), Edinburgh: Elsevier.

Richards, J., Thewlis, D. and Selfe, J. (2008) 'Measurement of muscle function and physiological cost', in J. Richards (ed.), *Biomechanics in Clinic and Research* (pp. 128–151), Edinburgh: Elsevier.

References

Akyildiz, I.F., Su, W., Sankarasubramaniam, Y. and Cayirci, E. (2001) 'Wireless sensor networks: A survey', *Computer Networks*, 38(4): 393–422.

Avesani, P., Massa, P. and Tiella, R. (2005) 'A trust-enhanced recommender system application: Moleskiing', in *Proceedings of the 20th ACM Symposium on Applied Computing* (pp. 1589–1593), Santa Fe, USA. New York: ACM.

Baca, A. (2003) 'Computer science based feedback systems on sports performance', *International Journal of Computer Science in Sport*, 2(1): 20–30.

Baca, A. (2013) 'Methods for recognition and classification of human motion patterns – A prerequisite for intelligent devices assisting in sports activities', *Mathematical Modelling*, 7(1): 55–61.

Baca, A. and Kornfeind, P. (2006) 'Rapid feedback systems for elite sports training', *IEEE Pervasive Computing*, 5(4): 70–76.

Baca, A. and Kornfeind, P. (2007) 'Mobile coaching in sports', in J.E. Bardram et al. (eds) *Adjunct Proceedings of UbiComp 2007* (pp. 172–179), Innsbruck, Austria. Weßling: Dt. Zentrum für Luft- und Raumfahrt.

Baca, A. and Kornfeind, P. (2008) 'A feedback system for coordination training in double rowing', *The Engineering of Sport*, 7(1): 659–668, New York: Springer.

Baca, A., Kornfeind, P., Preuschl, E., Bichler, S., Tampier, M. and Novatchkov, H. (2010) 'A server-based mobile coaching system', *Sensors*, 10(12): 10640–10662.

Broker, J.P. and Crawley, J.D. (2001) 'Advanced sport technologies: Enhancing Olympic performance', in *Proceedings of the XIXth ISBS Symposium* (pp. 323–327), San Francisco, USA. Konstanz: IBIS.

Chi, E.H. (2005) 'Introducing wearable force sensors in martial arts', *IEEE Pervasive Computing*, 4(3): 47–53.

Chi, E.H. (2008) 'Sensors and ubiquitous computing technologies in sports', in P. Dabnichki and A. Baca (eds) *Computers in Sport* (pp. 249–267), Southampton: WIT Press.

Collins, D.J. and Anderson, R. (2004) 'The use of a wireless network to provide real-time augmented feedback for on-water rowing', in *Proceedings of the American Society of Biomechanics 28th Annual Conference* (pp. 590–591), Portland, USA.

Ekblom, M.M. and Eriksson, M. (2012) 'Concurrent EMG feedback acutely improves strength and muscle activation', *European Journal of Applied Physiology*, 112(5): 1899–1905.

Graumnitz, J. (2011) 'Erhöhung der Antriebsleistung beim Startsprung im Sportschwimmen – Eine quasiexperimentelle Untersuchung', dissertation, Leipzig: University of Leipzig.

Guang-Zhong, Y. (ed.) (2006) *Body Sensor Networks*, New York: Springer.

Hill, H. (2002) 'Dynamics of coordination within elite rowing crews: Evidence from force pattern analysis', *Journal of Sports Sciences* 20(2): 101–117.

Holthouse, S. (2012) 'Advances in athlete tracking technology', in *Proceedings of the 30th International Symposium on Biomechanics in Sports* (pp. 84–86), Melbourne, Australia.

Kornfeind, P. (2006) 'Development of a mobile measurement system to acquire biomechanical parameters in elite rowing', diploma thesis, Vienna: University of Applied Science (Technikum Wien).

Kranz, M., Holleis, P., Spiessl, W., Schmidt, A. and Tusker, F. (2011) 'The Therapy Top measurement and visualization system – An example for the advancements in existing sports equipments', *International Journal of Computer Science in Sport*, 5(2): 76–80.

Kusserow, M., Amft, O. and Tröster, G. (2009) 'BodyANT: Miniature wireless sensors for naturalistic monitoring of daily activity', in *Bodynets 2009: Proc. 4th International Conference on Body Area Networks* (pp.1–8), Brussels. New York :ACM;

Kusserow, M., Amft, O. and Tröster, G. (2013) 'Modeling arousal phases in daily living using wearable sensors', *IEEE Transactions on Affective Computing*, 4(1): 93–105.

Lames, M. (2008) 'Coaching and computer science', in P. Dabnichki and A. Baca (eds) *Computers in Sport* (pp. 99–120), Southampton: WIT Press.

Larsson, P. (2003) 'Global positioning system and sport-specific testing', *Sports Medicine*, 33(15): 1093–1101.

Lyons, E., Tate, D., Ward, D., Bowling, J., Ribisl, K. and Kalyararaman, S. (2011) 'Energy expenditure and enjoyment during video game play: Differences by game type', *Medicine & Science in Sports & Exercise*, 43(10): 1987–1993.

Moeslund, T.B., Hilton, A. and Krüger, V. (2006) 'A survey of advances in vision-based human motion capture and analysis', *Computer Vision and Image Understanding*, 104(2–3): 90–126.

Nolan, L. and Halvorsen, K. (2007) 'Ground reaction forces during long jump take-off for transtibial amputees', in *Proceedings of the XXVth International Symposium on Biomechanics in Sports* (pp. 310–313), OuroPreto, Brazil. Konstanz: IBIS

Novatchkov, H. and Baca, A. (submitted), 'Pervasive computing in sport', *IGI Global*.

Paul, M. and Garg, K. (2012) 'The effect of heart rate variability biofeedback on performance psychology of basketball players', *Applied Psychophysiology and Biofeedback*, 37(2): 131–144.

Perl, J. (2004) 'PerPot – A meta-model and software tool for analysis and optimisation of load-performance-interaction', *International Journal of Performance Analysis of Sport*, 4(2): 61–73.

Perl, J. (2005) 'Dynamic simulation of performance development: Prediction and optimal scheduling', *International Journal of Computer Science in Sport*, 4(2): 28–37.

Perl, J. (2008) 'Physiologic adaptation by means of antagonistic dynamics', in M. Khosrow-Pour (ed.) *Encyclopaedia of Information Science and Technology,* 2nd edn, (pp. 3086–3092,_ Hershey, PA: IGI

Rauter, G., Sigrist, R., Baur, K., Baumgartner, L., Riener, R. and Wolf, P. (2011) 'A virtual trainer concept for robot-assisted human motor learning in rowing', *BIO Web of Conferences*, 1: 1–4.

Roantree, M., Whelan, M., Shi, J. and Moyna, N. (2009) 'Using sensor networks to measure intensity in sporting activities', in N. Bartolini et al. (eds) *Quality of Service in Heterogeneous Networks*, (pp. 598–612), New York: Springer.

Smith, R.M. and Loschner, C. (2002) 'Biomechanics feedback for rowing', *Journal of Sports Sciences*, 20(10): 783–791.

Smith, S.W. (1997) *Scientist and Engineer's Guide to Digital Signal Processing*, New York: California Technical Publishing.

Stevens, G., Wulf, V., Rohde, M. and Zimmermann, A. (2006) 'Ubiquitous fitness support starts in everyday's context', *The Engineering of Sport*, 6(3): 191–196, New York: Springer.

Tampier, M., Baca, A. and Novatchkov, H. (2012) 'E-coaching in sports', in *Proceedings of 2012 Pre-Olympic Congress* (pp. 132–136), Liverpool, UK. Edgbaston: World Academic Union.

Wiemeyer, J. (2010) 'Serious games – The challenges for computer science in sport', *International Journal of Computer Science in Sport*, 9(special issue 2): 65–74.

Witte, K., Emmermacher, P., Lessau, M., Hofmann, M., Potenberg, J. and Bystrzycki, S. (2007) 'Technikdiagnostik im Karate', in P. Emmermacher and K. Witte (eds) *Karanostik 2007 – Aktuelle Tendenzen im Sportkarate* (pp. 33–42), Magdeburg: Otto-von-Guericke-Universität Magdeburg.

Zitzewitz, J., Wolf, P., Novaković, V., Wellner, M., Rauter, G., Brunschweiler, A. and Riener, R. (2009) 'Real-time rowing simulator with multimodal feedback', *Sports Technology*, 1(6): 257–266.

5 Motion tracking and analysis systems

Roland Leser and Karen Roemer

Motion analysis and *game analysis* are major working fields of sport informatics. A key element of both fields is motion tracking. This chapter outlines the functionality and capabilities of state-of-the-art motion tracking methods and systems, and describes general analysis systems in these two areas. The topic embraces *biomechanical* operating principles including specific calibration and filter routines and available methods for the detection of kinematic parameters as well as the issues *accuracy testing* and *time-motion analysis* in *game analysis*.

Introduction

The main topics of this chapter are *motion tracking* and *analysis systems* in the biomechanical setting and in game analysis, which are two major working fields of sports informatics. Therefore, the chapter is split into the sub-chapters *motion analysis* and *game analysis*. The first sub-chapter introduces motion tracking systems and the process of motion analysis for biomechanical analyses and thus includes the issues *marker sets*, *calibration* and data *post-processing*. The second sub-chapter describes the main types of systems used for game analysis and discusses player tracking routines in particular. The most essential functionalities and capabilities of game analysis systems are outlined. Thus, it is a basis for Chapter 7 'Game Analysis', where this issue is discussed in more detail. Furthermore, the focus of this sub-chapter is on time–motion analysis, while Chapter 7 addresses all tactical analysis issues.

Motion analysis

The focus of analysing any human movement is the ability to quantify movement. Kinematic and kinetic analysis can be performed to study human movement. This part of the chapter will focus on kinematic motion analysis systems. Different parameters such as joint angles, absolute or relative positions, movement velocities, or impacts with high accelerations can be of interest while analysing human movement. There are a wide variety of tools available to analyse movement kinematics, starting from a simple video camera or a smartphone to highly sophisticated lab mounted systems. The chapter will give an overview of technologies that are most commonly used to quantify human movement kinematics. Furthermore, different concepts will be discussed for the post-processing of the data as well as some of the limitations of the systems in lab and field tests.

In general, motion analyses systems rely either on markers – active or passive – or on the detection of body landmarks or of body shapes.

Historically, motion analysis was performed using images taken of a movement. Photo cameras were utilized to take either single pictures or serial photographs. Later on video cameras were used to capture movement sequences. Initially, it was a major challenge to capture high speed movements with video cameras. Nowadays, digital cameras offer high spatial and temporal resolution, which allow the capture of full body movements. Even high-speed movements, such as impacts from a tennis ball on a raquet, can be captured accurately. However, the capability of the equipment requires knowledge about an optimum rather than a maximum of temporal and spatial resolution to measure a given movement. In-depth knowledge about signal processing and the impact of measurement frequencies in combination with pixel size relative to marker size on kinematic data and their derivatives is necessary to gain valid data.

The accurate detection of movement kinematics, as well as the signal processing, is a key feature of motion analysis software tools. In the following a variety of motion capture approaches such video based and infrared systems will be discussed.

Visual tracking systems

Motion analyses are performed as either two-dimensional (2D) or three-dimensional (3D).

Using a single video camera is sufficient to perform a 2D motion analysis. This type of analysis will deliver accurate results in particular while analysing postures or simple planar movements such as a flexion in the knee joint. However, the accuracy of 2D analyses will decrease with increasing movement complexity. The human gait is a planar motion when we consider the whole body movement. Nevertheless, several joint actions involved are three dimensional, such as hip abduction/adduction. Therefore, the decision on performing 2D or 3D motion analysis has to be based on a thorough understanding of the movement itself and the parameters used to quantify the movement. The camera setup is critical to get the most accurate results (Chiari et al., 2005). In a 2D setup the camera should be perpendicular to the movement plane. To avoid image distortions, the camera should be placed as far away as possible while moderately using the zoom to focus on the area of interest.

3D analyses allow quantifying more detailed information about a movement. Movements that occur in more than one direction and in particular movements with rotational components require 3D analyses. The addition of a dimension considerably increases the technology needed to capture the movement. The simplest setup would just require one additional camera that should be positioned

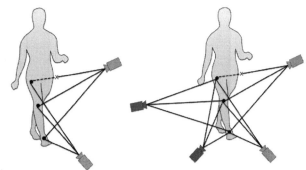

Figure 5.1 Setup of cameras for a 3D gait analysis

perpendicular to the first one. However, the likelihood of 'hidden points' increases with more complex movements. To gain appropriate results, at least two cameras have to 'see' the point of interest. No position information can be obtained if other body parts such as an arm swinging by a hip marker cover a point (Figure 5.1). This problem will be avoided by adding cameras. Furthermore, with additional cameras the accuracy of the obtained data will increase due to the redundancy of information.

However, when using a video based system, adding more cameras requires not only more hardware, but also more resources – computational and human – in processing the data.

Video based 3D motion analysis

Video based systems can be used with standalone cameras. However, it is desirable to use cameras that are directly connected to a computer. If standalone cameras are used for a 3D analysis, it will be important to define a unique trigger – most often a visual clue like a flash – that can be clearly identified by each camera. This trigger will allow defining a distinct starting point for the data analysis. Synchronizing the information of all cameras also needs to be addressed using standalone cameras because of a potential time lag between pictures taken (Tresadern and Reid 2008). It has to be expected that the pictures will not be taken at the exact same time point if each camera is started individually. This problem will increase with decreasing camera frequency. The less pictures taken per second, the larger is the potential time lag between data points of two or more cameras. The necessity of a trigger as well as the time lag can be avoided by using cameras that are connected to a computer and are fully controlled by the motion analysis software.

Markerless video analyses

Video based systems are often used as 'offline' systems, where the identification of landmarks will be performed after the motion capture is finished. An advantage

Figure 5.2 Example of manual digitization: analysis of a volleyball spike captured during a European League game

of video based systems is that they can be used in settings that do not allow the usage of markers, such as performing a motion analysis during a competition like the Olympic Games or European Championships (Escamilla et al., 2001; Hanley, Bissas and Drake, 2013). The markerless tracking can be performed manually or automatically. The manual process requires the visual identification of body landmarks – such as joints or segment endpoints – that will be tracked by individual mouse clicks. Those landmarks used in manual digitization are usually the estimated joint centres (Figure 5.2).

Kinematic information obtained by this method requires a lot of manpower. The digitization process can be monotonous and takes a lot of time. More effort is needed to ensure good quality data using this method. The trade-off between enhancing accuracy – i.e. using multiple cameras – and increasing post-processing times as well as manpower due to the manual digitization process has to be counterbalanced carefully. However, the video based approach without markers is the only way to gather 'real life' data and is therefore extremely valuable. The 100 m world record of Usain Bolt in Beijing 2008 is not repeatable in a lab setting and multiple kinematic analyses have been performed on video material (Beneke and Taylor, 2010; Eriksen et al., 2009).

A new development in markerless motion tracking is the automated identification of body shapes. The outline of a person will be identified in each camera based on local contrasts between the subject (foreground) and the background in the picture. The accuracy of the initial results depends – beside camera calibration and setup – on the resolution of the camera and the amount of contrast between neighbouring pixels. A kinematic model of the human being will be fitted into the detected shape to quantify the human movement. Boundary conditions – such as an anatomical defined range of motion – can be defined for the model to avoid unnatural joint positions if the shape of single segments cannot be detected accurately. The complexity of the kinematic models can vary from simple stick figures to complex individualized multi-body systems with articulated rigid bodies (Corazza et al., 2010). This new approach could change the way in which motion analysis is currently performed.

Marker based video analyses

Marker sets are used to standardize the identification of specific body landmarks. Markers are designed to maximize the contrast between neighbouring pixels. In general markers can be classified into passive and active markers. Active markers send out a signal such as light or sound, while passive markers do not send out a signal and usually consist of either reflective tape or the use of high contrast colours. Most often black and white markers are used to allow the greatest efficiency in automatic tracking. After a marker has been identified in one frame, the software will use the information of the identified pixel area and the contrast to its surrounding pixels as a reference. The software will search for the known contrast in a given diameter around the previous marker position in the next frame. Best data quality will be reached if a marker is visible in an array of pixels so that the shape of the object can be identified (Hedrick, 2008). Then the object's centroid can be used to determine the coordinates of this marker. Therefore, it is important to know the pixel size in relation to the marker size to gain the most accurate data. If a marker is too big relative to the pixel size, it will be hard to determine which pixel(s) and therefore which coordinate actually represents the location of the marker. If the marker size is too small it will result in discontinuities in the raw data which has to be subsequently corrected by filtering techniques (see Figure 5.3).

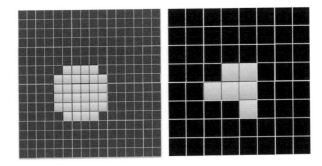

Figure 5.3 Difference in marker identification due to pixel-to-marker ratio

Kinematic models are often linked to specific marker sets, which enhances the accuracy of identifying the markers. Assumptions of relative movement or non-movement between markers are used as boundary conditions in identifying single markers or marker clusters.

The so-called infrared motion analysis systems optimized the marker-based approach to maximize the efficiency of automatic tracking. The infrared systems are often referred to as the 'gold standard' when evaluating motion analysis approaches (Krosshaug et al., 2007; Najafi et al., 2002).

Infrared systems

Infrared systems use specialized cameras to capture the reflection of infrared or near infrared light off reflective markers. These systems work best in controlled environments without too much sunlight and other reflective surfaces. Therefore, the standard setup is in a lab setting, where the environment can be well controlled.

The cameras of these systems are connected to a box that controls the camera synchronization as well as the synchronization with other equipment such as force plates, acceleration sensors, video cameras or an electromyography system. Therefore, the data acquisition of these systems is fully controlled by the software and no post-processing is needed to synchronize or trigger any data points. Camera features such as frequency, shutter speed, or strobe intensity are adjustable using the software.

Each camera is equipped with an infrared light-ring around the lens. The strobe light illuminates the reflective markers and the camera sensor detects its reflections. The signal is pre-processed within the camera and sent back to the computer where a real-time animation of the marker movement can be observed (see Figure 5.4).

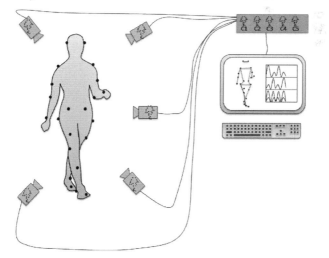

Figure 5.4 Typical setup for gait analysis: each camera detects the marker reflections and sends the information to the computer, where 3D coordinates are calculated

The application of camera systems – video or infrared – allows the analysis of complex human movements. Even the movements of multiple people and objects can be tracked accurately depending on the number of cameras. The capture volume can be defined based on specific needs, which make these systems very adaptable. Camera based systems can be found in various settings: gait laboratories, movie studios, car crash labs, ergonomics, virtual reality, etc.

Motion analysis software links the marker information to kinematic models and calculates kinematic parameters such as joint angles or movement velocities in real time. The accuracy of kinematic results can be optimized by carefully determining the degree of freedom of the associated kinematic model.

Marker sets

Marker sets are applied to the human being to measure the movement. The measured coordinates are used to fit the movement to a virtual kinematic model. Then, the information of the kinematic model is used to calculate relevant kinematic parameters. The idea of using kinematic models to calculate movement parameters is based on the assumption that the human being can be represented as a set of rigid bodies. Those rigid bodies are thought to represent the actual movement of the underlying bones. However, the human body does not consist of rigid bodies and therefore using markers that are attached to the skin will move relative to the bone. In general it is recommended to use multiple markers per segment to increase the accuracy of the estimated segment movement. Redundant information allows the minimization of the influence of marker movements relative to the bone. Distinct body landmarks such as medial and lateral malleolus are used to place markers that help to determine joint axes. However, in particular rotational angles are highly dependent on marker placement and are very sensitive to the proper identification of body landmarks (Della Croce et al., 2005). To minimize the above-mentioned effects several standardized marker sets such as the Helen Hayes Marker Set, Cleveland Clinic Marker Set, and Vicon Plug-in Gait are used, but a wide variety of optimized or individualized marker sets are also utilized (McGinley et al., 2009). Another approach is to use the point cluster technique that accounts for the marker movement relative to the bone and corrects for it. This method uses a cluster of markers surrounding the segment and the markers are weighted according to the deformation of the segment, for example due to muscle contraction (Alexander and Andriacchi, 2001). Therefore, the kinematic results obtained by motion analyses systems do not only depend on how well the cameras are set up and how well they can detect the markers, but even more so on how well the movement of a body segment can be represented by a set of markers. Another important step in obtaining accurate motion analysis data is the camera system calibration.

Calibration

The camera systems have to be carefully calibrated prior to any measurement. If only a 2D calibration is performed, it is sufficient to take one picture showing the 2D reference frame. Reference points will be digitized and the information of at least four points with known coordinates can be used to calculate the direct linear transformation (DLT) coefficients (Brewin and Kerwin, 2003). Using more than the minimum number of reference points will increase the accuracy of the calibration. The DLT method is based on the assumption that the reality is captured on a small scale without image distortions, for example due to a wide-angle lens.

The process of 3D calibration is more complex. The first step in the calibration process is to define the reference coordinate system. If a force plate is used in the laboratory, the origin of the reference system is usually defined on one of the corners of the force plate. The next step is to define the orientation of the reference system. Depending on the post-processing of the data different orientations of the coordinates might be considered. The recommendation of the International Society of Biomechanics is to define the global coordinate system as a right-handed system with the y-coordinate representing the vertical direction, the x-coordinate the anterior-posterior direction, and the z-coordinate representing the medio-lateral direction. The above-mentioned DLT method can also be applied to 3D camera calibration using a calibration cage. Using the DLT method requires covering the volume of interest – the area where the movement will take place – with a 3D calibration cage. The calibration cage is often a set of cubes with reference markers on the corners. This method is very accurate; however, setting up the cage and making sure that it really covers the whole volume of interest can be time-consuming (Pribanic, Peharec and Medved, 2009). Therefore, a calibration wand is often used for 3D calibration. For this method, the first step of defining the reference coordinate system is used to define an initial set of camera parameters for the system calibration. The second step is to refine those values using the calibration wand to reach maximum accuracy of the 3D calibration. The calibration wand is equipped with two markers that clearly define the wand's length plus one marker that is asymmetrically positioned between the two endpoints. This wand has to be moved through the volume of interest. The number of pictures in which each camera has to 'see' the wand can be individually defined. Most manufacturers recommend 1,000–2,000 pictures, which requires about 60–120 seconds depending on the camera frequency. It is important that the volume of interest is well covered by the wand movement to ensure an accurate camera calibration. Both the DLT and the wand method produce comparable results (Shin and Mun, 2012).

The previous section of this chapter covered markerless motion analysis and systems that detect passive markers. In the following part systems using active markers will be described. Active markers either send out signals that will be detected by specific sensors such as microphones or the marker itself contains the sensor.

Ultrasonic systems

An ultrasonic system uses markers providing an ultrasonic sound that will be captured by multiple microphones (Huitema, Hof and Postema, 2002). When a marker sends out the ultrasonic signal, it will be detected by each microphone with a specific time lag that depends on the distance of the microphone from the sensor. Using three microphones the exact position – i.e. 3D coordinates – of the marker can be determined by projecting the location at which the marker matches the respective distance to each microphone (Huitema, Hof and Postema, 2002).

In general the frequency of these systems is relatively low at about 50 Hz per marker. Increasing the number of markers reduces the measurement frequency because multiple markers sending their acoustic signal at the same time has to be avoided. The markers are wired to the computer and the software controls which marker pulses at which time point. This setup ensures the correct matching of a detected signal to a specific marker (Huitema, Hof and Postema, 2002). The number of microphone units depends on the type of movement captured. The acoustic signal can only be detected correctly if nothing blocks the direct transmission to the microphones. If for example a gait analysis is performed with markers on the lateral side of both legs, two microphone units are required so that the signal can be captured on each side of the person. A reference measurement with markers positioned in predefined spots defines the global coordinate system and calibrates the unit.

The range of the system is relatively small, therefore the major application of this system is the analysis of movements that are performed stationary, such as gait on a treadmill, a range of motion tests of single joints, or postures.

Inertial measurement unit (IMU)

The combination of gyroscopes and accelerometers and sometimes magnetometers is a newer approach in motion analysis. Accelerometers are very small units with a size of around 5 mm^2 and weighing less than 1 gram. The accelerometer is equipped with a proof mass that is connected on multiple points to a spring-like structure. The mass will move depending on the applied acceleration and the spring-like structure will detect the amount of movement and quantify the acceleration (Ang, Khosla and Riviere, 2007). The sole use of accelerometers to quantify parameters such as angles or positions can be problematic due to numeric integration. Therefore, accelerometers have been combined with gyroscopes in order to enhance the accuracy of the results. Gyroscopes quantify angular velocities using Coriolis forces and the combination of measured acceleration and velocities have proven to be comparable to the 'gold standard' infrared system (Mayagoitia, Nene and Veltink, 2002). The calibration of this system requires the equipped subject to assume defined postures so that reference coordinate systems for each joint of interest can be defined (Cutti et al., 2010).

An advantage of using IMU for the detection of joint postures and angles is that no cameras or other units are necessary to capture the motion. Therefore, one has not to worry about hidden sensors using this approach. The sensors are often embedded into a specific suit that predefines the proper positioning of the sensors on the body. However, while the quantification of the acceleration is very accurate, the position data can contain a drift due to small numeric integration errors that will sum up over time.

Another application of IMU in motion analysis is the detection of movement patterns over long time periods. Single sensors can be used to detect different types of movements and the information of several hours or even days can be stored on the sensor. This approach can be particularly valuable in monitoring the activity of the elderly throughout the day and could also be used to detect falls (Najafi et al., 2009).

A further application of accelerometers on their own is impact analyses, for example in sports equipment testing (Newman et al., 2005). More recently these systems have been adopted to monitor impacts in sports and the most prominent application is the Head Impact Telemetry (HIT) system. The HIT system is used to monitor the amount and number of high accelerations on the head in American football (Funk et al., 2012).

Post-processing

After any of the discussed systems capture kinematic data, post-processing of the data is required. The first step is often to filter the data to get rid of artefacts. The source of artefacts can be the motion detection itself or skin movement. Camera based motion analysis systems can generate artefacts or so-called gaps if the movement cannot be detected accurately, for example due to hidden markers or bad lighting. A gap will appear in the coordinate data if a marker could not be detected for one or multiple pictures, i.e. no information exists on the marker location for a specific amount of time (see Figure 5.5). The data can be interpolated and the gap can be filled if the time frame without information is not too large. Automated routines such as linear interpolation (Figure 5.5: line a) or spline interpolation (Figure 5.5: line c) can be applied and will lead to good results if the gap is short. Another possibility to fill a gap is to use information from other markers (Figure

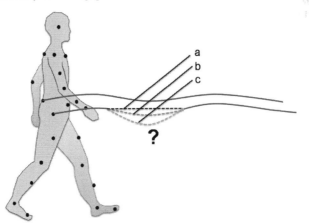

Figure 5.5 Example of the effect of different interpolation methods for a larger gap in a hip marker

5.5: line b). If multiple markers are used for one segment, the information about the movement pattern of the redundant markers can be applied to fill the gap.

Furthermore, skin movements due to an impact can produce peaks in the data that represent the movement of the marker relative to the underlying bone rather than the segment itself. Here it is again beneficial to use multiple markers and generate redundant information. If multiple markers are used to describe the movement of one segment, the influence of the inaccuracy of one single marker is reduced. Motion analysis software often has kinematic models implemented. The software algorithms are designed to fit the movement of the model with its rigid segments into the marker cloud and therefore to minimize the effect of artefacts of single markers. This approach has already had a filtering and dampening effect on the kinematic data because the inaccuracy of single markers have a reduced impact on the final result. Furthermore, motion analysis software employs standard filter routines such as a Woltring filter or Butterworth filter. The specific setting for filtering the kinematic data depends on the quality of the raw signal, the frequency of data acquisition and on the captured movement (Erer, 2007; Molloy et al., 2008). It is critical to have prior knowledge about impacts that might occur and therefore higher frequencies in a specific movement. If the filter is not adapted to the expected movement frequencies, important information might be cut off the data.

Therefore, performing motion analyses requires expert knowledge about the movement itself, about motion analysis systems, as well as about post-processing tools and filtering techniques in order to gather valid and reliable data.

Game analysis

State-of-the-art systems

In this section annotation systems, player tracking systems and visualization systems are outlined – as those are the main types of software tools used in the field of game analysis. Regarding the topic of motion tracking, player tracking systems are explained in more detail, while the other two kinds of systems are only introduced at a general level. The components and the workflow of annotation systems described in Chapter 7 'Game Analysis' are very detailed and, in particular, focus on tactical parameters, while the reader can find a rather general introduction in this chapter.

Annotation systems

Collecting relevant metadata of sports performance is a key issue of sports diagnostics and of game analysis in particular. Whilst some rough data is often captured live using simple notation techniques during a sports competition (Hughes and Franks, 1997), detailed analyses of sports behaviour can only be managed by means of post-event observations and by using video and annotation methods. Therefore, an observation system (Lames, 1994) has to be defined, including all the behavioural categories and events which are necessary for the game analysis (Hughes and Bartlett, 2002). To collect the relevant performance data this observation system, combined with interactive video, is used for indexing and describing the sports performance of interest. For example, Leser and Baca (2008) describe the process of video annotation for applied video and game analysis in table tennis.

The authors developed a video annotation system for entering the start and end time codes for each rally of an analysed game. Additionally, the player name of the winner of the rally and the type of error (e.g. net ball, out) are added. Information such as a set and rally number or the current score is gathered automatically after the game is initialized. The player's name, the laterality (forehand, backhand), type (topspin, flip, etc.) and impact position of each stroke can be complemented if detailed information about all player actions is intended. Thus, all relevant information for quantitative analyses of a table tennis match is available. Since all rallies of the game can be replayed, user-driven, qualitative analyses can also be performed (Leser, Baca, Baron and Kain, 2007).

Game analysis software packages using interactive video have been available for everybody since about 2000. Since then a high number of commercial software systems (e.g. Holzer, 2001) for the academic context (e.g. Gabin, Camerino, Anguera and Castaner, 2012), and freeware tools (e.g. Alastruey, 2008) have been developed. This progress has resulted in a high standard of functionality and usability in game analysis systems. The main requirements for these systems are listed below.

Due to the common process of game analysis (Leser, 2006), contemporary software tools provide data collection, data analysis and data presentation modes. Usually all three operating modes have a video interface supplying the following functionality:

- Play, freeze, variable playing speeds (forward and backward), jump to time function;
- Switch between small video window and full screen;
- Shortcuts for all video functions;
- Free-floating video window for watching on a secondary screen.

The data collection mode is usually operated by experienced users (e.g. sport scientists or notational analysts). Therefore, the capability and availability of operating features is more important than an easy to use program interface.

Before starting to observe and to collect game related data, a notation system has to be defined. The software used should be capable of simple video labelling (so-called 'tagging') up to applying more complex notation systems (so-called 'category systems'; Lames, 1994). The latter is exemplified in Table 5.1 for tennis. A tennis match can be described by a sequence of strokes. Furthermore, each stroke can be characterized by entering the performing player's name, the stroke type, the kind of rotation, the direction, technique and outcome of the stroke. Thus, to describe a tennis stroke one attribute from each of the six categories is chosen. When a stroke does not require a category attribute, then 'N.A.' is entered.

Table 5.1 Notation system for tennis by means of categories and attributes

Player	Type	Rotation	Direction	Technique	Effect
Player A	Service	Drive	Longline	Volley	Ace
Player B	2nd Service	Topspin	Cross	Smash	Winner
	Forehand	Slice	Centered	Lob	Double fault
	Backhand	N.A.	N.A.	Dropshot	Fault
				Passing shot	Unforced error
				N.A.	None

The notation system in Table 5.1 does not include spatial information. This could be added by directly clicking on a bitmap of the tennis field at the position from where a stroke is performed.

The annotation software should allow the storage of constructed notation systems as templates in order to use those later for further projects. Furthermore, the software should be linked to a database. The templates and other recurring information (team names, squads) as well as all analysis projects should be stored in this database.

The data collection starts by creating a new data set for the analysed match. The home and away team as well as other frame data (final score, competition type, weather conditions, etc.), and the video source are entered. When a live observation is performed, a digital clock should be available in order to synchronize the annotated data with the match video later. Good analysis software also allows the direct capture of the match video during the live annotation. In this case, the data and video are automatically linked to each other. The match data is collected by entering the start and end time codes of each video sequence of interest, which are labelled or described by the category system. The most important functions for the data collection mode are:

- One mouse click action for entering a new record;
- Predefined lengths for pre- and post-times after the mouse action for each type of observation unit (therewith the length of each video sequence can be defined only per one mouse action);
- Shortcuts for each type of observation unit;
- Graphical input interface (buttons instead of text lists; bitmap of the field for entering the position of game actions);
- Flexible removal or amendment of entered observation units or their start and end times;
- Colouring of collected records in order to have visual feedback about the type of observation unit.

Developing an analysis mode for sports annotation programs is most challenging, because the requirements of many, usually quite different, users have to be considered. If the software is to be used in different sports, it becomes even more difficult, because the common way of presenting match data differs from sport to sport. Therefore, an export function for the quantitative data is most important in order to analyse it with spreadsheet software or statistical packages. Additionally, a proper video analysis mode is essential for the users' qualitative match analyses. For those analyses some sophisticated filter and playlist functions are needed in order to adequately recall all collected video sequences.

When annotation software for game analysis is not only used for analytical purposes (e.g. by coaching staff), but also to convey the results to others (e.g. players), a proper presentation mode is mandatory. Whilst quantitative data (numbers, tables, graphs, figures) can be shown using conventional presentation software, proper video presentation functions are very important for the analysis of the software itself. The video window should be independent from the main application interface to present the video information in full screen mode on a second monitor. Playlist functions are necessary to organize selected video sequences for the presentation. These sequences must be available via shortcuts. Additional shortcuts are needed for stop and go, time jumps, slow motion and for activating a graphical sub-mode. In this graphic mode, elements such as lines, rectangles or arrows can be used to focus on specific aspects in the video and to illustrate tactical analyses in particular.

Player tracking systems

(Automatic) player tracking systems have been the most important technical innovation for performance analysis in game sports in the last decades. They enable sophisticated time–motion analyses (Leser, Baca and Ogris, 2011) and open new possibilities for tactical analyses (Lames, Siegle and O'Donoghue, 2012). Alongside the benefits of tracking data for training evaluation and game analysis, position information is also extensively used in TV coverage, on the Internet and in print media. Viewers and readers are informed about the performance data of players, such as covered distances or speeds.

For the purpose of game analysis, three player tracking technologies are available, which are explained below.

Global Positioning System (GPS) tracking is the most common tracking method because of the lowest costs. GPS receivers are worn by the players in special belts on the upper arm or the back. By means of GPS signals, the position of the GPS receiver-wearing player, covered distances since starting and the current speed can be calculated. This information is monitored and stored by a clock worn by the players or wirelessly transferred to a computer. The conventional GPS signal has an update rate of only 1 Hz, which is fairly low for proper performance data. Current GPS receivers also provide sample rates of 5 and 10 Hz, but the price for those devices is significantly higher. A couple of systems are additionally combined with accelerometer measurements, which are used to improve the GPS data. However, one has to be mindful of whether the product information of a 5, 10 or even 15 Hz sample rate refers to real GPS measurements or if this is as a result of accelerometer calculations. Data based on accelerometer measurements is normally not as precise as data from good GPS signals.

The main advantages of GPS sports systems are their low price (compared to radio wave and vision basing systems) and their full automation. The drawbacks are that they only work outdoors, depend on weather conditions and become noisy when measuring close to high buildings. Furthermore, GPS receivers sometimes obstruct athletes during sports activities. In general, a couple of studies (e.g. Barbero-Alvarez, Coutts, Granda, Barbero-Alvarez and Castagna, 2010) document that GPS tracking systems are sufficiently accurate for analysing covered distances and mean speeds in game sports but are not able to estimate speed at a given moment in time, acceleration and deceleration reliably.

Radio wave based player tracking systems work similar to GPS but are restricted to a certain location (e.g. soccer pitch). The players wear transponders, which answer to a conventional radio signal with an ultra-wide band pulse (UWB). The UWB signals are received by base stations (sensors) mounted around the observation field and are eventually transferred to a computer. By means of time-difference-of-arrival and/or angle-of-arrival measurements of the UWB signals at the base stations the location (x-, y-, z-coordinates) of the transponders can be calculated. These electronic systems have sample rates up to 2,000 Hz in total, which have to be shared among all active transponders. The accuracy is much higher than for GPS systems (Ogris, Leser, Horsak, Kornfeind, Heller and Baca, 2012) and some systems also allow good estimates for speed at a given moment in time, acceleration and deceleration. Similar to GPS, a full automatic operating mode is possible. Besides the relative high costs the main drawback of this type of tracking system are the obtrusive transponders. Due to these, radio wave based tracking systems are not allowed in many competitions under official rules (e.g. soccer).

The third approach of player tracking is based on images shot by calibrated video cameras. Since no devices have to be worn by the players, this approach can be used for tracking in all game sports during training sessions as well as during competitions. Although moving cameras can also be used, most video tracking systems use fixed cameras to reduce the number of possible calibration problems (Beetz et al., 2009). Depending on the pitch size, 1 to 16 cameras are mounted high in a central location or around the sports court. Each camera covers a certain section of the field and is usually calibrated in 2D by means of the field markings. When objects (like players or a ball) move into the calibrated pictures they can be detected and are assigned to the relevant video pixels. Due to the calibration the pixel coordinates can be converted into real world coordinates (location on the pitch).

In contrast to biomechanical analyses, position tracking in game sports does not necessarily need information about human posture and gait; only information about large-scale human motion is required (Pers, Bon, Kovacic, Sibila and Dezman, 2002), which simplifies the tracking process. Video based human motion tracking in team sports is mainly based on (1) player segmentation (Figure 5.6) and (2) temporal correspondences. The second is the process of associating the

Figure 5.6 Image and corresponding background image with segmented foreground (VisTrack®)

person detected in the current image with the one detected in the image before. For the first step, there are a couple of established, sophisticated methods (Pansiot, 2009). Region based approaches aim to distinguish between different fields in a picture, where each region shares similar properties. The segmentation can be realized by edge detection algorithms, based on similar colours or texture. Among several different approaches for background segmentation and due to the almost changeless pitch, in team sports the representation of the background pixel by one or more Mixed Gaussian Models became a proven method (Moeslund, Hilton and Krüger, 2006). Based on a model for the statistical colour distribution of the pixel representing the background, a significant sudden change in colour and intensity in subsequent images implies that this pixel has become part of the foreground and is a part of a player. When the contrast between the players and the playing field is sharp, this method works very well (Figure 5.6). However, a common problem for tracking under outdoor conditions is a sudden change of light conditions due to weather. Therefore frame based segmentation can be used, applying a couple of different background models (Stauffer and Grimson, 1999). In practice it is common to apply a combination of the aforementioned segmentation approaches.

Once the pixels representing the players are separated from the background, several algorithms can be used to classify team identity. Please note that if it comes to real time tracking, an exact player determination still remains a big challenge nowadays due to the extremely high computational effort. However, assuming that the vertical movements of a player are negligible and an initial supervised player assignment was applied followed by a subsequent automated spatial positioning over time, well working player tracking system can be realized. In general, the bottom-centre coordinates of the detected foreground object are taken as the position of the corresponding player. This method works very well as long as two or more players are not too close to each other. Because of the interacting character of game sports, however, collisions between players occur frequently. These overlaps have prohibited automatic player tracking. Thus, commercial tracking systems still require a considerable amount of operator interventions to provide complete tracking data (Barris and Button, 2008).

To overcome the overlapping problem a couple of strategies are pursued at present. First, a greater number of cameras installed around the playing field provide additional perspectives to identify individual objects. Second, the detection rate of players increases with the increasing resolution of the video footage. However, if two or more players are very close to each other, e.g. during goal celebrations, the identities of the players still get lost. In such cases the main strategy is to identify the players as soon as possible after those events and to individually track the objects back as far as necessary. Furthermore, the colour of the skin, the hair, and even of the boots can give hints for player identification.

Another approach is to detect the shirt number or to identify players by means of individual body models. However, both methods (in particular the latter) require video images with very high resolution and the processing power and time will increase significantly. This is an important aspect because often tracking data is provided almost in real time. The last approach for assisting full automatic player tracking is a probabilistic one. Depending on the positional role of a player in a team, specific areas of the field are covered. Furthermore, he/she has a typical profile of actions and interactions. Hence, the probability for a player being an unknown object can be calculated based on data from the past.

In line with the expectations for future hardware development and the above-mentioned approaches, full automatic vision based player tracking in team sports can be expected in the next 10 to 15 years.

Visualization systems

Visualizing key factors of sports performance has become an important part of applied game analysis (see 'Annotation systems') and for sports broadcasting in particular (Figure 5.7). Nowadays TV stations do not only entertain people and broadcast images from sport events, but also provide in-depth information on athletes' and teams' performances. The requirements for proper visualization systems are very high, because they have to handle professional video footage, should work very efficiently (the analyses are often used immediately post-event) and provide attractive graphics. Due to the working procedures and the necessary capabilities listed below, the systems used are high-performance software tools, which require powerful computational hardware:

- By means of available field markings in the video images a 2D calibration of the pitch is performed. Some tools even realize 3D calibrations with additional vertical calibration points. Based on this information a virtual stadium is calculated and can be visualized from each perspective and viewpoint.
- Within the virtual stadium the players and the ball can be tracked using only the images of TV cameras and no additional infrastructure. Thus, entire match scenes can be transformed into an animated 3D environment. However, visualization tools are constrained to rather short video sequences – usually

Figure 5.7 Analysis of a match situation in soccer by means of a visualization tool (VizLibero®) (image courtesy of Vizrt/LiberoVision AG/ Teleclub AG)

not longer than a minute – and thus are not able to replace player tracking systems.

- The standard drawing tools for highlighting (tactical) performance aspects are (offside) lines, rectangles, circles and arrows. All elements are visualized in line with the calibration and therefore have virtual effects.
- All tracked objects (players, referees and ball) can be highlighted dynamically with a light cone, a circle or other graphical elements. In addition the trajectories of the objects can be shown.
- Measurements can be performed from freeze images as well as from video sequences: time intervals (e.g. from offensive attempts), distances (e.g. between players), speeds (e.g. from shots).
- Depending on the available camera perspectives, specific game situations can be viewed in real pictures from different angles. To pan from one perspective to another, so-called camera flights are calculated. They give the impression of flying around the field from one viewpoint to another to have a better view of the scene.
- Contemporary systems process full high-definition footage and, therefore, have additional features like zooming.

Analysis and visualization systems as described above are used in the sports coverage of TV stations. For the day-to-day work in sports teams these software tools are most often too expensive and too complex to operate. However, visualization functions are also desirable for the presentation mode of annotation systems. Thus, most annotation systems have available (uncalibrated) easy to use graphic features which enable game tactical information to be conveyed.

Accuracy testing

The accuracy of the data collected by analysis systems as described above in 'State-of-the-art systems' is crucial to assess the systems' quality. Regarding annotation systems, aspects of inter-rater reliability have to be considered. For a detailed view on this methodological issue see Hughes, Cooper and Nevill (2004). For visualization applications, only a little value is put on their precision, because these systems basically provide vivid graphics for qualitative analyses and their accuracy is secondary. However, a rather technical aspect and a central issue of sports informatics is the accuracy of player tracking. Quite a lot of validation and reliability studies have been performed for several types of sports: court-based sports (Duffield, Reid, Baker and Spratford, 2010), field-based sports (Roberts, Trewartha and Stokes, 2006) and team sports (e.g. Gray, Jenkins, Andrews, Taaffe and Glover, 2010). A series of other investigations focused on the accuracy of specific types of sports: Australian football (e.g. Edgecomb and Norton, 2006), cricket (Petersen, Pyne, Portus, Karppinen and Dawson, 2009), field hockey (MacLeod, Morris, Nevill and Sunderland, 2009), football (e.g. Frencken, Lemmink and Delleman, 2010) and futsal (Dogramaci, Watsford and Murphy, 2011). A third type of studies examined the issue for general sports purposes (e.g. Varley, Fairweather and Aughey, 2012).

Results with respect to the accuracy of player tracking systems are available for video based systems (e.g. Di Salvo, Collins, McNeill, and Cardinale, 2006), GPS systems (e.g. Barbero-Alvarez et al., 2010) and radio wave based systems (e.g. Frencken et al., 2010). All papers listed analysed the accuracy of positioning systems, with reference to time–motion analyses in particular. Although the movements performed in each sport and the requirements of time–motion analysis are specific to that sport, most studies claim to have general validity in game sports.

In addition to the above used classification, reliability and validation studies for position detection systems can be categorized by means of the used reference system and the examined parameters. A common choice for testing systems' accuracy is to define runs, prescribed movements or standard circuits with known distances, and to compare the distance calculated by the positioning system with the reference value (e.g. Duffield et al., 2010). In a couple of studies (e.g. Frencken et al., 2010) timing gates were used for time measurement of straight runs and running courses. Herewith also average speeds can be calculated to be used for accuracy detection. The main shortcoming of this approach is that the data is not gathered under ecologically valid conditions. Straight runs are very rare in real match play of game sports, whereas specific running courses try to overcome this disadvantage. However, real match play or simulated games would be much more suitable to detect the accuracy of tracking systems.

Another approach is pursued by Siegle, Stevens and Lames (2012). They used laser devices in order measure the actual position data for straight runs. This position data is compared to the data of the player tracking systems. Since position values (x-, y-coordinates) are the raw data of the tracking systems, this approach is the most accurate validation method for game sports. However, the comparison of position data to their respective reference values should not only be done for straight runs but also for other movements performed in game sports. This is realized by Randers et al. (2010), who compare the position measurements of four different systems used concurrently in match play. The drawback of this method is the lack of accurate reference data.

The high number of studies concerning the accuracy of player tracking methods and systems is of significant relevance to the topic of sports informatics. However, the impression cannot be avoided that the high activity around this issue is a consequence of the available technology (in particular of low cost GPS systems) and the practicability of performing this kind of study, rather than an in-depth scientific interest. Therefore, some standards for designing appropriate accuracy studies are outlined hereafter. The key criterion for choosing a specific study design is the choice of a proper reference system and of proper reference parameters. If accurate position data (x/y- or $x/y/z$-coordinates) is necessary, then actual position data gained by the system has to be considered for the accuracy tests. If a system is used for time–motion analyses, measuring parameters like distances or speeds, then it is sufficient to check the accuracy of those parameters. This can be much less work-intensive than methods comparing each position measurement with an adequate reference value. Thus, the method for testing the accuracy of a player tracking system should be chosen depending on the requirements the specific system is to be used for.

In the simplest case a time–motion study is performed by analysing only covered distances and average speeds. For this, Leser, Schleindlhuber, Lyons and Baca (2014) introduce a valid, replicable and easy to use method for investigating the accuracy of a player tracking system. The authors used their method for validation in basketball. Therefore, a regular five versus five game was played. One additional player, not participating actively in the match, led a trundle wheel and followed one of the ten players. A trundle wheel is a measuring device for distances with an accuracy of about 99.50 per cent. The wheel is held by a handle which is attached to the axle. The measured units were started and stopped via an acoustic signal. Afterwards total and percentage differences between the distance and average speed estimations of the player tracking system and the reference values of the trundle wheel were calculated. By performing the measurements in simulated match play, the data is gathered under highly ecologically valid conditions. Furthermore, no expensive equipment is necessary and the effort for conducting the study is low. The drawbacks of the method are that no actual position data is processed and the analysis is restricted to two basic parameters (distance, average speed).

If a player tracking system is used for analyses processing x-, y- coordinates (e.g. for tactical assessments), then the system's validation should also refer to this type of data. For this purpose Ogris, Leser, Horsak, Kornfeind, Heller and Baca (2012) recorded soccer based games with small sides concurrently with a tracking system and a Vicon motion analysis system. The motion analyses system has a very high accuracy and thus can be used as a reference. Actual position data as well as parameter estimations (distance, speed) were compared between the systems.

The availability of a motion analysis device as a proper reference system may be the main hindrance to researchers for deploying the above described gold standard for accuracy investigations. A suitable motion analysis system is very expensive. Additionally, the effort for manually post-processing the captured motion data can be very high, depending on the quality of the position recordings. Thus, the before mentioned study design by Siegle et al. (2012), using a much cheaper laser device, can be used. With this device the x-, y-coordinates of straight movements can be gathered with a high sampling rate and accuracy. Using a standard running protocol, the effort for data post-processing is relatively low as the coordinates of the laser device and the player tracking system are compared. The accuracy of the investigated system can be quantified by a comprehensible parameter such as the root mean square error for the x- and y-coordinates. The main disadvantage of this approach is that only straight movements can be captured.

Leser et al. (2011) underline that positioning systems in game sports are used for a major portion of time–motion analyses. Osgnach, Poser, Bernardini, Rinaldo and Di Prampero (2010) stress the importance of more sophisticated analyses of acceleration and deceleration. Therefore, investigations testing the accuracy of player tracking systems should also adequately consider those parameters. Consequently, the approach with the motion system as reference is the only method, which sufficiently handles these requirements.

In summary, the approach by Ogris et al. (2012) using a very accurate motion analysis system as the reference, widened by a sport specific running protocol in order to focus on acceleration and deceleration aspects, should be used as the gold standard to examine the accuracy of player tracking systems. If a time–motion analysis is performed and the only interests are in covered distances and average speeds, then the approach by Leser et al. (2014) can alternatively be used.

Time–motion analysis

Annotation systems and player tracking systems, as described above, are used in game sports for analysing tactical aspects and for time–motion analysis. All issues concerning tactical parameters are covered in Chapter 7 by Peter O'Donoghue. The systems' application for time–motion analysis is outlined in this section.

The term 'time–motion analysis' concerns the application of annotation and player tracking systems for analysing the extent and intensity of motions performed in training or in match competition. Referring to Carling, Bloomfield, Nelsen and Reilly (2008) time–motion analysis research can be split into the fields (1) overall work rate analysis, (2) analysis of categories of movements, (3) analysis of positional demands, (4) analysis of fatigue, and (5) other uses of motion analysis. The results of time–motion investigations can be used to design fitness programmes for specific game sports, positional roles and individual players. Moreover, the physical preparation for match play and the development of specific strategies for competitions can be purposefully pursued.

Table 5.2 Categories of movement depending on speed

Category of movement	Range of speed
Standing	0.00 – 1.99 km/h
Walking	2.00 – 5.99 km/h
Jogging	6.00 – 10.99 km/h
Low-speed running	11.00 – 13.99 km//h
Moderate-speed running	14.00 – 18.99 km/h
High-speed running	≥ 19.00 km/h

The high number of available papers on time–motion data proves its significance for sport science. The biggest amount of papers addresses either overall work rate analyses or analyses of movement categories (e.g. Gabbett and Mulvey, 2008). Typically, the overall work load is expressed as distance that is covered in a game or during specific periods of a game (e.g. first/second half). The movement categories are often expressed based on intensities (speeds). Table 5.2 shows a common categorization which can be used for time–motion research.

A series of other studies examine time–motion data combined with the physical load of individuals. Therefore, measures of heart rate (e.g. Mallo and Navarro, 2008), lactate (e.g. Bangsbo, Norregaard and Thorso, 1991), oxygen uptake (e.g. Murias, Lanatta, Arcuri and Laino, 2007) and rating of perceived exertion (e.g. Hill-Haas, Dawson, Coutts and Rowsell, 2009) are correlated with the work rates of game players. A further interest of sport science is the role of playing positions. Thus, profiles for different playing positions are established by means of time–motion data (e.g. King, Jenkins and Gabbett, 2009). Other studies concern the differences in physiological performances between different performance levels (e.g. Sirotic, Coutts, Knowles and Catterick, 2009) or different leagues (e.g. Andersson, Randers, Heiner-Moller, Krustrup and Mohr, 2010), between different formats of games (e.g. Petersen, Pyne, Dawson, Portus and Kellett, 2010), between training and match performances (e.g. McLellan, Lovell and Gass, 2011) and between match performance and the results of diagnostic test data (e.g. Castagna, Manzi, Impellizzeri, Weston and Barbero-Alvarez, 2010). Time–motion analyses also often address the issue of fatigue (e.g. Aughey, 2010). In such studies, the change (decrease) of performance parameters like covered distances or moving intensities are observed over the progress of time in competition.

In summary, the most important issues in sports science investigating positional data with respect to time–motion analysis in game sports are workload analyses in training and match play as well as analyses of physiological responses to workloads measured by heart rate, lactate and other metabolic parameters. This kind of work rate data is also used as an alternative to diagnostic measurements, to quantify fatigue and to gain insight into the demands of different positional roles in game play. This kind of research requires very sophisticated time–motion analyses. Therefore player tracking systems are usually used because annotation systems are only capable of gathering categorical data (like standing, walking, running and sprinting).

Conclusions

Motion analysis systems provide access to kinematic information about human movements. Movements can be captured in various environments, and each approach – camera based, marker based, markerless, ultrasonic, accelerometers – has advantages which make it most applicable to specific environments. The accuracy of kinematic data depends on the chosen approach, the system calibration, the measurement frequency and the definition of appropriate marker sets – if applicable.

The future of motion analysis might head towards markerless approaches, which are already implemented in video games as a gesture based user interface.

For game analysis, annotation systems are often used to observe matches and to gather information about game behaviour. Rather simple graphic software as well as complex visualization tools are used by coaching staff and broadcasting companies to illustrate the results of game analysis. The most expensive game analysis tools are player tracking systems, which are based on video, radio wave or GPS technology. Therewith, sophisticated time–motion analyses can be performed, which provide essential information for the physical preparation of athletes. Tests for investigating the accuracy, reliability and objectivity of the mentioned systems range from inter-rater reliability tests up to position reference measurements.

Study tasks

1   Read the section 'Motion analysis'. Research gait laboratories that offer professional gait analyses and list the equipment they use for their motion analyses.
    • What systems are being used and how are they combined?
    • Is their equipment optimized to do the measurements in a lab setting?
    • Are they able to take the equipment outside the lab?
2   Read the section 'Motion analysis'. How would you equip a motion analysis lab?
    • Why would you choose a specific setup and favour it over another system?
3   Read the section 'Motion analysis'. Discuss the benefits of a mobile motion analysis system using gait or running analysis as an example.
4   Read the section 'Motion analysis'. Discuss the benefits of a lab mounted motion analysis system using gait or running analysis as an example.
5   Read the section 'Annotation systems'. Define a notation system for a sport of your choice.
    • Which functions should be available for a good annotation system using this notation system?
    • Discuss how these notation and annotation systems could be used for analysis by coaching staff.
6   Read the section 'Player tracking systems'.
    • What types of player tracking systems are available?
    • Discuss the advantages and drawbacks of each system.

7   Read the section 'Player tracking systems' and explain the basic principles of vision based player tracking systems.
8   Read the section 'Accuracy testing'. How can the accuracy of player tracking systems be determined?
   •   Discuss the different options.
   •   Which method should be chosen for which purpose?
9   Read the section 'Accuracy testing' and explain the subject 'time–motion analysis'.
   •   What are the sub-areas of time–motion analysis?
   •   How can time–motion analyses be performed with an annotation system?

Recommended further reading

Cappozzo, A., Della Croce, U., Leardini, A. and Chiari, L. (2005) 'Human movement analysis using stereophotogrammetry – Part 1: Theoretical background', *Gait & Posture*, 21(2): 186–196.

Carling, C., Williams, A.M. and Reilly, T. (2005) *The Handbook of Soccer Match Analysis*, London: Routledge.

Hughes, M. and Franks, I. (2004) *Notational Analysis of Sport*, London: Routledge.

Leardini, A., Chiari, L., Della Croce, U. and Cappozzo, A. (2005) 'Human movement analysis using stereophotogrammetry – Part 3: Soft tissue artifact assessment and compensation', *Gait & Posture*, 21(2): 212–225.

Mautz, R. (2012) 'Indoor positioning technologies', habilitation thesis, University ETH Zurich.

O'Donoghue, P. (2010) *Research Methods for Sports Performance Analysis*, London: Routledge.

References

Alastruey, A. (2008) 'LongoMatch: A sports video analysis tool based on free software', diploma thesis, University of Rome.

Alexander, E. and Andriacchi, T. (2001) 'Correcting for deformation in skin-based marker systems', *Journal of Biomechanics*, 34(3): 355–361.

Andersson, H., Randers, M., Heiner-Moller, A., Krustrup, P. and Mohr, M. (2010) 'Elite female soccer players perform more high-intensity running when playing in international games compared with domestic league games', *The Journal of Strength & Conditioning Research*, 24(4): 912–919.

Ang, W., Khosla, P. and Riviere, C. (2007) 'Nonlinear regression model of a low-g MEMS accelerometer', *IEEE Sensors Journal*, 7(1): 81–88.

Aughey, R. (2010) 'Australian football player work rate: Evidence of fatigue and pacing?', *International Journal of Sports Physiology and Performance*, 5(3): 394–405.

Bangsbo, J., Norregaard, L., and Thorso, F. (1991) 'Activity profile of competition soccer', *Canadian Journal of Sports Science*, 16(2): 110–116.

Barbero-Alvarez, J.C., Coutts, A., Granda, J., Barbero-Alvarez, V. and Castagna, C. (2010) 'The validity and reliability of a global positioning satellite system device to assess speed and repeated sprint ability (RSA) in athletes', *Journal of Science and Medicine in Sport*, 13(2): 232–235.

Barris, S. and Button, C. (2008) 'A review of vision-based motion analysis in sport', *Sports Medicine*, 38(12): 1025–1043.

Beetz, M., Hoyningen-Huene, N., Kirchlechner, B., Gedikli, S., Siles, F., Durus, M. and Lames, M. (2009) 'ASPOGAMO: Automated sports games analysis models', *International Journal of Computer Science in Sport*, 8(1): 4–21.

Beneke, R. and Taylor, M. (2010) 'What gives Bolt the edge – AV Hill knew it already!', *Journal of Biomechanics*, 43(11): 2241–2243.

Brewin, M. and Kerwin, D. (2003) 'Accuracy of scaling and DLT reconstruction techniques for planar motion analyses', *Journal of Applied Biomechanics*, 19(1): 79–88.

Carling, C., Bloomfield, J., Nelsen, L. and Reilly, T. (2008) 'The role of motion analysis in elite soccer: Contemporary performance measurement techniques and work rate data', *Journal of Sports Medicine*, 38(10): 839–862.

Castagna, C., Manzi, V., Impellizzeri, F., Weston, M. and Barbero-Alvarez, J. (2010) 'Relationship between endurance field tests and match performance in young soccer players', *The Journal of Strength & Conditioning Research*, 24(12): 3237–3243.

Chiari, L., Della Croce, U., Leardini, A. and Cappozzo, A. (2005) 'Human movement analysis using stereophotogrammetry – Part 2: Instrumental errors', *Gait & Posture*, 21(2): 197–211.

Corazza, S., Mundermann, L., Gambaretto, E., Ferrigno, G. and Andriacchi, T. (2010) 'Markerless motion capture through visual hull, articulated ICP and subject specific model generation', *International Journal of Computer Vision*, 87: 156–169.

Cutti, A., Ferrari, A., Garofalo, P., Raggi, M. and Cappello, A. (2010) '"Outwalk": A protocol for clinical gait analysis based on inertial and magnetic sensors', *Medical & Biological Engineering & Computing*, 48(1): 17–25.

Della Croce, U., Leardini, A., Chiari, L. and Cappozzo, A. (2005) 'Human movement analysis using stereophotogrammetry – Part 4: Assessment of anatomical landmark misplacement and its effects on joint kinematics', *Gait & Posture*, 21(2): 226–237.

Di Salvo, V., Collins, A., McNeill, B. and Cardinale, M. (2006) 'Validation of Prozone®: A new video-based performance analysis system', *International Journal of Performance Analysis in Sport*, 6(1): 108–119.

Dogramaci, S.N., Watsford, M.L. and Murphy, A.J. (2011) 'The reliability and validity of subjective notational analysis in comparison to global positioning system tracking to assess athlete movement patterns', *Journal of Strength and Conditioning Research*, 25(3): 852–859.

Duffield, R., Reid, M., Baker, J. and Spratford, W. (2010) 'Accuracy and reliability of GPS devices for measurement of movement patterns in confined spaces for court-based sports', *Journal of Science and Medicine in Sport*, 13(5): 523–525.

Edgecomb, S.J. and Norton, K.I. (2006) 'Comparison of global positioning and computer-based tracking systems for measuring player movement distance during Australian football', *Journal of Science and Medicine Sport*, 9(1): 25–32.

Erer, K. (2007) 'Adaptive usage of the Butterworth digital filter', *Journal of Biomechanics*, 40(13): 2934–2943.

Eriksen, H., Kristiansen, J., Langangen, O. and Wehus, I. (2009) 'How fast could Usain Bolt have run? A dynamical study', *American Journal of Physics*, 77: 224–228.

Escamilla, R., Fleisig, G., Zheng, N., Barrentine, S. and Andrews, J. (2001) 'Kinematic comparisons of 1996 Olympic baseball pitchers', *Journal of Sports Sciences*, 19(9): 665–676.

Frencken, W.G.P., Lemmink, K. and Delleman, N. (2010) 'Soccer-specific accuracy and validity of the local position measurement (LPM) system', *Journal of Science Medicine and Sport*, 13(6): 641–645.

Funk, J., Rowson, S., Daniel, R. and Duma, S. (2012) 'Validation of concussion risk curves for collegiate football players derived from HITS data', *Annals of Biomedical Engineering*, 40(1): 79–89.

Gabbett, T. and Mulvey, M. (2008) 'Time-motion analysis of small-sided training games and competition in elite women soccer players', *The Journal of Strength & Conditioning Research*, 22(2): 543–552.

Gabin, B., Camerino, O., Anguera, T. and Castaner, M. (2012) 'Lince: Multiplatform sport analysis software', *Procedia – Social and Behavioral Sciences*, 46: 4692–4694.

Gray, A.J., Jenkins, D., Andrews, M.H., Taaffe, D.R. and Glover, M.L. (2010) 'Validity and reliability of GPS for measuring distance travelled in field-based team sports', *Journal of Sports Sciences*, 28(12): 1319–1325.

Hanley, B., Bissas, A. and Drake, A. (2013) 'Kinematic characteristics of elite men's 50 km race walking', *European Journal of Sport Science*, 13(3): 272–279.

Hedrick, T.L. (2008) 'Software techniques for two and three-dimensional kinematic measurements of biological and biomimetic systems', *Bioinspiration & Biomimetics*, 3(3): 1–6.

Hill-Haas, S., Dawson, B., Coutts, A. and Rowsell, G. (2009) 'Physiological responses and time-motion characteristics of various small-sided soccer games in youth players', *Journal of Sports Sciences*, 27(1): 1–8.

Holzer, C. (2001) 'Simi Scout – Ein Softwareanalyse-System zur freien Spielbeobachtung', in P. Lange (ed.), *Leistungsdiagnostik und Coaching im Fußball* (pp. 103–110), Hamburg: Czwalina.

Hughes, M. and Franks, I. (1997) *Notational Analysis of Sport*, Padstow: TJ International.

Hughes, M. and Bartlett, R. (2002) 'The use of performance indicators in performance analysis', *Journal of Sports Science*, 20(10): 739–754.

Hughes, M., Cooper, S. and Nevill, A. (2004) 'Analysis of notation data: Reliability', in M. Hughes and I. Franks (eds), *Notational Analysis of Sport* (pp. 189–204), London: E & FN Spon.

Huitema, R., Hof, A. and Postema, K. (2002) 'Ultrasonic motion analysis system – Measurement of temporal and spatial gait parameters', *Journal of Biomechanics*, 35(6): 837–842.

King, T., Jenkins, D. and Gabbett, T. (2009) 'A time-motion analysis of professional rugby league match-play', *Journal of Sports Science*, 27(3): 213–219.

Krosshaug, T., Nakamae, A., Boden, B., Engebretsen, L., Smith, G., Slauterbeck, J., Hewett, T. and Bahr, R. (2007) 'Estimating 3D joint kinematics from video sequences of running and cutting maneuvers – assessing the accuracy of simple visual inspection', *Gait & Posture*, 26(3): 378–385.

Lames, M. (1994) *Systematische Spielbeobachtung*, Münster: Philippka.

Lames, M., Siegle, M. and O'Donoghue, P. (2012) 'Space creation and restriction in elite soccer', *World Congress of Performance Analysis of Sport IX, 25–28 July 2012, Book of Abstracts*, University of Worcester, UK. http://www.sportsci.org/2012/WCPAS_IX_Abstracts.pdf (accessed 25 August 2014)

Leser, R. (2006) 'Systematisierung und praktische Anwendung der computer- und digitalvideo-gestützten Sportspielanalyse', doctoral thesis, University of Vienna.

Leser, R. and Baca, A. (2008) 'Practice oriented match analyses in table tennis as coaching aid', in A. Lees, D. Carbello and G. Torres (eds), *Science and Racket Sports IV*, London: Routledge.

Leser, R., Baca, A., Baron, R. and Kain, H. (2007) 'Qualitative game analysis in table tennis', *Proceedings of the 10th Anniversary International Table Tennis Sports Science Congress*, Zagreb, Croatia. Lausanne: ITTF

Leser, R., Baca, A. and Ogris, G. (2011) 'Local Positioning Systems in (game) sports', *Sensors*, 11(10): 9778–9797.

Leser, R., Schleindlhuber, A., Lyons, K. and Baca, A. (2014) 'Accuracy of an UWB-based position tracking system used for time-motion analyses in game sports', *European Journal of Sport Science*. Retreived from <http://www.tandfonline.com/doi/abs/10.108 0/17461391.2014.884167> (accessed on 1 April 2014).

MacLeod, H., Morris, J., Nevill, A. and Sunderland, C. (2009) 'The validity of a nondifferential global positioning system for assessing player movement patterns in field hockey', *Journal of Sports Sciences*, 27: 121–128.

Mallo, J. and Navarro, E. (2008) 'Physical load imposed on soccer players during small-sided training games', *The Journal of Sports Medicine and Physical Fitness*, 48(2): 166–171.

Mayagoitia, R., Nene, A. and Veltink, P. (2002) 'Accelerometer and rate gyroscope measurement of kinematics: An inexpensive alternative to optical motion analysis systems', *Journal of Biomechanics*, 35: 537–542.

McGinley, J., Baker, R., Wolfe, R. and Morris, M. (2009) 'The reliability of three-dimensional kinematic gait measurements: A systematic review', *Gait & Posture*, 29: 360–369.

McLellan, C., Lovell, D. and Gass, G. (2011) 'Performance analysis of elite rugby league match play using global positioning systems', *The Journal of Strength & Conditioning Research*, 25: 1703–1710.

Moeslund, T., Hilton, A. and Krüger, V. (2006) 'A survey of advances in vision-based human motion capture and analysis', *Computer Vision and Image Understanding*, 104: 90–126.

Molloy, M., Salazar-Torres, J., Kerr, C., McDowell, B. and Cosgrove, A. (2008) 'The effects of industry standard averaging and filtering techniques in kinematic gait analysis', *Gait & Posture*, 28: 559–562.

Murias, J., Lanatta, D., Arcuri, C. and Laino, F. (2007) 'Metabolic and functional responses playing tennis on different surfaces', *The Journal of Strength & Conditioning Research*, 21: 112–117.

Najafi, B., Aminian, K., Loew, F., Blanc, Y. and Robert, P. (2002) 'Measurement of stand-sit and sit-stand transitions using a miniature gyroscope and its application in fall risk evaluation in the elderly', *IEEE Transactions on Biomedical Engineering*, 49: 843–851.

Najafi, B., Helbostad, J., Moe-Nilssen, R., Zijlstra, W. and Aminian, K. (2009) 'Does walking strategy in older people change as a function of walking distance?', *Gait & Posture*, 29: 261–266.

Newman, J., Beusenberg, M., Shewchenko, N., Withnall, C. and Fournier, E. (2005) 'Verification of biomechanical methods employed in a comprehensive study of mild traumatic brain injury and the effectiveness of American football helmets', *Journal of Biomechanics*, 38: 1469–1481.

Ogris, G., Leser, R., Horsak, B., Kornfeind, P., Heller, M. and Baca, A. (2012) 'Accuracy of the LPM tracking system considering dynamic position changes', *Journal of Sports Sciences*, 30: 1503–1511.

Osgnach, C., Poser, S., Bernardini, R., Rinaldo, R. and Di Prampero, P. (2010) 'Energy cost and metabolic power in elite soccer: A new match analysis approach', *Medicine & Science in Sports & Exercise*, 42: 170–178.

Pansiot, J. (2009) 'Markerless visual tracking and motion – analysis for sports monitoring', doctoral thesis, University of London.

Pers, J., Bon, M., Kovacic, S., Sibila, M. and Dezman, B. (2002) 'Observation and analysis of large-scale human motion', *Human Movement Science*, 21: 295–311.

Petersen, C., Pyne, D., Portus, M., Karppinen, S. and Dawson, B. (2009) 'Variability in movement patterns during one day internationals by a cricket fast bowler', *International Journal of Sports Physiology and Performance*, 4: 278–281.

Petersen, C., Pyne, D., Dawson, B., Portus, M. and Kellett, A. (2010) 'Movement patterns in cricket vary by both position and game format', *Journal of Sports Sciences*, 28: 45–52.

Pribanic, T., Peharec, S. and Medved, V. (2009) 'A comparison between 2D plate calibration and wand calibration for 3D kinematic systems', *Kinesiology*, 41: 147–155.

Randers, M., Mujika, I., Hewitt, A., Santisteban, J., Bischoff, R., Solano, R., Zubillaga, A., Peltola, E., Krustrup, P. and Mohr, M. (2010) 'Application of four different football match analysis systems: A comparative study', *Journal of Sports Sciences*, 28: 171–182.

Roberts, S., Trewartha, G. and Stokes, K. (2006) 'A comparison of time-motion analysis methods for field-based sports', *International Journal of Sports Physiology and Performance*, 1: 388–399.

Shin, K. and Mun, J. (2012) 'A multi-camera calibration method using a 3-axis frame and wand', *International Journal of Precision Engineering and Manufacturing*, 13: 283–289.

Siegle, M., Stevens, T. and Lames, M. (2012) 'Design of an accuracy study for position detection in football', *Journal of Sports Sciences*, 31: 166–172.

Sirotic, A., Coutts, A., Knowles, H. and Catterick, C. (2009) 'A comparison of match demands between elite and semi-elite rugby league competition', *Journal of Sports Sciences*, 27(3): 203–211.

Stauffer, C. and Grimson, W. (1999) 'Adaptive background mixture models for real-time tracking', *Proceedings IEEE Conf. on Computer Vision and Pattern Recognition* (pp. 246–252), Fort Collins, CO. Washington, DC: IEEE Computer Society Press.

Tresadern, P. and Reid, I. (2008) 'Camera calibration from human motion', *Image and Vision Computing*, 26(6): 851–862.

Varley, M.C., Fairweather, I.H. and Aughey, R.J. (2012) 'Validity and reliability of GPS for measuring instantaneous velocity during acceleration, deceleration, and constant motion', *Journal of Sports Sciences*, 30(2): 121–127.

6   Modelling and simulation

Jürgen Perl

Introduction

Modelling does not need to be learned. Every thought, every impression generates models. Every insight, every decision uses models.

Therefore the central question is, if and how such an extremely reflexive term like model, which we use for thinking in order to understand it, can be seen through and universally defined.

Obviously, we cannot claim to understand modelling as a monolithic and binding paradigm. Modelling has developed differently in different contexts, has developed specific traditions and in particular created bases for pragmatic applications. Exemplarily, natural sciences represent such a pragmatic understanding and use of models. In particular, the models of 'laws of nature' help in finding efficient and effective descriptions of natural interaction systems, making diagnoses of systems' states and calculating prognoses of future development and behaviour.

In the field of sports science, the utility of that pragmatic modelling approach is impressively well proven, for example in the areas of medicine, physiology and biomechanics.

It has to be noted that 'pragmatic' does not mean 'low level' or 'non-scientific'. It only means that the focus of that kind of modelling is less philosophical but more technical in order to calculate useful results. Following this understanding, modelling in computer science is even more pragmatic and orientated mainly in computers and their quantitative properties like speed and storage, together with high demands on efficiency and effectiveness. In contrast, the precision of computer-based calculation is only an apparent one if not based on an appropriate and well-designed model. This means: if we do not understand what is happening in a complex system even the best computers and programs cannot help to calculate better diagnostic and prognostic results.

Following those preliminary considerations, a chapter on modelling first of all has to define what idea of model and modelling will be dealt with, followed by some systematic of types of models.

Furthermore, the specific orientation on sports means to focus the presentation on athletes – their internal physiologic dynamics as well as their external behaviour – and teams of athletes with their group- and interaction-oriented dynamics. Therefore dynamic systems will play an important role in dealing with modelling in sports.

Some case studies will demonstrate ways of designing models and how to apply them in practice.

Basics of modelling

Following the pragmatic approach that has been discussed in the introduction, the term 'model' briefly can be defined as (Perl, Lames and Miethling, 1997: 43): 'A model is an abstract mapping of a system. It supports the diagnosis of the system's state and the prognosis of the system's behaviour.'

In this definition 'system' means a real world construct consisting of interacting partners or components, which in turn interacts with its environment. Such systems can be extremely complex, like, for example, the physiology of an athlete. Therefore the model has to reduce or abstract the system, which normally results in major distortions, for example disregard of components, their interactions or interactions between system and environment.

Obviously, such distortions cannot be completely avoided. Therefore a well-designed model has at least to map the most important parts of the system as precisely as possible – which in practice often is a most difficult task that requires a lot of information and experience. And, of course, the designed model has to be checked: whether it maps the real system in an adequate way. Normally it does not in the first step; a second step is necessary and so on. This means that model designing is an iterative process, even more so because the model normally has to be adjusted to changing context conditions during its lifetime.

Despite those problems with abstraction and precision, the described way of modelling is well supported by countless approaches in natural sciences: based on observed data, mathematical equations describe interactions of the involved objects and so help in predicting their future behaviour – as is successfully done for instance with planets, comets or satellites.

In this type of modelling a deterministic behaviour of the modelled system is assumed – i.e. the laws are given and only have to be detected and formulated by means of the model. But this assumption cannot be generalized and has to be carefully considered. Three examples may make plain that not all real world systems meet that strong precondition of universal laws and/or deterministic behaviour:

1   Newton's laws modelled the mechanical behaviour of real world objects seemingly perfectly – until the beginning of the twentieth century. Then the Michelson experiments showed that c, the speed of light, is a universal limitation of any speed. In direct consequence this meant that the mass of an object – i.e. its resistance against acceleration – is not an invariant property of an object but increases to an infinite value if its speed approaches c. Based on those findings, the relativistic model of mechanics was developed, which contains the classic model as a borderline case of small speed.

Nowadays, satellite journeys to distant planets are planned using relativistic models, while for the analysis of a 100-metre race the classic model (normally) is sufficient.

2   In the 1950s the skills of the first electronic computers were that fascinating that people spoke of 'electronic brains' and dreamt of 'artificial intelligence'. The extremely simple computers with bit-oriented user interfaces were taken as quantitative as well as qualitative models of human thinking – although their abilities were poor compared to today's smartphones or even pocket calculators.

Artificial neural networks – today indisputably extremely helpful and successful tools in the area of pattern recognition or fast calculation of high dimensional functions – forty years ago were developed in order to model natural brains and to understand the laws of human thinking. The problem is: even if the behaviour of artificial networks, often in an astonishing way, is similar to that of networks of natural neurons it cannot be a model of human thinking as long as the dynamics of human thinking is not completely understood – and as long as artificial neural networks work with some hundreds of neurons while natural ones usually contain some billions of them.

3   In the 1970s the 'Club of Rome' developed so-called world models, consisting of a complex system of coupled equations, which, briefly stated, were thought to predict the balance between supplies and consumption of natural resources ('Limitations of Growth'). Doubtless this was a first important step in order to understand the global phenomenon of resource flow and distribution. Nevertheless, from today's point of view the approach was naïve. To understand and validate the behaviour of such a lot of coupled equations is as difficult as it is to understand and predict the behaviour of the modelled system. Artefacts and numeric inaccuracy can distort the results down to complete uselessness (for the basics of system dynamics see Forrester, 1968).

These examples give a first impression of what is important for adequate modelling.

The structure and dynamics of the system to be modelled has to be understood – at least in the parts the focus of diagnosis and prognosis is on.

Models cannot be developed in one step but have to be approached by an iteration of checks and improvements. Therefore, modelling not only means mapping a system for calculating its state or predicting its future behaviour. The procedure of modelling itself helps to aid a better understanding of the system's structure, dynamics and behaviour. However, most of the real world systems are so complex that a satisfying model seems extremely difficult if not impossible. A spectacular example is that of the above mentioned 'Limitations of Growth': although the political utility – namely the recognition of basic global problems – was indisputable, the predictions in detail were doubtful because of two reasons. The global structure of supplies and consumption is much too complex for a comparably simple differential equation model. And, moreover, those structures are not at all stable but vary depending on political dynamics.

Nevertheless, abstraction, i.e. reduction of complexity, is a basic concept in modelling, because it is the only chance to get a model at all.

Therefore, modelling means to bridge a gap: although models have to be as complex as necessary in order to represent reality, they also have to be kept as simple as possible in order to be able to validate their accuracy, adequateness and usability.

Take the complex dynamic system 'game' as an example. It often is reduced to numbers, frequencies and distributions of events or actions – neglecting, however, determining factors like interaction and time-depending dynamics. Although it can be helpful, of course, to know what the success rate of a player was, more informative is why it was so low or high – i.e. what particular behaviour, interactions and tactical processes were the reasons for it. Obviously, here the above mentioned discrepancy is as follows. On the one hand, reducing the game to a model of countable events produces numbers but offers only little information about the playing processes and dynamics. On the other hand, preserving all available data from sensors, observation and video overlays can hide important information about dynamics.

As will be discussed in 'Unconventional modelling' and 'Pattern analysis by means of SOMs', patterns can help to solve this problem by aggregating players to tactical groups and events to simplified patterns of behavioural processes.

Finally there is one problem that appears in social and/or behavioural systems like in sports and cannot be handled using mathematical equations only. Human beings act in a very individual and often not predictable way. If they appear as members of big crowds, the behaviour normally can be described by stochastic distributions. If not, as is the case in sports, modelling has to change from exact mathematical equations to paradigms that are able to describe vagueness, complex patterns or time-depending evolutions (regarding the debate on voluntarism versus determinism see for instance Burrell and Morgan (1985)).

Three of those paradigms, namely fuzzy models, artificial neural networks and evolutionary algorithms, will be introduced briefly. In particular the usability of self-organizing maps, a special type of artificial neural networks for pattern recognition in sports, will be demonstrated in a case study.

Further reading

Bossel, 1994; Bungartz, Zimmer, Buchholz and Pflüger, 2009; Burrell and Morgan, 1985; Forrester, 1968; Kastens and Kleine Büning, 2005; Spriet and Vansteenkiste, 1982.

Particular aspects of modelling in sports

Modelling plays an important role in nearly all human activities, and therefore and in particular in the area of sports, where precise recognition of the situations and selection of adequate actions often decide on win or loss. There are, however, a huge number of concepts and methods, approaches and applications in modelling, which makes it a problem to select a small number of representative ones.

While the areas of biomechanical and stochastic (quantitative) modelling are quite well presented in literature, a lot of open questions and problems are still left in the areas of the qualitative and behavioural modelling of dynamic systems.

Whenever complex system behaviour has to be analysed – in case of technical systems as well as in case of biological systems – the main problem is that of modelling its structure and the interaction of its components. A reduction to just comparing input data to output data is not sufficient, neither for qualitative nor for quantitative analyses. If the aim is to predict future system behaviour based on present state and planned activities, the system's dynamics have to be transparent and well understood. Only under these conditions modelling and simulation can help aid a better understanding of system behaviour in general and additionally allows for finding and optimizing training schedules or competition strategies.

Activities in sports are normally characterized by time-depending processes. Therefore process orientation is a most important aspect of modelling in sports, where 'process-orientated' means that not just one isolated activity causes an isolated change of a state, but sequences of activities or events cause sequences of states, where in particular buffers and transfers play an important role for delayed effects. It is of particular importance that such delayed effects are driven by internal system dynamics and, therefore, very often cannot properly be measured by statistical methods.

Finally, the difference between data and information has to be taken into consideration.

Data can (automatically) be recorded from the athletes' activities. Data provides the basis for analyses, and only the result of such analyses is useful information – assuming that the analyses are well designed and successful. However, as the following example, which is taken from Perl (2008), may make plain, data can be relevant, highly redundant or in strong correlation to each other, depending on the particular type of analysis:

> As a first example, motion data of an athlete can be recorded automatically, hundred times a second, containing positions, angles, speed of articulations and much more. On the one hand, those data are useful for the bio-mechanist to find out specific striking features of a single articulation over time. On the other hand, if the process of moving as a whole is of interest, many of the data and also their precision are of minor meaning, because they are strongly correlated to a complex pattern of moving. I.e. the information connected to the data can be quite different and obviously depends on the aim of investigation.

Further reading

Lames 1998, 2000; McGarry and Perl, 2004; Perl, 2008; Perl, Lames and Glitsch, 2002.

Simulation and prediction

Simulation

The original meaning of 'to simulate' is 'to imitate' or 'to make sth. similar to sth.' and therefore at first seems to be related to the process of modelling. However, the specific aspect of simulation in the context of modelling becomes transparent if looking at the dynamic behaviour of time-variant systems:

> Simulation basically helps in getting model behaviour to work. A major aim of simulation is to predict the behaviour of the simulated model and/or the modelled system. One motivation for doing such prediction by means of simulation is that often the observation of the original system is difficult or not possible at all. But even if such observation were possible it would not allow seeing the future development.
>
> (Perl, Lames and Miethling, 1997: 65, translated from German)

In sport, training is a process for individuals or teams in order to improve their performance or skills. Normally, a training concept is based on a 'mental model', taking into account information about the athlete's or the team's state and performance potential as well as a lot of experience. That can help the coach to predict the success of the planned training steps in order to find the optimal training strategy – but unfortunately often fails if the modelled system is too complex or if not all of the necessary information is available.

Nowadays, computerized modelling is not much limited by system's complexity, and also access to information is much easier for computers than for coaches. Therefore it is a good idea to support 'mental models' with computer based ones, giving the coach more time for developing ideas, methods and concepts and leaving the work of calculating, checking and predicting to the computer.

Further reading

Baca and Hinterleithner, 2000; Fishwick, 1991; Perl, 2002a, 2008; Perl and Endler, 2012; Wiemeyer, 2000a

As the following example demonstrates, simulation can help to understand models and systems and to check the correctness of models.

Example 1: transportation model 1

The following very simple example models the transport of goods from a source container, S, to a target container, T. At every point in time, t, $S(t)$ and $T(t)$ mean the levels of S and T, respectively, and $R(t, t + \Delta t)$ means the transport rate from S to T during the time interval from t to $t + \Delta t$. The maximum capacity of the transport channel is denoted by C.

The simplest model is the greedy one ('all you can eat'):

$$R(t, t + \Delta t) = C \tag{0}$$
$$S(t + \Delta t) = S(t) - R(t, t + \Delta t) \tag{1}$$
$$T(t + \Delta t) = T(t) + R(t, t + \Delta t) \tag{2}$$

Starting with initial values of S and T, e.g. $S(0) = So$, $T(0) = 0$, the behaviour of the model can be predicted by means of a step by step calculation of the equations. However, whether or not this calculation is really an adequate simulation of the modelled transport system depends on whether or not the equations model the system in an adequate way.

Easy transformations of the equations from above lead to the following equations, which show that after $t > So / C$ steps the source level becomes more and more negative while increases in T are unlimited:

$$S(t) = So - t \times C \tag{1a}$$
$$T(t) = \quad t \times C \tag{2a}$$

This result does not in any way meet experience and expectations. Even if S and T meant bank accounts the bank office would stop the transfers after a finite number of steps.

Obviously the reason for that strange behaviour is the missing control of the remaining source level. Taking the remaining source level into consideration leads to

$$R(t, t + 1) = \text{if } S(t) \geq C \text{ then } C \text{ else } S(t) \tag{0b}$$

and changes the S and T equations (1a), (2a) to

$$S(t) = \text{if } So \geq t \times C \text{ then } So - t \times C \;\; \text{else } 0 \tag{1b}$$
$$T(t) = \text{if } So \geq t \times C \text{ then } \quad t \times C \quad \text{else } So \tag{2b}$$

Of course, a lot of different ways of control is possible – depending on the real system that has to be modelled. Therefore, a simulation based check is necessary, if the developed model really maps the transport system in question.

Finally, a remark regarding differential equations seems to be necessary. Natural scientists tend to replace difference equations like that in (1) and (2) by differential equations, where the time interval Δt approaches zero, hoping to solve and calculate them directly without the need of iterative calculation. If it works it is very helpful for understanding the modelled dynamics and simplifies the handling a lot. However, in the case of (0b), (1b) and (2b) this would not work without problems because those equations are 'non-linear', i.e. they contain contextual conditions. In such cases of limited capacities – like in human physiology or in time- and space-limited games – it is recommended to use the difference equations approach, i.e. to work with 'algorithmic' equations like those from (0b), (1b) and (2b) and to calculate the solutions numerically. If, in particular, the input is not functionally determined but unpredictable like in real-time-systems (for example see the load performance system in 'Case studies: interactive dynamic systems') then stepwise calculation is the only way to get useful results.

Exercise 1

It is suggested checking the model above by means of a simple Excel application and to compare the behaviours of the two versions of the transport model.

Task 1

Try to find out how the algorithm above reacts to different parameter values and under what circumstances the process jumps from one behavioural phase into another. If available you can use a program like the Excel application from Exercise 1.

Prediction

Often systems consist of objects the states of which are time-dependent real numbers like in the transport system above. Simulation and prediction then can mean finding the functions with which the changing state values can be calculated for any given point in time.

Figure 6.1 (top graphic) shows the simplest case of such a system. A single object with a state value $p(x)$ that depends on the time value x. System analysis resulted in the assumption that the system behaviour could be described by a parabola $p(x) = a \times x^2$, where by an appropriate calibration the parameter, a, could be optimized to about 2.95. The deviations at the given points are very small. The interpolation between the given points is fully satisfying.

So far, the parabola model seems to be correct and in any case can be used for diagnosis – i.e. for calculating state values in the presented time range.

The problem is that the model only uses the surface of the system – i.e. the observable data – without understanding the underlying dynamics – i.e. the functional structure of the modelled system. Looking closer at the dynamics, it turns out that actually the system behaviour is described by the well-known catenary (see any collection of mathematical formulas, e.g. Bronstein et al., 2008), which describes the figure of a hanging chain and is a combination of e-functions (Figure 6.1, bottom graphic). The surprising effect is that only a few time steps outside the observed time range, the difference between the parabola model and the original chain system becomes enormous.

Therefore, the model does not allow extrapolation and so is not usable for any kind of prediction.

The simple conclusion is:

> Prediction not only requires careful observation of the system's data but also needs a deeper understanding of the system's dynamics.

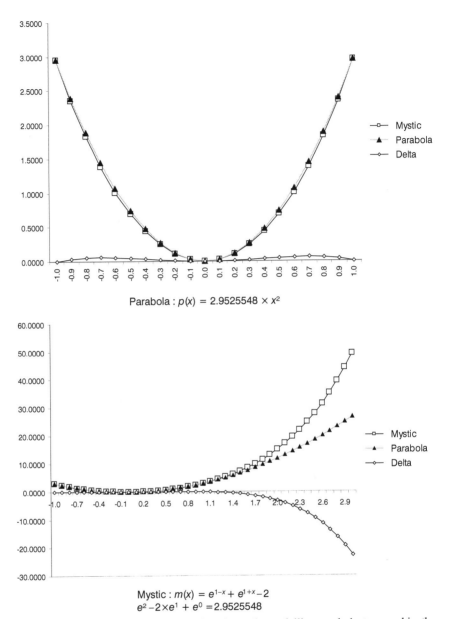

Parabola : $p(x) = 2.9525548 \times x^2$

Mystic : $m(x) = e^{1-x} + e^{1+x} - 2$
$e^2 - 2 \times e^1 + e^0 = 2.9525548$

Figure 6.1 Comparison of a 'mystic' e-function and a modelling parabola: top graphic: the small range of modelling with excellent results, i.e. small deviation (see the lowest part of the parabola); bottom graphic: a large area of extrapolation with extremely high deviation (see negative values).

Example 2: performance prediction

Following the conclusion above it immediately becomes clear how difficult it is to predict the performance development of an athlete or even a team compared to that of a technical device like a car. While a car and its components are constructed under the aspect of predictability an athlete normally is not – or at least the type of performance the athlete is adapted to and is expected to produce in daily life is quite different from the particular performance that has to be produced in sports. Therefore it is an important task of science in sport to better understand the dynamics of producing and improving performance as well as predicting the effect of training regarding performance development.

As has been outlined in (Perl, 2008),

> 'More and better training causes increasing performances' on the one hand seems to be a convincing approach – since it seems to meet most of our experiences from short term as well as from long term training. On the other hand, too much training can reduce performance. Therefore, of course, it is quite clear that simple rules like that above can only give a first orientation.
>
> Due to the fact that an athlete is a complex system with limited capacities and feasibilities, which moreover is embedded in a complex interaction of external impacts, the athlete's reaction on training can be complicated and, at least in details, unpredictable. So the problem of predictability is a central one in particular in the field of adaptation, where the test person forms a dynamic system with time-dependent dynamic states. Therefore in sport, particularly in training and motor learning in order to optimize training and learning strategies and schedules, the problem is not only to evaluate the status of an athlete but also to understand his specific dynamics.
>
> This obviously can hardly be done by sporadically and unsystematically recording isolated values but only by the systematic recording of complete time series.
>
> Even more complicated is the situation in case of games if one tries to predict the result of a future game, based only on past results or other statistical data and without taking dynamic state fluctuations of the teams into consideration. In a similar way, most of the so-called performance models of players as well as of teams are useless if they are based only on past values. Those values of course are necessary. But they are helpful for a workable prediction only if they are used on the basis of an adequate model, which the data are compatible with. Often prediction fails because there is no model at all or the recorded data do not meet the requirements of the model.

Dynamic systems

Introduction

Modelling a dynamic system like a car or an athlete means mapping not only its components and input–output behaviour but also and in particular its components' interactions. The example of a car shows that not only the power of the motor predicts the maximum speed of the car. The way the power is transferred to the wheels, the size of the wheels, the grip of the wheels, and the surface of the street are extremely important too. Moreover, interaction normally is delayed and so needs time. If one tries to accelerate an old and weakly motorized car uphill, the effect of activating the accelerator can be delayed dramatically. Additionally, such delays are not static but can depend on the point in time and the situation the system is in. A marathon runner, for instance, can immediately increase his speed at the start, with some delay if running through an applauding crowd, with a long delay after a phase of fatigue, and normally not at all in his finishing phase.

This means that a system input – depending on the respective internal status – can cause quite different dynamics and outputs, which makes it extremely difficult to predict the system behaviour by only taking static pairs of input and output values into consideration. Accordingly, stochastic analysis methods like correlation or trend analysis based on past values in dynamic systems are normally neither sufficient nor adequate for an acceptable prediction. This is quite obvious in cases like game analysis or rehabilitation but also holds true for motor analysis and training and performance analysis.

Continuous modelling versus discrete modelling

As has been mentioned in connection with the transportation model, often the question is whether to use continuous models or to use discrete models. In dynamic systems this particularly means: differential equations or difference equation?

There are three main reasons for preferring differential equations:

1   The system to be modelled can have a continuous nature. This is the case for instance with flowing liquids. But the flow in discrete units can also look like a continuous one, and can be handled as such if the units are small, their number is high and the distance of the observer is large. Examples are bottles in a filling machine or cars on a crowded motorway. In cases like these, modelling by means of differential equations seems to be adequate, even if the system actually has a discrete nature.
2   If it is possible to describe the system's dynamics by means of a differential equation there is a certain expectation of finding functional solutions, which allow the recognition of the basic functional structures of the system and the easy calculation of simulations and prognoses. Natural laws, which are often derived from differential equations of observed phenomena, are convincing examples.
3   Mathematical tools are available, which help in solving differential equations or at least in numerically integrating them.

However, the disadvantages of the differential equations approach can be explained using the same aspects:

1   If the interacting objects of the system to be modelled are not small enough or if their number is too small then differential equations tend to idealize the type of the system, which can result in severe errors in the model and its simulation. Such errors also can appear if non-linear algorithmic aspects like limited capacities, case distinctions, conditional repetitions or external control have to be modelled. In such cases the system's state does not move continuously through only one set of state elements but jumps between different sets of state elements, where each set characterizes a specific situation and/or context of the system (compare the transport model above).

2   Based on experience gained since the beginning of the modelling of social systems, their structures and dynamics normally are too complex for a description by differential equations in order to find functional solutions. Not least, starting in the early 1950s, this was a reason for developing special simulation languages, which helped in computer based formulating and calculating the models of such complex dynamic systems. Nowadays, a lot of mathematical calculation tools are available. Even normal programming languages like Java or table calculation tools like Excel can be used for the same purpose.

3   If the differential equation model is not functionally solvable in a closed form it has to be solved iteratively by means of numeric integration. For this purpose the model has to be transformed into a system of difference equations – implicitly by the calculation tool used or explicitly by changing the model.

Further reading

Bossel, 1994; Bungartz, Zimmer, Buchholz and Pflüger, 2009; Kastens and Kleine Büning, 2005; Spriet and Vansteenkiste, 1982.

Example 3: transportation model 2

VARIABLES AND PARAMETERS

R: transportation rate; S: source level; T: target level; t: point in time; $(t, t + \Delta t)$: time interval; Δt: length of time interval; f: proportional factor of transportation (can be interpreted as transportation delay).

APPROACH AND DIFFERENCE EQUATIONS

The idea of the model is that, similar to transportation model 1, during the time interval, Δt, the transportation rate reduces the source level, S, by a certain amount and increases the target level, T, by the same amount. Different from model 1, the transported amount is not constant but depends on the source level, $S(t)$.

By easy transformations the model equations then can be transformed to difference quotients.

$$R(t, t + \Delta t) = \Delta t \times f \times S(t) \tag{0}$$
$$S(t + \Delta t) = S(t) - R(t, t + \Delta t) = S(t) - \Delta t \times f \times S(t) \tag{1}$$
$$T(t + \Delta t) = T(t) + R(t, t + \Delta t) = T(t) + \Delta t \times f \times S(t) \tag{2}$$

DIFFERENCE QUOTIENTS:

$$(S(t + \Delta t) - S(t)) / \Delta t = - \Delta t \times f \times S(t) \tag{1a}$$
$$(T(t + \Delta t) - T(t)) / \Delta t = \Delta t \times f \times S(t) \tag{2a}$$

The difference quotients on the left hand sides through $\Delta t \rightarrow 0$ are transferred into differential quotients, resulting in:

DIFFERENTIAL EQUATION:

$$dS(t) / dt = S'(t) = -f \times S(t) \tag{1b}$$
$$dT(t) / dt = T'(t) = f \times S(t) \tag{2b}$$

E-FUNCTIONS:

The solution (1c) of equation (1b) obviously is a reverse e-function, describing the situation of asymptotically losing substance with the level S starting with $S(0)$ and tending to 0, where the delay in that process is characterized by the factor f:

$$S(t) = S(0) \times e^{-f \times t} \tag{1c}$$

The solution (2c) of equation (2b) is a curbed e-function, describing the situation of asymptotically winning substance with the level T starting with 0 and tending to $S(0)$, where again the delay in that process is characterized by the factor f:

$$T(t) = S(0) - S(0) \times e^{-f \times t} \tag{2c}$$

CONSISTENCY ANALYSIS:

One can easily see that for

$t = 0$: $S(t) = S(0)$ and $T(t) = 0$,

$t \rightarrow \infty$: $S(t) \rightarrow 0$ and $T(t) \rightarrow S(0)$

for all $t \geq 0$: $S(t) + T(t) = S(0)$, i.e. the balance is always constant.

The example presented demonstrates why in the practice of modelling and simulation often the following simple approach is favoured. Single components of the system are separated and modelled by means of differential equations in a prototypical way. The advantage is that such reduced equations possibly can be solved functionally and therefore allow for mathematical analysis of the component's typical behaviour.

One example is the self-stabilizing physiologic dynamics of training-driven load and recovery. The main dynamics can be described by two complementary e-functions – but only in a rather small context-free area and as long as the natural capacity limitations are not approached. Otherwise, when stability is disturbed by approaching limitations or by external influences, behaviour is jumping through secondary phases until it reaches stability again or it collapses. In this case it is better to use the original difference equations and calculate the system's behaviour iteratively step by step, without reducing complexity and neglecting contexts and phase changes. In 'Case studies: interactive dynamic systems' an example (PerPot) is presented, which deals with the fatigue-recovery dynamics, using transportation processes like those above.

Quantitative versus qualitative models

In sports, performance and ranking orders are the focus. That means that performance has to be measurable by quantities and that those quantities have to be comparable in order to find ranking lists. Even if the phenomenon to be measured has a qualitative nature like, for example, the elegance or technical perfection of a motion, the subjective impression of referees is measured by numbers and so transformed to a pseudo-objective quantity.

In systems like games in which complex interaction as well as objectively measurable events are of importance the situation is different.

An attack can successfully end with scoring – without meeting the coach's expectations of a well done interaction process. Also adding quantitative information about the players involved, number of passes, or positions of the players and the ball is not sufficient in order to qualitatively measure the playing process, if the causal prognostic relationship between process quality and scoring success is of interest.

Analogously, the motion of a body is a complex interaction process of the components involved. The measurable success of a motion on the one hand depends on the optimization of each single component, on the other hand it depends on the optimization of their complex interactions.

The way out of this dilemma is given by state-event models, patterns and situational contexts.

The processes that characterize the interactions of a system are recorded and qualitatively identified by types (also see references above and 'Unconventional modelling'). These process types then can be combined with quantitative attributes like frequency, involved components or success.

The throw by a basketball player biomechanically can be described as a time sequence of the positions, speeds and accelerations of the throwing arm's segments. However, the amount of data of such a quantitative characterization makes it difficult to recognize and compare the process information behind the data.

Instead, the biomechanical data can be reduced to time-depending distribution of patterns that define phase-depending motion types like concentration, draw back, throw, finishing and relaxing. Quantitative attributes could be number of type, frequency and duration of the phases as well as of the complete throw.

Similarly, in the playing processes of games like soccer, individual players and their positions can be divided into tactical groups and their centroids (i.e. the mean value of the players' positions, also see 'Example 9: soccer' in 'Pattern analysis by means of SOMs'). This way, tactical behaviour and interaction can be described by the qualitative moving patterns of those centroids, completed as above by quantitative attributes like type number, frequency and success. Additionally, the situational context plays an important role in such behavioural processes. Whether or not, for instance, the goalkeeper's dribbling with the ball is dangerous or successful obviously depends on the opposition team's attacking players' positions.

These two examples lead to two central aspects of process modelling. Patterns are used to describe and characterize types of individual processes, while state-event models describe the processes of a dynamic system in its entirety.

Patterns

A sign consisting of a red octagon together with the white inscription 'stop' will be understood worldwide, independently of its exact size or quality in detail, i.e. the red octagon together with the white inscription builds a prototype or pattern.

Similarly, corresponding to the examples above, processes in sports build patterns. Such patterns can contain numerical attributes like the biomechanical ones of a throw. In this case the exact values don't characterize the pattern but the way the values form a time-depending sequence do. Or, as in games, a process can be characterized by rough positions like left or right and actions like pass or flank. So a tactical pattern in soccer could have the form <pass left, pass left, flank from left to right, pass right>.

Example 4: attacking processes in soccer

In Figure 6.2, six examples of approaching processes of attacking players against the opposition goal are presented. Taking only the *x*- and *y*-coordinates would not give that much information. By presenting them graphically, one can immediately see that there are two groups of processes, one on the right wing and the other on the left wing. At first glance the processes of the respective groups seem to be rather similar to each other. However, whether or not the groups form patterns of similar processes is not quite as easy to say. To understand and eventually to answer this question some aspects of similarity are discussed in the following.

In the end, the way to find an answer is to calculate the distance between the sequences of coordinates and – depending on a given similarity tolerance – the answer can be 'yes' or 'no'.

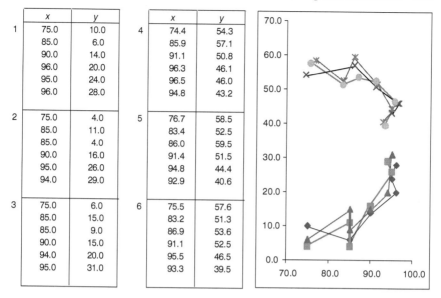

	x	y		x	y
1	75.0	10.0	4	74.4	54.3
	85.0	6.0		85.9	57.1
	90.0	14.0		91.1	50.8
	96.0	20.0		96.3	46.1
	95.0	24.0		96.5	46.0
	96.0	28.0		94.8	43.2
2	75.0	4.0	5	76.7	58.5
	85.0	11.0		83.4	52.5
	85.0	4.0		86.0	59.5
	90.0	16.0		91.4	51.5
	95.0	26.0		94.8	44.4
	94.0	29.0		92.9	40.6
3	75.0	6.0	6	75.5	57.6
	85.0	15.0		83.2	51.3
	85.0	9.0		86.9	53.6
	90.0	15.0		91.1	52.5
	94.0	20.0		95.5	46.5
	95.0	31.0		93.3	39.5

Figure 6.2 Two groups of three moving processes (graphs on the right-hand side) together with their position coordinates.

Similarity

(1) Two uncoloured triangles can be said to be similar, if the distances between each of the corresponding corners are below a given threshold. But then the question arises what are the corresponding corners?

The answer is given by the next example.

(2) If two coloured photographs are compared, for each pixel the colours have to be compared – in a given order, for example from top, row by row from left to right, to the bottom.

So the answer is 'predefined ordering'. The objects that have to be compared first of all have to be ordered identically with respect to their components. In the case of photographs the pixel colours are encoded by a sequence of vectors of coordinates

$$(c_{11}, \ldots ,c_{1n}), (c_{21}, \ldots ,c_{2n}), \ldots , (c_{m1}, \ldots ,c_{mn}),$$

where 'm' is the number of rows, 'n' is the number of columns, the first index means the row, the second index means the column and 'c' is the colour code. Therefore 'c_{34}' means the colour code of the pixel in the third row and the fourth column.

Simplified:

$$(c_{11}, \ldots ,c_{1n}, c_{21}, \ldots ,c_{2n}, \ldots ,c_{m1}, \ldots ,c_{mn})$$

This is called the (colour) pattern of the photograph.

Analogously, the corners of the triangle are ordered into a sequence A, B, C, where each corner has x- and y-coordinates, leading to the sequence $(A_x,A_y),(B_x,B_y),(C_x,C_y)$. Normally, the vector

$$(A_x,A_y,B_x,B_y,C_x,C_y)$$

would be taken as (corner) pattern of triangles.

Often in sports, constellations of players are of interest. Compared to the triangle, the players here play the roles of corners, and correspondingly

$$(P_{1x},P_{1y},P_{2x},P_{2y}, \ldots ,P_{kx},P_{ky})$$

can be taken as the pattern of a k-player constellation, where x and y are the coordinates of the player's position on the playing ground.

Once the order of the information is agreed, the similarity of two patterns can be measured by their distance. Usually and in particular in case of geometric patterns the Euclidian distance is chosen, which generalizes the distance of 2-dimensional geometric points to n-dimensional vectors:

$$\mathbf{A} = (a_1,a_2, \ldots ,a_n), \mathbf{B} = (b_1,b_2, \ldots ,b_n)$$
$$ED(\mathbf{A},\mathbf{B}) = \sqrt{((a_1 - b_1)^2 + (a_2 - b_2)^2 + \ldots + (a_n - b_n)^2)}$$

If the Euclidian distance, ED, of $\mathbf{A}$ and $\mathbf{B}$ is small, where 'small' has to be defined as a threshold, then $\mathbf{A}$ and $\mathbf{B}$ are called similar, otherwise non-similar.

Obviously, as the following three examples make plain, it does not matter whether the vectors $\mathbf{A}$ and $\mathbf{B}$ stand for geometric information or – for example – for biometric data or even time-dependent processes.

1   The vectors $\mathbf{A}$ and $\mathbf{B}$ contain the position coordinates of the same selection of players. The players form geometric constellations. The distance measures the similarity of the constellations.
2   The vectors $\mathbf{A}$ and $\mathbf{B}$ contain the angles of a leg's articulations, representing motion patterns. The distance measures the similarity of those motions.
3   The vectors $\mathbf{A}$ and $\mathbf{B}$ contain the positions of a player during a time interval, describing the moving processes of the respective players. The distance measures the similarity of those processes.

In the case of moving, the processes are given as sequences of 2-dimensional positions. Let P_1 and P_2 be two of such processes of length 6, as presented in Figure 6.2:

$$P_1 = ((x_{11},y_{11}), \ldots ,(x_{16},y_{16})) \text{ and } P_2 = ((x_{21},y_{21}), \ldots ,(x_{26},y_{26}))$$

(A) METHOD OF MEAN EUCLIDEAN POSITION DISTANCE

It seems to make sense to calculate the Euclidian distances of the corresponding positions,

$$\Delta_1 = \sqrt{((x_{11} - x_{21})^2 + (y_{11} - y_{21})^2)},$$

$$\dots,$$

$$\Delta_6 = \sqrt{((x_{16} - x_{26})^2 + (y_{16} - y_{26})^2)},$$

and to take the mean value of these Euclidean distances

$$\Delta P_1 P_2 = (\Delta_1 + \dots + \Delta_6) / 6$$

as a measure for the similarity.

In the given constellation, processes 5 and 6 are rather similar with a distance of 2.51, while process 4 has a distance of 5.49 to process 5 and a distance of 4.98 to process 6. From this it follows that processes 5 and 6 are similar, while process 4 is not as similar to 5 and 6.

(B) METHOD OF EUCLIDEAN PROCESS DISTANCE

The similarity analysis above is orientated in the player's positions but does not compare the 12-dimensional x–y-sequences as a whole. In the same way as the distance of two 2-dimensional points can be measured, the distance of two 12-dimensional x–y vectors can be calculated. In order to do so we understand $\mathbf{P}_i$ and $\mathbf{P}_j$ as follows, i.e. without separating the pairs:

$$\mathbf{P}_i = (x_{i1}, y_{i1}, \dots, x_{i6}, y_{i6}) \text{ and } \mathbf{P}_j = (x_{j1}, y_{j1}, \dots, x_{j6}, y_{j6})$$

and calculate the difference between P_i and P_j by

$$\Delta \mathbf{P}_i \mathbf{P}_j = \sqrt{((x_{i1} - x_{j1})^2 + (y_{i1} - y_{j1})^2 + \dots + (x_{i6} - x_{j6})^2 + (y_{i6} - y_{j6})^2)}.$$

Doing it this way results in $\Delta \mathbf{P}_4 \mathbf{P}_5 = 14.97$, $\Delta \mathbf{P}_5 \mathbf{P}_6 = 7.69$, $\Delta \mathbf{P}_4 \mathbf{P}_6 = 13.03$, confirming the result above.

In the second method positions and the metric interpretation of distances do not play a role. Therefore it is the more general method, which can also be used in the case of abstract processes, where the components are not necessarily coordinates but can be arbitrary values – for example the biomechanical ones recorded by sensors, as is dealt with in 'Example 5: throw'.

Exercise 2

Try to calculate the mean Euclidean distances between the processes 1, 2 and 3 from the table in Figure 6.2 and check whether the numerical results meet the subjective impression. Compare the two methods A and B. It is helpful to develop an Excel application, which makes it much easier to get comparable results with varying position data.

Task 2

What is the unit of measurement of the mean Euclidean distance in 'Example 4: attacking processes in soccer', and what does that mean? Is there any reason why the values of the first method are larger than those of the second method?

Example 5: throw

In the example of soccer processes the recognition of patterns is supported by the graphical presentation. Even without mathematical calculation one can get an initial idea of whether two processes are similar or not. If the process steps have three coordinates then we could use a 3-dimensional graphical representation. If the process steps have more than three coordinates then there is no way to produce a reasonable graphical representation. In case of biomechanical processes, at each point in time a number of data is recorded, which depends only on the number of installed sensors. Take for instance the example of a throw, where – restricted to the arm – mainly the shoulder, the elbow and the hand are involved. For each of those joints data regarding position, acceleration, speed, angle (and more) can be recorded, totalling (at least) eighteen attributes for each process step. Obviously it is a difficult job to recognize similarities and patterns in such multidimensional processes. There are mathematical and stochastic methods to do this job. In particular artificial neural networks are helpful in this difficult type of analysis.

Patterns reduce the huge amount of recordable data to a smaller amount of information. This can make analysing complex interaction processes much easier – assuming, of course, the selected information is sufficient for describing the important aspects of the processes in question.

In general, patterns are helpful in characterizing and recognizing types of behaviour, as, for example, are motions or tactical processes. The last two sections will demonstrate how patterns can easily be handled by means of artificial neural networks.

State-event models

The state is a snapshot of a system. In tennis, for example, a state could describe the positions of both of the players together with the position of the ball at the moment when it touches the ground. The event then normally is the action of the receiving player, with attributes like technique and direction of the stroke. The situational context can widely spread from the tactical phase and game score to spectators' behaviour or weather.

In general, for each state the state-event model describes which events are possible in the current context, and to which next state the system is being transferred by each of these events. Iteratively continuing this local state-event–state structure leads to a net structure of alternating states and events – where the events are coupled to corresponding context information – which represents all possible processes by the collection of connected state-event paths.

State-event models are adapted from technical systems, where such models are used to describe significant processes, critical points, possible bypasses, shortest paths or rare or most frequent ones. Note that the transportation model above obviously is a state-event model. There the states are the levels of the containers, the events are the rates between the containers and the contexts are given by the conditions.

Transferred to games they can help to recognize the basic tactical behaviour and the strengths and weaknesses of a player. Moreover, they can be used to simulate the players' behaviour. If the probabilities and the success values of the events in the corresponding states are known then the state-event model can be used for a Monte Carlo simulation (see below) of games. This method, for example, can be used to find out whether or not a new tactical concept promises to be successful.

Example 6: Monte Carlo simulation of tennis

A comparatively simple kind of simulation is given by a frequency–success simulation, the corresponding matrices for which are given in Figure 6.3.

Assume that the player analysed gets the ball on position BR (back right). The first matrix contains the frequencies of returns to the target positions on the opponent's half: 35 per cent to BR, 45 per cent to BL (back left), 15 per cent to FR (front right), and 5 per cent to FL (front left). By dividing the percentages by 100 and adding up the results to 1, the percentages are mapped to sub-intervals of the interval [0,1]: the frequency 35 per cent of the return (BR→BR) is mapped to the interval [0,0.35]. Correspondingly, the 45 per cent of (BR→BL) is mapped to [0.35,0.80], the 15 per cent of (BR→FR) to [0.80,0.95], and the 5 per cent of (BR→FL) to [0.95,1.00]. The same is done with the positions BL, FR and FL. The length of each interval now maps the probability of the corresponding return. The maximum values of theses intervals – i.e. 0.35, 0.80, 0.95, and 1.00 for BR – are given in the second matrix, called 'frequency Monte Carlo intervals'.

The way that simulation works is as follows: assume BR to be the starting position. A random number, r, in the interval [0,1] is generated, e.g. $r = 0.56$. The frequency Monte Carlo interval that r belongs to is [0.35,0.80]. The corresponding target position is BL. Hence, the generated return is (BR→BL).

In a similar way the success of that return is calculated: the success probability of (BR→BL) is 0.90, as can be taken from the third matrix called 'success probability'. This means: if a random number smaller than 0.90 was generated, then the return was successful, otherwise it was not.

Depending on the goal of the simulation, different scenarios can be developed. The simplest one is to simulate actions as long as a player is successful, then changing to the opponent player and so on. Of course, this simple version has not much to do with tennis but helps to understand how it works and is easy to implement as a simple Excel application.

The simulated processes and their success depend on the entries in the matrices. The idea is to analyse how changes in these entries change the overall results. This could answer questions about whether shifts in the target positions of returns would improve the success of the process.

Frequency [%]					
	BR	BL	FR	FL	sum
BR	35	45	15	4	100
BL	30	55	5	10	100
FR	30	65	0	5	100
FL	60	30	5	5	100

Frequency Monte Carlo intervals				
	BR	BL	FR	FL
BR	0.35	0.80	0.95	1.00
BL	0.30	0.85	0.90	1.00
FR	0.30	0.95	0.95	1.00
FL	0.60	0.90	0.95	1.00

Success probability				
	BR	BL	FR	FL
BR	0.80	0.90	0.70	0.80
BL	0.80	0.70	0.70	0.70
FR	0.60	0.90	0.80	0.70
FL	0.90	0.70	0.60	0.80

Figure 6.3 Probability and success matrices for a Monte Carlo simulation of tennis

Note that in practical application all frequencies and probabilities had to be taken from games observed, and the simulated results actually hold only if the characteristics of the corresponding players meanwhile have not changed (too much).

In conclusion, the examples make clear that the quantitative level-rate models like the transportation model are special types of the more general qualitative state-event models. The big advantage of state-event models is that they do not need quantitative numbers. In turn, the big disadvantage is that they do not necessarily allow for calculating numerical results – which, however, can be compensated for by numeric attributes like frequency and success, as has been done in the tennis example.

Exercise 3

Try to calculate some steps of the simulation based on matrices like those from Figure 6.3. If no random generator is available a dice can be used but needs some transfer. In any case it is helpful to develop an Excel application, which makes it much easier to get comparable results with changeable data.

Task 3

Develop a model which is closer to real tennis than that from the example above. Discuss what features had to be added and what tasks seem to be too complicated for a simple simulation.

Case studies: interactive dynamic systems

Model of sprint

Every motion of a body is an example of an extremely complex system together with the also extremely complex interactions of its components. If information is needed about future behaviour, a model has to be built which is able to transform the complex dynamics into simple equations. If, for example, it is of interest how fast a sprinter could be under optimal conditions it would not help to only model the interactions of muscles. More helpful are biometric information about length, height and frequency of steps, which in turn could influence training and performance. At the high level of top sprinters who have already optimized all those technical details, the question could remain whether the speed profile – consisting of the acceleration phase, maximum speed and deceleration phase – is optimal or could be improved.

The example in Figure 6.4 on the left-hand side models the 100 m speed profile of a top sprinter (let's call him 'Speedy') using a rather simple model assuming the acceleration and deceleration rates to be constant: in the first 10 m Speedy speeds up from 0 km/h to a maximum speed of 46.3 km/h with an acceleration rate of 1.17 m/s². On the next 80 m Speedy keeps the constant speed of 46.3 km/h, meaning an acceleration rate of 0. On the last 10 m Speedy loses speed with a deceleration rate of –0.5 m/s² and finishes in a remarkable time of 9.68 s. That seems to be extremely fast and difficult to improve upon. However, during the same event Speedy finishes 200 m in 19.27 s (right graphic). This is remarkable, too. More remarkable is that his constant speed phase reaches from 10 m to 150 m

Distance [m]	Acceleration [m/s²]	Deceleration [m/s²]	Max. speed [km/h]	Mean speed [km/h]	Speed time needed [s]
Left graphic					
100	1.17	-0.50	46.3	37.2	9.68
100	1.17	-0.20	46.3	37.7	9.56
100	1.17	0.00	46.3	37.9	9.50
Right graphic					
200	1.17	-0.16 last 48 m	46.3	37.4	19.27
200	1.17	-0.16 last 40 m	46.3	38.9	18.50

Figure 6.4 Models of a 100 m sprint (left) and a 200 m sprint (right): profiles (graphics above) and values (tables below) of speed, acceleration/deceleration and time needed

– meaning that the deceleration phase in the 100 m contest was not caused by fatigue. Taking into consideration that in the finishing phase speed almost always is reduced a little bit, the run modelled was calculated with a reduced deceleration rate of -0.20 m/s^2, predicting a finishing time of 9.56 s. Speedy's coach said 'he can', and not much later Speedy did it. Was this the last word? The model says 'no': with full concentration like in the 200 m run Speedy should be able to do it in 9.50 s, without increasing his speed or improving his general performance. Even a 200 m finishing time in less than 19 s could be possible if his fatigue phase is reduced to about 40 m.

Although the sprint model is rather simple it helps to understand the interactions between phases in a dynamic process and their role in order to predict future behaviour. One aspect that could have been neglected in this particular example but is very important in most kinds of sports is that of fatigue, which temporarily can reduce performance a lot. Therefore, if not sprinting short distances but running longer distances, the schedule of the speed profile is of importance in order to keep fatigue and recovery in balance. The next example presents a model that deals with the dynamic interaction of fatigue and recovery on a high and abstract level, but nevertheless can be used for quite realistic demands of performance optimization.

Exercise 4

Try to calculate some similar simulations using different parameters for the values and lengths of accelerations and decelerations. Find out how sensible the simulation is to small changes of the values and length. If possible, develop an Excel application for easier calculation and comparison of the simulations.

Task 4

Develop a model for a 400 m run. Does it make sense to linearly extrapolate the dynamics from 100 m and 200 m? Are there any reasons to change the structure of the model, and if so, how? What about the physiological aspects of fatigue?

PerPot

The transportation model demonstrated how internal states – i.e. the contents of the levels – together with external events or transitions – i.e. the flow control between the levels – can define the dynamics of a system.

Although this sounds rather technical, one can find such dynamics in a lot of natural systems like continental drift, weather development, predator–prey systems and age distributions in populations. Also physiologic dynamics like interactions between human organs can be described by such level-rate models, as will be described in the following.

If an athlete is loaded with training, then his internal components are activated to produce, transmit and use up substances. This process can be described by

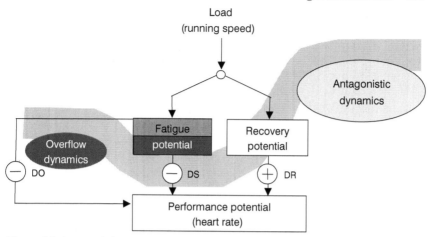

Figure 6.5 Antagonistic structure of the basic performance-potential metamodel (source: Perl and Endler 2012)

a level-rate model. On the external level of detection, training plays the role of transition between the states of being relaxed and being tired. Moreover, and this naturally is the reason for training, it is a transition between the states of lower performance and higher performance. Summed up, an athlete together with training forms a dynamic system that can be described by a complex model combining state-event and level-rate components. As discussed above, state-event models need numerical interpretations in order to be calculated. The Performance-Potential-Metamodel (PerPot) describes training dynamics in a very easy way, combining level-rate equations with state-event interpretations (see Perl, 2002a). As is shown in Figure 6.5, the central idea of this approach is that of antagonism, meaning that a load input has negative as well as positive effects, which in their delayed combination will result in a time-depending change of performance.

The term 'metamodel' is used because of the fact that PerPot is not restricted to athletes and their training but can be used whenever systems are controlled by antagonistic dynamics. One spectacular example is stock dynamics, where increasing rates on the one hand motivate buying, expecting increasing wins, and on the other suggest selling, in order to avoid the risk of suddenly decreasing rates.

Finally, the question can be discussed whether an approach like PerPot should be designed as a continuous or as a discrete model. In physiology, the basic dynamics of course are a continuous and could be described by differential equations, as several approaches show. As discussed above, the problem is the limitation of the capacities of physiologic components, leading to different phases with different attractors, which makes it extremely difficult to find functional solutions. Moreover, the determinism of such closed solutions would make it difficult to adjust the model's behaviour to external influences. Therefore the design decision for PerPot was to use discrete difference equations, enabling iterative calculation and flexible response to external influences.

Basic structure and behaviour

Antagonism has been used as the basic concept in PerPot Each load impulse feeds a strain potential as well as a response potential. These buffer potentials in turn influence the performance potential, where the response potential increases the performance potential (delayed by delay of response – DR) and the strain potential reduces the performance potential (delayed by delay of strain – DS), of course depending on the maximum capacities and on the current states of the potentials involved (see Figure 6.5).

The behaviour of PerPot mainly depends on the delay values, that is, on the relation between DS and DR, and on the capacity limitations.

When starting to develop PerPot in the late 1990s, two fundamental questions had to be answered by the model approach, namely 'Does the super-compensation effect really exist?' and 'Can linearly increasing load cause a performance profile like a reverse u-function?'

Both questions could easily be answered by PerPot, which is shown in Figure 6.5. The dark grey part of the fatigue potential represents the amount of accumulated fatigue, while the medium grey part means the available reserve. If the reserve is reduced to zero an overflow of fatigue reduces the performance potential with a small delay, possibly causing a sudden break down, which cannot be compensated by the slow recovery flow. (The curved pattern in the background just symbolizes the super-compensation effect.)

Whether or not the super-compensation effect appears depends only on the relation between DS and DR. If DS is smaller than DR, i.e. if fatigue is faster than recovery, then the effect can be seen as is illustrated in Figure 6.5. This often is the case if an athlete is well trained but not at the top level. The reason is that because of the small load delay the load causes fast tiring and is only later compensated by the slower response. The smaller the difference between DS and DR, like in the case of top level athletes, the more the effect disappears and the load causes a continuous asymptotic increase to maximum performance.

The inverse u-function is shown by the performance profile if for instance the load is increasing continuously, causing first a strongly increasing performance, followed, however, by an overflow effect and a sudden break down (see explanations above).

Collapsing and how to predict and prevent it is of high importance not only in top level sports. The following example demonstrates how this phenomenon, by taking capacity limitations into consideration, is integrated in PerPot and how it can help to make endurance sports safer.

Strain overflow and reserve

As can be shown, a simplified PerPot without the capacity limitation of the fatigue potential always becomes stable after a couple of steps, independent of how high the load is. Biological systems do not behave this way but collapse if the load becomes too high. The reason is – from the structural point of view – that the

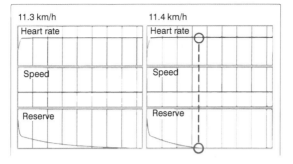

Figure 6.6 In both graphics the graph on the top shows the heart rate profile over the marathon distance caused by constant speed (graph in the middle); the graph on the bottom shows the profile of the simulated reserve – increasing the constant speed by only 0.1 km/h causes early negative reserve (i.e. a sudden break down) represented by immediately switching from the aerobe to the anaerobe heart rate area (source: Perl and Endler 2012)

capacities of biological potentials are always limited and so are in the habit of overflowing under overload. Figure 6.5 shows how this restriction is integrated in the model structure: the strain potential capacity is limited. If for instance the load level is too high or the load is increasing too long or too much, the strain potential is fed over its upper limit and an overflow is produced, which reduces the performance potential immediately, i.e. with a rather small delay of overflow (DO).

In particular, the concept of potential overflow allows the introduction of a reserve: overflow starts when the current strain level becomes greater than the strain potential capacity. So the reserve (= strain potential capacity – current strain level) indicates how close the system is to collapsing – i.e. how 'dangerous' the next load steps are.

Figure 6.6 demonstrates how sensible the dependency between small overload and break down can be: both graphics show the simulated results of a run with constant speed of 11.3 km/h (left) and 11.4 km/h (right). The corresponding heart rate curves have changing shades, symbolizing low (light grey), medium (medium grey) and high (dark grey) rates. The highlighted spot represents the area of 'beyond individual anaerobe threshold (IAT)'. The simulation shows that even an only very small increase of speed can cause a reduction of reserve below zero and, therefore, cross the IAT line.

This correspondence between reserve and IAT, together with some adjustments, can be used to calculate IAT by simulation, using only speed and heart rate data of the athlete.

Finally the example of strain overflow answers a frequently asked question – namely why the PerPot model does not use differential equations and their solutions but difference equations with iterative calculations: in the moment when reserve falls below 0, the state of the system changes to a different phase and therefore demands a different calculation. This can be compared to specific phases and their attractors in technical systems, which can make it extremely difficult to calculate the system's behaviour by means of differential equations: each phase can have its own behaviour and then therefore needs its own model and model equations, which have to be constantly changed when changing the phases.

In PerPot, which has three limited capacities and, therefore, $2^3 = 8$ different phases, the situation is even more complicated because of changing context conditions which additionally affect the equations. This should make it clear that PerPot cannot be calculated in one piece but has to be adapted iteratively to changing situations.

Further reading

Perl, 2002a, 2008; Perl and Endler, 2012.

Exercise 5

Assume $L(t)$ to be the load at time, t, and $FP(t)$, $RP(t)$ and $PP(t)$ the potentials of fatigue, recovery and performance at time, t, respectively. The somewhat simplified dynamic equations of PerPot are given as follows.

Rate equations that describe the flow during the time interval from t to $t+1$:

- flow from the fatigue potential to the performance potential, which decreases *PP*:
  $$RFP(t, t+1) = \min(FP(t), \max(0, PP(t))) / DS \text{ (R1)}$$

- flow from the recovery potential to the performance potential, which increases *PP*:
  $$RRP(t, t+1) = \min(RP(t), \min(PPmax, PPmax - PP(t))) / DR \text{ (R2)}$$

  PPmax is the capacity limit of *PP*,

  in this normalized form can be taken as '1'.

Level equations that describe how the potential levels have to be replaced at the step from t to $t+1$ by means of the respective rate flows:

$$FP(t+1) = FP(t) + L(t) - RFP(t, t+1) \text{ (L1)}$$

$$RP(t+1) = RP(t) + L(t) - RRP(t, t+1) \text{ (L2)}$$

$$PP(t+1) = PP(t) + RRP(t, t+1) - RFP(t, t+1) \text{ (L3)}$$

A simulation starts with initial potential values $FP(0)$, $RP(0)$ and $PP(0)$ (between 0 and 1) and then iteratively calculates the rates and the levels according to the given equations.

Try to calculate some simulation steps. If possible design an Excel application and compare variant simulations with different delay values and different initial values.

Task 5

Discuss the model equations above and try to understand how the dynamics work. Try to find out what 'delay' really means. If a program is available (e.g. an Excel application) try to verify your ideas on model behaviour by simulation runs.

Unconventional modelling

Artificial intelligence and soft computing

A short history of the development of artificial intelligence and soft-computing is given in Perl (2008) as follows:

> Since the 1950s, Artificial Intelligence has been one of the most challenging areas of Computer Science. The aim was to understand and model human thinking by means of computers. Finally, in the 1980s, it became clear that neither could human thinking be understood in a simple algorithmic way nor were the computers powerful enough for an appropriate simulation of complex neural systems.
>
> Soft-computing, as an important new area of Computer Science, is developing the ideas of Artificial Intelligence in a modern and more pragmatic way. It is dealing with new approaches and concepts of handling complex dynamic systems – which means a change of paradigms according to biologic systems, where determinism is replaced by randomness, precision by fuzziness and completeness by flexibility and adaptability. This way patterns of motions or tactical patterns in games can be analysed and compared more easily by means of artificial neural networks; interaction and communication in games can better be described by means of fuzzy modelling; solutions in high-dimensional problem spaces like optimal tracks of motions can be found much faster by means of evolutionary algorithms.
>
> (Perl, 2008)

In particular in processes – i.e. the time-dependent event based change of systems' states – analyses might not be restricted to single states or events but have to take into consideration present states and changing events as well as past ones. As has been pointed out above, future behaviour cannot be predicted without understanding the past, and therefore cannot be calculated by means of statistical probabilities alone.

Moreover, behaviour and interacting like in sport games show a certain contradiction between rule based or convergent types (tactics, strategies) and spontaneous or divergent ones like situation based decisions or creative actions.

Further reading

Perl, 1996, 1999; Quade, 1996.

The following examples may demonstrate what the major approaches of soft computing are and how they can work in practice.

Fuzzy modelling

Fuzzy modelling first of all has to do with understanding and describing a problem rather than with finding a solution. As one example from games, the attempt to find a useful optimal strategy for a specific situation might fail because of unsuitable problem descriptions and/or unreasonable demands on the results – e.g. too high numerical accuracy: although from the technical point of view it is possible to appoint a player's position on the ground with a deviation of only some centimetres, it makes no sense to use such numeric information in order to describe 'optimal' behaviour in a way like 'take the first serve on position [–0.25; +1.57]'.

Instead of such apparent precision, fuzzy modelling tries to use imprecise terms like human communication does – which by the way is the very reason we understand each other. In the case above, the coach for instance could suggest taking the serve about a foot behind the baseline and about a long step right from the centre line. In terms of fuzzy modelling 'a foot behind the baseline' could read 'a range from +0.10 to –0.60 with a degree of membership varying from 0.1 for "+0.10" up to 0.7 for "–0.30" and down to 0.1 for "–0.60"'.

Note that the range of degrees of membership does not mean a stochastic distribution. The difference is as follows. The stochastic distribution gives information about the frequencies of past events belonging to disjunctive classes, suggesting an expectation for the probability of future events belonging to those classes. In contrast, fuzzy classes like 'a foot behind the baseline' are not disjunctive (+0.10 also belongs to the class 'a foot before the baseline'), and the degree of membership does not mean a probability but a rating of how much the respective value or corresponding event is the focus of the class. If, for example, the position +0.10 has '0.4' as the degree of membership in the class 'a foot before the baseline', then it has the two degrees '0.1' and '0.4' of membership, respectively, to the corresponding classes – meaning it is mainly 'before' but also a little bit 'behind'.

At first glance this seems to be a bit confusing, but reflects human thinking and behaviour much better than mathematic precision, because in the dynamics of a game process nobody can control their motions on centimetres but only can orientate on more or less fuzzy patterns. The idea of reducing precision in order to obtain more information appears in a lot of approaches where event interactions (rather than a single event) during a dynamic process are of major interest. One very important example is given by communication, where only the fuzziness of the transfer objects (like words or pictures) enables the interpretation and understanding of the semantics of communication patterns.

Neuro-fuzzy clustering fuzzifies accurate information of patterns and so can improve reading and understanding of complex processes like those from motions or games. (Note as one example that word based communication processes work *because* and not *although* words have fuzzy meanings.) Let, for instance, the technical description of an attacking process in a soccer game be the time series of ball coordinates. Obviously, the number of different processes is very high and their frequencies are very small, which means poor conditions for stochastic analyses. By replacing the precise positions by fuzzy intervals the different processes become blurred to fuzzy patterns which can be grouped into types – as self-organizing neural networks do very reliably. As a very simple example, such process patterns then could be given as 'right, forward right, cross left, backward right, ...', which much better transfers an impression of the game than precise coordinates could do.

Further reading

Demant, 1993; Kosko, 1992; Schiebl, 1999; Zadeh, 1965; Zimmermann, 1991.

Exercise 6

A basketball coach needs a tall player. You know that 2.20 m is tall, but what about 1.90 m, and where are the borders between 'tall' and 'medium' or 'medium' and 'short'? Try to design profiles of the fuzzy variable V = 'belongs to' using numbers between '0 = does not belong to' and '1 = belongs fully to'. Example: '$V(1.80) = 0$' meaning does not belong to 'tall', ... , '$V(1.95) = 0.5$' meaning belongs gradually to 'tall', ... , '$V(2.20) = 1$' meaning belongs fully to 'tall'.

Task 6

Design fuzzy profiles of the fuzzy variables 'belongs to "excellent"', 'belongs to "medium"', 'belongs to "poor"' for the finishing times in swimming, running and biking in triathlon. Design some athletes with their best finishing times, assign them to the fuzzy variables and find a way to compare them and to find the optimal candidate. What is the difference to a rating based ranking-list method?

Another unconventional way of strategic analyses in the following is described from the perspective of evolutionary algorithms.

Evolutionary algorithms

The technical abilities of computers like quantity and speed of data analysis in particular are of importance in algorithmic solutions of mathematical problems. For example the characteristic input data of a problem – i.e. attributes of a player's situation like position, technical perfection and situational context – by means of a system of algorithmic statements are transformed to output data like best player's activity. Such algorithms are normally conventional in the sense that they are correct, verifiable and, in particular, deterministic – i.e. repeating the same input results into an unchanged output.

At first glance these criteria seem to be reasonable and necessary. But if analysing human behaviour or the movements of molecules in a gas, often the stochastic Monte Carlo method is helpful, where probabilistic quantitative characterizations replace not-existing or unknown deterministic effects. In this case the stochastic number generator prevents the repetition of the same solution again and again, which makes sense if finding an unknown solution in an unknown area of solutions is the problem.

This, in an intelligent and optimized way, is exactly what evolutionary algorithms are doing.

Nature has developed an extremely successful method of optimally adapting populations dynamically to changing environmental conditions. In detail, there are some basic steps in order to find (almost) optimal solutions: generating new properties by crossing over the given ones (for example genes or playing processes); selecting unsuitable individuals ('survival of the fittest', avoiding unsuccessful playing processes); and generating random changes (mutations, creative playing processes).

The results of such an evolutionary algorithm are not predictable because of its stochastic elements in crossing and selection. Therefore, the transformation of input into output cannot be followed in a logical and structural way. Nevertheless, because of their optimum-oriented combination of stochastic and generic search, they are able to find even rare and hidden solutions in huge amounts of possibilities and so are very useful in cases of detecting optimal individuals or processes.

A not too simple example dealing with a kind of tennis may illustrate how the evolutionary approach could work in the practice of sports.

Assume that a playing process in tennis, after having been started with a service, S, runs through phases of baseline playing, B, and phases of half court playing, H. Assume further that B and H have different technical or tactical types of being played – for example say $B1$, $B2$, $B3$; $H1$, $H2$ – and the two orientations, forehand side, F, and backhand side, B. Finally restrict the number of phases of the processes to five, excluding the service.

Two examples of such processes are given by:

$P1 = (S, B3F, B1F, H2B, B1B, H1F)$

$P2 = (S, B1F, B2B, B3F, H1F, H2B)$

It easily can be calculated that there are $10^5 = 10,000$ processes altogether, but it obviously is not quite as easy to calculate which one might be the most successful in the context of the opponent's actions.

The way an evolutionary algorithm tries to find a solution is as follows.

1   Initialization: a comparably small number of basic processes (for instance 100) is stochastically generated and ordered with respect to their success values.
2   Selection: a percentage (for instance 10 per cent) of the best value processes is selected.

3   Crossing: the selected processes are crossed pair-wise with stochastic crossing points as is illustrated in the following example using *P1* and *P2*:

$P1' = (S, B3F, B1F, \textbf{\textit{B3F}}, B1B, \textbf{\textit{H2B}})$

$P2' = (S, B1F, B2B, \textbf{\textit{H2B}}, H1F, \textbf{\textit{H1F}})$

4   Completion and mutation: the processes generated by crossing are completed by processes from the old basis, building the new basis for the next steps. With a small mutation rate (for instance 5 per cent) processes are stochastically selected and changed in one or more components. Finally the new basic processes are ordered with respect to their success values.

If the best of these basic processes is good enough, the procedure is finished.

Otherwise the procedure is repeated with the selection and so on.

Assuming an iteration rate of about ten repetitions, which is reasonable in the situation described, the number of calculations steps totals (10 repetitions) × (10 × 10 crossings) = 1,000, while the systematic checking would need 10,000 steps. The reason for the advantage of the evolutionary approach against the systematic search is, briefly stated, that selecting and crossing finds paths from worse to better solutions, while mutations help to avoid dead ends.

However, in practice it sometimes is difficult to find the optimal tuning – i.e. the rates of selection, crossing and mutation – which requires a very careful adjustment to the problem situation. In particular the meaning of 'success', which has not been discussed in the example at all, is of central importance in effective evaluating and ranking the processes.

Further reading

Fruh, Korczak and Vanderwalle, 2000; Seifriz, 2001.

Neural networks

When, in the early 1960s, computers came into commercial and scientific use, their abilities in speed and data handling seemed to be so unbelievable that they were called 'electronic brains'. The slogan of 'artificial intelligence' was born and the idea arose to use computers for modelling human brains and their processes of thinking. Nowadays normal smartphones would be massively undersupplied if their power was restricted to that of those first computers. But even now there is not the slightest chance of modelling the brain and its inconceivable complexity and dynamics by means of computer science and technology approaches.

Nevertheless, the idea of modelling local structures of human brains by means of neurons and impulse channels has been shown to be useful.

Neurons have states; these states can be taken as the neuron's information. Incoming impulses change the neuron's state and information provoking outgoing

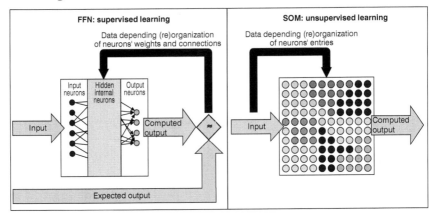

Figure 6.7 Comparison of the methods of unsupervised learning and supervised learning: a SOM organizes the input data into clusters of corresponding neurons on its own; a FFN learns a relation of input and output values by comparing computed and expected results together with a stepwise rearrangement of the internal representation (source: Perl and Memmert 2013)

impulses, which in turn affect neurons that are connected by impulse channels as well as the channels themselves. This means that specific input to such a neural network can change the states of its neurons and channels in a specific way – i.e. a stream of input data is mapped to a changing sequence of state patterns. This effect can be taken for targeted training, where input data from a complex data space influences the network in a way that the state patterns reflect the specific areas or properties of the input data space.

Today, two approaches are mainly in use, which can complement each other in particular in decision making processes that occur in team sport: unsupervised or self-organizing maps (SOMs) or networks can learn and recognize the patterns of match situations on their own (Figure 6.7, right graphic), whereas supervised or feed forward networks (FFNs) learn by supervision and recognize the best solution for a situation (Figure 6.7, left graphic); see also Kohonen (1995) and Hopfield (1982).

A brief definition of these two types of network can be given as follows.

Feed forward network (FFN)

A FFN consists of neurons which are connected by weighted edges. The neurons are grouped into a sequence of layers. The input layer transfers the input data to the hidden layers from which the output layer gets the result data. During the learning process, the neurons of each layer 'feed forward' their information to the neurons of the following layer in order to change their entries. The calculated result of a learning step depends on the weights of the connecting edges. It is compared to the expected result, and the deviation is used for adjusting the connection weights in the completing phase of 'feedback' and/or 'back propagation'.

After the learning phase, i.e. as soon as the calculated results are satisfactorily accurate, the network can be used as an algorithmic model for the relation between input and output data – e.g. the relation between situations and normally following actions in a game.

In general, the approach of FFNs is useful if dealing with complex relations between input data and output data.

Self-organizing map (SOM)

A SOM consists of neurons, which are arranged in a matrix. As in FFNs, the neurons of a SOM can be connected, where, different from FFNs, a connection does not mean a data pathway but a topological neighbourhood.

During the learning process, the input information triggers the particular target neuron the entry of which is closest to the input. The entries of the target neuron and, with decreasing weight at decreasing degree of neighbourhood, the entries of neighbouring neurons are moved to the new input. Due to those similarity-controlled neuron movements, eventually the distribution of the neuron entries is topologically similar to the distribution of the input data.

After the learning phase, clusters of neurons represent classes of similar input data and so can classify types of data. This way, the great variety of data can be reduced to a small number of characteristic types – e.g. the enormous variety of attacking processes in soccer could be reduced to about twenty characteristic patterns.

In general, the approach of SOMs is useful if the aim is the typing and clustering of complex data spaces as for instance in motions or in games.

Further reading

Bauer and Schöllhorn, 1997; Edelmann-Nusser, Hohmann and Hennberg, 2002; Hopfield, 1982; Kohonen, 1995; Lees, Barton and Kershaw, 2003; Leser, 2006b; Maier, Wank, Bartonietz and Blickhan, 2000; Memmert and Perl, 2006, 2009a, 2009b; Perl and Dauscher, 2006; Perl and Memmert, 2012; Pfeiffer and Perl, 2006; Schöllhorn, 2004; Wiemeyer, 2000b.

Pattern analysis

Inherent to the analysis of complex processes like games or motions in sports there is a conflict between quantitative numeric and qualitative descriptive approaches. In order to get measurable and valuable data, numbers are the main interest, which, because of their complexity, normally are reduced to statistical data like frequencies, mean values or distributions, verified by means of evaluation criteria. This way, however, the dynamics of a process are neglected and cannot be understood. If describing the process qualitatively, the understanding of the dynamics is much better. The results, however, are mostly neither specific nor can they be generalized. They are informative but without quantitative significance.

Patterns can help to bridge the gap between the microscopic level of counting quantitative details and the macroscopic level of understanding qualitative phenomena. Basically, a pattern consists of a number of quantitative components – e.g. players of a tactical group – together with a qualitative description – e.g. groups moving through phases of particular tactical meaning. Patterns on the one hand are connected with the microscopic level, i.e. they contain all information about their components and, thereby, enable the calculation of statistics if necessary. On the other hand they are connected to the macroscopic level as components of the complex processes. This way, they enable the calculation of process oriented statistics, where the patterns are the items.

In summary, patterns in sport can be taken as tactical patterns from a game, as motor patterns from movements or as training or performance patterns in training analysis. Such patterns reduce the complex original information to the most relevant parts – e.g. trajectories of a time-dependent process – and so allow for easier analyses (Perl, 2002a).

Exercise 7

Try to describe tactical patterns in games like tennis, badminton or squash.

Task 7

Take some tactical patterns from the exercise above: what happens in the interaction of tactical patterns of the opponent players? What do you think is the difference between tactics and strategy? Based on your experience, discuss the coordination between techniques, tactics and strategy from the aspect of patterns.

Completing or even replacing *quantitative modelling focusing on numbers* by *qualitative modelling focusing on patterns and types* can be done using artificial neural networks.

Pattern analysis by means of SOMs

Pattern recognition

If we speak of patterns, we normally think of graphical and/or coloured compositions, natural structures or surfaces like landscapes or faces, or typical types of behaviour. Even these few examples show that there are two different dimensions where patterns can spread: space and time. In the area of sports, both kinds of patterns are of importance. In soccer, for example, the coordinates of a group of players at one point in time form a spatial pattern, which can characterize the current task, interaction or tactical plan. The change of that pattern over time builds a temporal pattern, which can characterize how tasks are carried out or how interaction or tactical plans work.

Obviously, neither spatial nor temporal patterns can be handled by computer programs without being transformed to numbers.

There are quite different techniques to do this. In the easy case of simple geometric patterns like a coloured triangle, the coordinates of the corners and the code of the colour are necessary. In the more difficult case of a photograph, the coordinates and colour code of each pixel is needed. But such transformation is just the first step. The second and much more important step is 'recognition', and that means finding a pattern in a collection of patterns, which is identical or at least the most similar to a given one. Normally one would not expect to find the exactly identical exemplar but to detect the most similar one in a group of similar ones. Such a group of similar patterns is called a 'cluster' or 'type', and one important meaning of pattern recognition, therefore, is to identify the type of a given pattern. In turn that means that we need a collection of patterns and a procedure that is able to separate the totality of those patterns into clusters of similar ones.

Immediately it can be seen what the problems are: what does 'similar' mean? How can clusters be built?

The first question was dealt with in 'Dynamic systems', where the Euclidian distance was introduced: if the Euclidian distance of two patterns is smaller than a given threshold of accuracy they are said to be similar.

The second question is similarly simple if a collection of representative patterns is given: each new pattern is compared to each representative and added to the representative's cluster to which it is most similar– i.e. where its distance to the representative is smallest.

The situation is more difficult if such a system of representatives is not known. In this case the patterns have to organize themselves, finding their representatives on their own. This is exactly the way in which self-organizing neural networks are doing it in the phase of training.

Iteratively, the neurons of the network represent patterns as entries – i.e. vectors of numbers in the way described in 'Dynamic systems'. A new pattern is compared to all neurons to find the best fitting one – i.e. the one with the most similar entry. Adding the new pattern to that neuron means changing the collection of the corresponding patterns, and therefore the neuron's entry has to be changed, too. Moreover, the particular idea of self-organizing neural networks is that not only the selected neuron changes but also a region of neighbouring neurons. This way, step by step, clusters as regions of similar neurons are arranged. There are standard procedures for those learning and clustering steps, which are used in the common network tools.

After the training, each cluster represents a type of pattern, and the neurons of the cluster represent variant shapes of that type.

Pattern recognition then can be done by comparing the number vector of the pattern, P, to all neurons, N, to find the most similar neuron, No. The cluster, Co, which No is a member of, then is called the type of P, while No represents the corresponding shape of P. Note that normally the vector of P and the entry of No are not identical but only most similar. This is, as explained above, because each neuron, N, represents not just one but a collection of similar patterns.

As is explained in more detail in the examples below, configurations of players, for example, can by typed by means of neural networks, reducing the large amount of possible shapes to a handful of representative types, which makes tactical analyses much easier.

Moreover, process analysis of complex games becomes easier if the time-depending situation patterns are reduced to types and the process is understood as a sequence of situations or activity type numbers.

Further reading

Grunz, Memmert and Perl, 2012; Perl, 2002a, 2004a, 2004b; Perl, Grunz and Memmert, 2013; Witte, Emmermacher, Langenbeck and Perl, 2012.

Applications and examples

The importance of artificial neural networks in sports can be seen from the wide variety of applications in different areas, as for instance in individual sports (see references in 'Unconventional modelling').

A number of applications of SOMs in sport, which stretch from game analysis over biomechanics to rehabilitation, can be taken from Perl and Dauscher (2006). The most complex challenge regarding process analysis and pattern recognition in sport obviously can be found in games. Therefore three example of how SOMs can support such analyses are dealt with below.

Example 7: handball

In this example a SOM is used in order to analyse types of tactical structures in team handball. Therefore a process oriented observation model of offensive play was developed on the basis of offensive attempts. Fifteen matches (twelve teams) of the Women's Junior World Championship 2001 were observed. Afterwards a prepared neural network was trained with 2,900 offensive attempts (processes) from all teams to identify offensive attempt patterns. In Pfeiffer and Perl (2006) it is shown that the neural network can be used in order to identify the typical tactics of different teams.

In the first step, offensive attempts were identified on the network. One part of the network classified attempts in the position attacks of type 4:2, while the remaining network represented attempts in the position attack of type 3:3. Within this area clusters of neighbouring neurons were identified, indicating the similarity of the corresponding entries.

In the next step, the neurons and clusters identified by the network were specified and analysed with regard to tactical behaviour. In particular, teams could be analysed and compared regarding the similarity of their tactical behaviour. As an example the offensive attempts of the three best teams were isolated from the training data and tested afterwards with the network. As could easily be seen, the basic structural frame was identical for the three teams, while the individual areas of major importance and frequency were quite different. As is analysed in more detail in Pfeiffer and Perl (2006), the tactical behaviour of Hungary, Russia and Germany could briefly be characterized as follows.

The activities of type 'fast attack' could be identified in a particular corner of the net. They were not identical but rather similar for the three teams. In contrast, the activities of type 'position attack' differed a lot. The tactical concept of Hungary was dominated by the formation '3:3' and individual actions (large central cluster), while the Russian team additionally showed the formation '2:4', transitions and other actions, which could be identified by particular clusters. In the German tactical concept dominating tactical types could hardly be identified. The offensive attempts were distributed over the entire network area, indicating a diversified tactical behaviour.

A similar approach was developed by Leser (2006a), who focused on processes as sequences of tactical events in soccer (also compare Perl and Lames (2000) for volleyball).

The next example deals with the question of how positioning movements of players in a game can be recognized as tactical elements.

Example 8: volleyball

The aim of the approach was to identify the tactical concepts of the teams by means of a net-based analysis of the team configurations – i.e. the set of positions of every player of a team on the playing field.

The analysis of team configurations with SOMs allows the detection of patterns as well as their changes and variability. This has a strong practical relevance, since variable attack and defence configurations are supposed to be necessary for successful teams. The analysis of those aspects by means of networks is done by mapping the time-depending sequences of configurations onto the 2-dimensional grid of the neurons net. This reduction of complex information helps to understand the structural as well as dynamical properties of the processes.

One of the projects dealt with the defence preparation in volleyball, i.e. the phase of preparation in expecting the opponents attack. The position data was taken from videos recorded at twenty-five frames per second. The six player positions per frame lead to a 12-dimensional constellation vector per frame, containing the x- and y-coordinates of each player. A SOM was trained with some thousands of those constellation vectors, resulting in a net where the neurons were grouped into clusters representing types of constellation and each neuron of a cluster represented a variant of that type (also see 'Example 9: soccer').

First of all it could be seen that different teams had different preferences regarding those defence types, which gave interesting information about technical skills and/or preferred tactical variants. Moreover, the variability of a team could be seen from the number of defence types that were used in a game. Finally, the preparation processes themselves could be analysed in greater depth.

Each frame of the video corresponded to its representing neuron, showing how long a team stayed in the same cluster, only changing the neuron to adjust positions, or changing the type to adjust the whole constellation. One interesting result from one of the games was the way that team A very quickly concentrated on one cluster, only changing the neurons, while team B tended to change the clusters. This means that team A very quickly anticipated the forthcoming action of team B, immediately taking the best fitting constellation and then adjusting corresponding to the evolving situation. In contrast, team B did not recognize the attacking situation well, and so was looking for the best constellation.

More information about modelling and net based analysis of volleyball can be found in Perl and Lames (2000).

In general, there are several different approaches for analysing players' positions in games, for instance:

- by means of artificial neural networks, recognizing patterns in the interaction of squash players (Perl, 2002b).
- by means of a hierarchical cluster analysis, identifying volleyball teams (Westphal and Schöllhorn, 2001) or studying opponent specific defence patterns (Jäger, Schöllhorn and Schwerdfeger, 2003).
- from a dynamic systems perspective, analysing stable and unstable phases in the positions of two squash players (McGarry, Khan and Franks, 1999). In particular the technique of combining single patterns to trajectories – i.e. sequences patterns – is very helpful in order to analyse processes. As was explained earlier, the use of clusters related to pattern types simplifies such analyses by far and allows the recognition of tactical behaviour and its strong and weak points.

The last example deals with soccer and demonstrates how net based trajectory analysis and conventional data analysis can be combined to a deeper analysis of the strengths and weaknesses of a team.

Example 9: soccer

As in volleyball, configurations of players are of interest in soccer. However, one difference to volleyball is that the playing field in soccer is much larger. Also the number of players is greater and the players are not separated by a net. Therefore the configuration patterns in soccer would be much more difficult than those in volleyball, and in particular the number of patterns would be much too large for cluster analysis. Two measures can be taken to reduce that number dramatically. First, the configurations can be restricted to tactical groups like offense or defence, which have a smaller number of members. Second, the spatio-temporal configuration can be separated from its location on the playing field, in this way reducing it just to a temporal formation, keeping the position information (i.e. the mean value of the players' positions, also called 'centroid') separately for further analyses.

Formations are sufficient data for net training. The result of such training is the set of neuron clusters, which represent types of formation patterns, as described above. The types can be encoded by numbers. Feeding these numbers back to the process–time axis completes the transformation from the original spatio-temporal process of original position data to a process, where the position data is replaced by formation data – i.e. the types and positions of the tactical groups involved (also see Memmert and Perl, 2009a, 2009b; Perl and Memmert, 2012).

This significantly simplified process now allows for a lot of process analyses, three of which are briefly introduced in the following examples.

a. Distribution and success analyses: assume that the interactions of the offense group of team A against the defence group of team B is of interest. First of all the frequencies of the formation patterns of A and B over the game can be determined, resulting in frequency distributions over the formation types, which can be completed by the rates of successful action corresponding to those types. This, for example, gives information like '35 per cent of the A formations were of type 4 and 60 per cent of them were successful'. Combining the distributions of A and B leads to information like: '18 per cent of all interactions were A type 4 against B type 2, where B was successful for 65 per cent'.

    Statistical analysis is helpful for an initial recognition of normal and of seldom or striking situations. In order to recognize the role they play in the game process, statistical analysis can be combined with animated process analysis.

b. Combined quantitative and qualitative process analysis: as mentioned above, the formation data can be completed by semantic data like technical or tactical aspects and success. The following example deals with evaluating the success of a team in a given formation interaction. Assume team A is playing offense formation 3 against defence formation 5 of team B. The success rate is rather small, and it seems A is having serious problems in this type of interaction. However, a second glance might make evident that the absolute numbers of those actions and interactions are very small, significantly reducing their importance. In turn, the small numbers could be a hint that those actions could be spontaneous creative attacks in order to surprise the opponent defence – although without being immediately successful but giving the opposing team a feeling of uncertainty.

c. Net based tactics analysis: tactics analysis is done by net based trajectory analysis. The idea is that at each point in time the formations of tactical groups are identified and can therefore be encoded by a corresponding number and/ or colour. After training, the network can recognize the formation and the formation type contained in each data set of the original position data, and is therefore able to map the original process to a trajectory, as is presented in Figure 6.8.

In the example presented the position data sets of the game process activate corresponding neurons of the network, starting with the one with the grey mark. The process then runs through some light grey neurons followed by some medium grey and some dark grey ones and so on. Reduced to the significant types

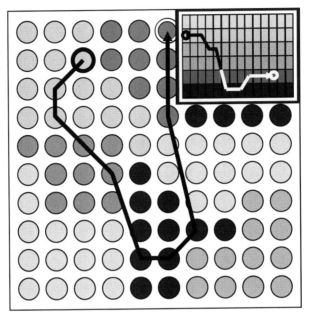

Figure 6.8 A trajectory of formations on the net and its reduction to a formation type trajectory: starting with the marked neuron, the trajectory runs through a sequence of neurons of different shades, which represent different types of situations; the small embedded graphic on top right shows the reduction of the trajectory to the sequence of the type-representing shades (or numbers) – such a sequence can be taken as the type of the corresponding process (source: Perl and Memmert 2013)

represented by the corresponding shades, the trajectories become much simpler and therefore represent the specific behaviour of the corresponding tactical group (see the small embedded graphic on top right in Figure 6.8).

Such a trajectory describes the formation process of a tactical group by a sequence of the corresponding formation type numbers. Two corresponding tactical groups like offense A and defence B build corresponding trajectories. Normally, such trajectories show typical repeating parts that are also driven by typical and repeating activities on the playing field. Those parts can be taken as temporal tactical patterns and hence can be trained to a new network in order to recognize what the typical tactical patterns of a team are.

Such a tactics analysis then on a second level of complexity can be handled as is described in (a) and (b).

Exercise 8

Take a video of a team game and select a tactical group like defence or offense of one of the teams. Try to follow and describe their tactical patterns using a handful of types. Try to describe the behaviour of that group by a type profile like that from the small graphic in Figure 6.8.

Task 8

Based on the exercise above, develop the pattern type profiles of two interacting groups like offense team A and defence team B and compare them. Are there any repeated correspondences, and how many of such typical interactions can be observed? What about infrequent patterns and interactions?

Recommended further reading

Baca, A. and Hinterleithner, T. (2000) 'Animation sportlicher Bewegungsabläufe', in A. Baca (ed.) *Informatik im Sport II*, Wien: öbv and hpt.

Bauer, H.-U. and Schöllhorn, W.I. (1997) 'Self-organizing maps for the analysis of complex movement patterns', *Neural Processing Letters*, 5: 193–199.

Bossel, H. (1994) *Modellbildung und Simulation: Konzepte, Verfahren und Modelle zum Verhalten dynamischer Systeme*, Braunschweig: Vieweg.

Bungartz, H.-J., Zimmer, S., Buchholz, M. and Pflüger, D. (2009) *Modellbildung und Simulation: Eine anwendungsorientierte Einführung*, Berlin: Springer, eXamen. press.

Demant, B. (1993) 'Eine Einführung in die Fuzzy-Theorie und Gedanken zu ihrer Anwendung im Sport', in J. Perl (ed.) *Sport und Informatik III*, Köln: Strauß.

Edelmann-Nusser, J., Hohmann, A. and Henneberg, B. (2002) 'Modeling and prediction of competitive performance in swimming upon neural networks', *European Journal of Sport Science*, 2 (2) 1–10.

Fishwick, P.A. (1991) 'Methods for qualitative modeling in simulation', in P.A. Fishwick and R.B. Modjeski (eds) *Advances in Simulation*, vol. 4 (Knowledge-Based Simulation), New York: Springer.

Fruh, G., Korczak, J. and Vandewalle, H. (2000) 'Determination of physiological parameters determining the running performance by using a genetic algorithm', in A. Baca (ed.) *Informatik im Sport II*, Wien: öbv and hpt.

Grunz, A., Memmert, D. and Perl, J. (2012) 'Tactical pattern recognition in soccer games by means of special self-organizing maps', *Human Movement Science*, 31: 334–343.

Kastens, U. and Kleine Büning, H. (2005) *Modellierung: Grundlagen und formale Methoden, München*, Wien: Hanser.

Lames, M. (1998) 'Modellbildung und Simulation in der Sportwissenschaft' in J. Mester and J. Perl (eds) *Informatik im Sport*, Köln: Strauß.

Lames, M. (2000) 'Modellbildung in den Sportspielen – Stand und Herausforderungen', in A. Baca (ed.) *Informatik im Sport II*, Wien: öbv and hpt.

Lees, A., Barton, B. and Kerschaw, L. (2003) 'The use of Kohonen neural network analysis to establish characteristics of technique in soccer kicking', *Journal of Sports Sciences*, 21: 243–244.

Leser, R. (2006b) 'Prozessanalyse im Fußball mittels Neuronaler Netze', *Human Performance and Sport*, 2: 199–202.

Maier, K.D., Wank, V., Bartonietz, K. and Blickhan, R. (2000) 'Neural network based models of javelin fight: prediction of fight distances and optimal release parameters', *Sports Engineering*, 3: 57–63.

McGarry, T. and Perl, J. (2004) 'Models of sports contests – Markov processes, dynamical systems and neural networks', in M. Hughes and I.M. Franks (eds) *Notational Analysis of Sport*, London and New York: Routledge.

Memmert, D. and Perl, J. (2006) 'Analysis of game creativity development by means of continuously learning neural networks', in *The Engineering of Sport*, 6 (3), New York: Springer.

Perl, J. (1996) 'Grundlagen der Modellbildung und Konzepte der Umsetzung', in K. Quade (ed.) *Anwendungen der Fuzzy-Logik und Neuronaler Netze*, Köln: Strauß.

Perl, J. (1999) 'Aspects and potentiality of unconventional modeling of processes in sporting events', in B. Scholz-Reiter, H.-D. Stahlmann and A. Nethe (eds) *Process Modelling*, Berlin and Heidelberg: Springer.

Perl, J. (2004a) 'Artificial neural networks in motor control research', *Clinical Biomechanics*, 19 (9): 873–875.

Perl, J. (2004b) 'A neural network approach to movement pattern analysis', *Human Movement Science*, 23: 605–620.

Perl, J. and Endler, S. (2012) 'PerPot: Individual anaerobe threshold and marathon scheduling', *International Journal of Computer Science in Sport*, 11 (2): 52–60.

Perl, J. and Lames, M. (2000) 'Identifikation von Ballwechselverlaufstypen mit Neuronalen Netzen am Beispiel Volleyball', in W. Schmidt and A. Knollenberg (eds) *Schriften der dvs*, 112, Hamburg: Czwalina.

Perl, J., Lames, M. and Glitsch, U. (eds) (2002) *Modellbildung im Sport*, Schorndorf: Hofmann.

Quade, K. (ed.) (1996) *Anwendungen der Fuzzy-Logik und Neuronaler Netze,* Köln: Strauß.

Schiebl, F. (1999) 'Fuzzy-Bewegungsanalyse', in W.-D. Miethling and J. Perl (eds) *Sport und Informatik VI*, Köln: Strauß.

Schöllhorn, W. (2004) 'Applications of artificial neural nets in clinical biomechanics', *Clinical Biomechanics*, 19 (9): 876–898.

Seifriz, F. (2001) *Simulation im alpinen Skirennsport: Ein Modell zur Analyse der biomechanischen Einflussgrößen und Optimierung der Fahrlinie auf realen Rennpisten mit Genetischen Algorithmen*, Berlin: dissertation.de.

Spriet, J.A. and Vansteenkiste, G.C. (1982) *Computer-aided Modelling and Simulation*, London: Springer.

Wiemeyer, J. (2000a) 'Animation and Simulation in Sport Science Education – Examples and Evaluation', in A. Baca (ed.) *Informatik im Sport II*, Wien: öbv and hpt.

Wiemeyer, J. (2000b) 'Artificial neural networks – simulations using a simple delta network', in A. Baca (ed.) *Informatik im Sport II*, Wien: öbv and hpt.

Witte, K., Emmermacher, P., Langenbeck, N. and Perl, J. (2012) 'Visualized movement patterns and their analysis to classify similarities – demonstrated by the karate kick Mae-Geri', *International Journal of Fundamental and Applied Kinesiology*, 44 (2): 155–165.

Zadeh, L. (1965) 'Fuzzy sets', *Information and Control*, 8: 338–353.

Zimmermann, H.-J. (1991) *Fuzzy Set Theory – and Its Applications*, 2nd edn, Boston, MA: Kluwer Academic Publishers.

References

Bronstein, I.N., Semendjajew, K.A., Musiol, G. and Muehlig, H. (2008) *Taschenbuch der Mathematik [Pocketbook of Mathematics]*, Frankfurt am Main: Deutsch.

Burrell, G. and Morgan, G. (1985) *Sociological Paradigms and Organizational Analysis: Elements of the sociology of corporate life,* Aldershot: Gower.

Forrester, J.W. (1968) *Principles of Systems*, Cambridge, MA: MIT Press.

Hopfield, J.J. (1982) 'Neural networks and physical systems with emergent collective computational abilities', *Proceedings of the National Academy of Sciences*, 79: 2554–2558.

Jäger, J.M., Schöllhorn, W.I. and Schwerdfeger, B. (2003) 'A pattern recognition approach for an opponent specific classification of tactical moves in volleyball', in E. Müller, H. Schwameder, G. Zallinger and V. Fastenbauer (eds) *Proceedings of the 8th Annual Congress of the European College of Sport Science*, Salzburg: Institute of Sport Science.

Kohonen, T. (1995) *Self-organizing Maps*, Berlin, Heidelberg and New York: Springer.

Kosko, B. (1992) *Neural Networks and Fuzzy Systems*, Englewood Cliffs, NJ: Prentice-Hall.

Leser, R. (2006a) 'Systematisierung und praktische Anwendung der computer- und digitalvideo-gestützten Sportspielanalyse' [Systematisation and practical application of computer and digital video supported game analysis]', doctoral thesis, University of Vienna.

McGarry, T., Khan, M.A. and Franks, I.M. (1999) 'On the presence and absence of behavioural traits in sport: An example from championship squash math-play', *Journal of Sports Sciences*, 17: 297–311.

Memmert, D. and Perl, J. (2009a) 'Analysis and simulation of creativity learning by means of artificial neural networks', *Human Movement Science*, 28: 263–282.

Memmert, D. and Perl, J. (2009b) 'Game creativity analysis by means of neural networks', *Journal of Sport Science*, 27: 139–149.

Perl, J. (2002a) 'Game analysis and control by means of continuously learning networks', *International Journal of Performance Analysis of Sport*, 2: 21–35.

Perl, J. (2002b) 'Adaptation, antagonism, and system dynamics', in G. Ghent, D. Kluka and D. Jones (eds) *Perspectives - The Multidisciplinary Series of Physical Education and Sport Science*, volume 4, Oxford: Meyer and Meyer Sport.

Perl, J. (2008) 'Modelling', in P. Dabnichki and A. Baca (eds) *Computers in Sport*, Southampton and Boston, MA: Wit Press.

Perl, J. and Dauscher, P. (2006) 'Dynamic pattern recognition in sport by means of artificial neural networks', in R. Begg and M. Palaniswami (eds) *Computational Intelligence for Movement Science*, Hershey, London, Melbourne and Singapore: Idea Group Publishing.

Perl, J. and Lames, M. (2000) 'Identifikation von Ballwechselverlaufstypen mit Neuronalen Netzen am Beispiel Volleyball [Identification of rally types with use of Neuronal Networks using the example of volleyball]', in W. Schmidt and A. Knollenberg (eds) *Sport - Spiel - Forschung* (pp. 211–216). Hamburg: Czwalina.

Perl, J. and Memmert, D. (2012) 'Network approaches in complex environments', *Human Movement Science*, 31 (2): 267–270.

Perl, J., Grunz, A. and Memmert, D. (2013) 'Tactics analysis in soccer – an advanced approach', *International Journal of Computer Science in Sport*, 12 (1): 33–44.

Perl, J., Lames, M. and Miethling, W. (eds) (1997) *Information Technology in Sport: A handbook*, Schorndorf: Hofmann.

Pfeiffer, M. and Perl, J. (2006) 'Analysis of tactical structures in team handball by means of artificial neural networks', *International Journal of Computer Science in Sport*, 5 (1): 4–14.

Westphal, N. and Schöllhorn, W. (2001) 'Identifying volleyball teams by their tactical moves', in J. Mester, G. King, H. Strüder, C. Tsolakidis and A. Osterburg (eds) *Proceedings of the 6th Annual Congress ECSS*, Cologne: Strauß..

7 Game analysis

Peter O'Donoghue

Introduction

Match analysis is used within coaching, infotainment, judging and academic contexts to study important tactical aspects of performance in individual or team games. Manual notation systems have been used in the past but now computerized match analysis systems that integrate video and match databases together are affordable to coaches from amateur level to elite squad. Computerized match analysis systems have followed advances in information technology, especially in the areas of human–computer interaction, multimedia technology and distributed systems. There have been previous reviews of the historical development of computerized notational analysis systems and how advances in technology have been exploited. However, the field is moving so rapidly that a recent chapter on match analysis written by this author (O'Donoghue, 2013) is already out of date. Figure 7.1 in the current chapter is an updated version of Figure 11.2 in O'Donoghue's (2013, p.167) chapter in a sports coaching text book. As well as the need to provide an up-to-date review of computerized match analysis systems, it is also important to consider the area from a computer science perspective. Previous reviews of computerized match analysis have all been written from the view of the application area.

Match analysis is an area of sports performance analysis that is concerned with strategy and tactics in games and the effectiveness with which skills are performed. There are other aspects of sports performance analysis such as work-rate analysis and analysis of technique that are outside the scope of the current chapter. Readers who are interested in work-rate analysis can find relevant material in Chapter 5 by Roland Leser and Karen Roemer. Match analysis is used within coaching to provide feedback to players and squads about areas of performance requiring attention. This is not merely done on an individual match basis, but also on sets of matches to produce performance profiles and to analyse trends in performance. Match analysis involves quantitative and qualitative analysis of sports performance data. Quantitative analysis is done on match event lists allowing areas requiring attention to be identified. Relevant video sequences can then be analysed in detail by coaches and players who can use their knowledge of the sport during in-depth analysis of the complex video information to explore reasons why events occurred and ways of improving performance.

The chapter commences with a discussion of general purpose and special purpose match analysis systems before a review of areas of computer science that are relevant to match analysis. The areas of computer science that are covered in this chapter are human–computer interaction, multimedia technology and software engineering.

General purpose match analysis systems

Advantages and disadvantages of general purpose systems

There are general purpose match analysis systems and special purpose match analysis systems. The general purpose systems can be tailored for use with any sports of the users' choice. Special purpose systems, on the other hand, are developed for use in particular sports. Examples of special purpose systems are Crickstat DV (CSIR, Pretoria, South Africa) which is used in cricket, Prozone's MatchViewer (Prozone Sports Ltd, Leeds, UK) which is used in soccer, the system used by Williams (2004) to analyse rule changes in rugby union and the tennis analysis system used by the author of the current chapter (O'Donoghue and Ingram, 2001). General purpose match analysis systems, on the other hand, were not developed to analyse a single sport. General purpose systems include software platforms such as Observer Pro (Noldus, Wageningen, Netherlands), Dartfish (Dartfish, Fribourg, Switzerland), sportscode (Sportstec, Warriewood, New south Wales, Australia), Focus X2 (Elite Sports Analysis, Delgaty Bay, Fife, Scotland) and Nacsport (Nacsport, Las Palmas de Gran Canaria. Spain). These systems integrate a match video with a timed event list. The main conceptual requirements of such systems are that they allow video to be captured and indexed (tagged) with event records, supporting event querying, statistical output and interactive video review. Event types are created by users to represent the sport being analysed. The advantages of using general purpose packages are:

- The packages can be used repeatedly for different sports with a common general interface and functionality.
- The systems are easier to develop because they do not have to be all things to all people.
- Sports governing bodies do not need to commission the development of special purpose software to analyse their sport.
- General statistical output is provided by cross-tabulating variables.
- Video sequences of interest can be viewed interactively within the package.
- Highlight movies containing relevant video sequences can be produced and viewed on other computers where the package is not installed.
- Event lists can be exported for analysis in general purpose data processing packages such as Microsoft Excel.

The main disadvantage of general purpose systems is that they cannot provide every specific function required by every sport. For example, there may be specific data presentation methods used in different sports that are well understood by practitioners in those sports. These include the worm diagram and wagon wheel diagram used in cricket (Kirkbride, 2013). In order to produce the required outputs for a sport when using a general purpose package, the analyst often needs to export data into a spreadsheet or other data analysis tool for further processing. This requires skilled analysts with the ability to undertake such analyses.

Data entry

There are two main ways in which match analysis packages represent match events. An event can be represented as an instantaneous event that has no duration, for example the point in time at which a football is kicked or the point in time at which a raquet strikes a ball. Video sequences of such events include a user-defined period before (pre-roll) and after (post-roll) the event so that viewers can consider the cause and consequences of the event. The other way of representing behaviour in sport is for events to have a non-zero duration which spans from the start point of the event to the end point of the event. For example, a possession in soccer is not an instantaneous event but lasts from a team gaining possession to losing possession or scoring. Similarly, a rally in a raquet sport is not performed in an instant but takes a period of time between the serve being made and the rally ending with a winner or an error. Some general purpose packages, such as Focus X2, use the first method, abstracting behaviour to a series of instantaneous events. Where it is necessary to represent states or behaviours that occur over a period of time, packages like Focus X2 can be used to represent the start and end points of these states as instantaneous events. Other packages, such as sportscode and Observer Pro, allow both instantaneous events as well as events that have a non-zero duration.

Users tailor the general purpose package so that it can be used for their sport by defining event types that occur within their sport. This is done by creating a code window in sportscode or a category set in Focus X2. The other packages can be tailored in similar ways for use with specific sports. Events are recorded through a data entry interface, such as the code window of sportscode. As events are logged, their time within the video is recorded; this could be an instantaneous time or, if the event has a non-zero duration, the start time and end time of the event could be recorded. This event list could be a simple table of events or represented graphically, for example the timeline in sportscode. Events can have other information about them recorded. For example, when a pass is made in a team game we can record the team and player making the pass, the area of the pitch where the pass was made from, the area of the pitch where the pass was received and the outcome of the pass. Another example is a point in tennis where we might also wish to record the serving player, whether the point emanated from a first or second serve, whether the point was served to the deuce or advantage side, the player winning the point and whether the point ended on a winner or an error.

There may be some behaviours in sport where some information is needed for some event types but not for others. For example, in tennis we may have a category 'point type' with seven values: ace, double fault, serve winner, return winner, server to net first, receiver to net first or baseline rally (O'Donoghue and Ingram, 2001). If a point is an ace, double fault, serve winner or return winner then we do not need to enter a value for whether a point finishes on a winner or error. This is an example of a variant record where the data structure for an event differs depending on the event type. In Focus X2, a value needs to be entered for every category. Therefore, it may be necessary to have some 'N/A' (not applicable) values for some categories. Other systems only require the users to enter the labels that they need to for any given event.

Some systems define behaviour in more sophisticated ways than others. For example, in sportscode sets of events can be defined as mutually exclusive so that only one event within the set of mutually exclusive events can be recorded at a time. This means that recording an instance of one event within the set will deactivate any instance of any other event in the set that is active at that time. Sportscode also allows activation links where some events can automatically trigger other events. For example, in a raquet sport, we may have two events representing forehand and backhand shots. When either of these events is recorded they can automatically trigger a more general shot event saving the user from having to enter it.

Analysis facilities

Once the video is indexed (or tagged) with a list of timed events, the data can be analysed and video sequences can be viewed interactively. Variables can be cross-tabulated to provide efficient quantitative information. For example, shot type (forehand or backhand) could be cross-tabulated with outcome (winner, error or rally continues) to see if one shot type leads to proportionally more errors than the other. In some packages, cells within this table (or matrix) can be clicked on directly on the computer screen to access video sequences for those recorded events. There are other ways of accessing video sequences such as direct manipulation of the event list or timeline. In Focus X2, the category set is used to enter events, when the system is in logging mode, and to display events, when the system is in review mode. In review mode, criteria for events of interest are established by the user and only those events satisfying these criteria are shown in the event list. For example, in soccer we may wish to see any passes from four specific areas of the nine defined pitch areas that were unsuccessful in the first half. When the relevant values of the categories are selected, the system provides a restricted view of the event list, only showing those events satisfying these criteria. These events can then be clicked on by the user to view the video sequences of them.

Creating highlight movies

As well as interactively viewing video sequences, it is also possible to save highlight movies. Highlights movies are standalone video files that can be played on computers that do not have the software package installed. Some packages have movie organizer facilities within them that allow titles and annotations to be added to the movie as clips are included. The advantages of creating highlights movies are that they can be viewed on coaches' computers where the package may not be installed and the movie can be played efficiently without user manipulation of the system interrupting briefing sessions. The highlights movie will also be rehearsed and the best clips of any candidate clips will have been selected. The disadvantage of creating highlights movies is that it takes time to do this and saving the video file requires the analyst's computer for a period of time, preventing other work.

The architecture of general purpose packages

Sportscode is used as an example of a general purpose match analysis package because it is the most sophisticated commercial package available at the time of writing. It has a 'statistical window' that can be programmed to inspect the timeline of events calculating performance statistics automatically which can be output during matches or afterwards. The system runs on Apple Macintosh computers and can communicate with iPads and iPhones during data entry, allowing remote data entry as well as remote real-time access to match statistics. Figure 7.1 shows the main components of the sportscode system and the human operation processes involved during the data capture and match analysis phases.

The sportscode system shown in Figure 7.1 contains a number of components. Simple systems can be developed to record events and associated value labels into the timeline, allowing an event by label matrix to be produced. Video clips can then be viewed interactively either by direct manipulation of the timeline or the matrix. A simple system like this does not require remote data entry, remote output, matrix organizers, statistical windows or output windows. The decision about which components of sportscode are to be used depends on system requirements and how often the system is to be used. For example, programming a statistical window may not be justified if the system is to be used for a single tournament of six matches, but may be justified if the system is to be used over one or more seasons of 30 or more matches per season. The components shown in Figure 7.1 are described as follows:

- Video capture window – the video capture window shows the match video frames as they are being recorded.
- Code window – the code window is used to input events and value labels during data capture as well as correct events and labels later.
- Timeline – the timeline in sportscode is a visual representation of the timed event list showing the start and end of each instance of each event type.
- Matrix – a matrix is a two dimensional table that has a row for each event type and a column for each label. The cells of the matrix show frequency of each value label recorded for each event type.
- Matrix organizer – sometimes it is not necessary to show all value label types in the matrix displayed to users. Furthermore, there are occasions where users wish to see the frequency of events containing different combinations of value

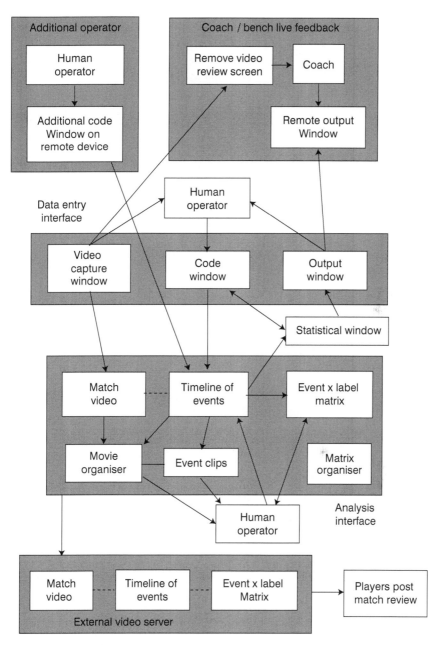

Figure 7.1 The main sportscode components

labels. For example, we might be interested in the frequency of some event performed in a given area of the pitch and which was performed successfully. The matrix organizer is used to define the value labels and combinations of value labels that we wish to display in the matrix.

- Label tree – there may be many different value labels that are used with different event buttons. A label tree defines a hierarchical menu structure with the value labels at the base of this hierarchy. This menu structure can be used during labelling of events to navigate through the menu structure to select the label needed rather than presenting users with a single list of all labels to choose from.
- Event clip – a video sequence for a given instance of an event. Video sequences can be accessed for events by direct manipulation of the timeline or the matrix.
- Statistical window – the statistical window can be programmed to determine information from the raw labelled events that have been recorded in the timeline. The information produced by the statistical window can be sent to a user-friendly output window.
- Script – a script is a sequence of executable instructions within the cell of the statistical window. The script is programmed to produce information using data from the timeline as well as values from other cells of the statistical window. The script typically produces a piece of information that is displayed in the particular cell. Other commands within the script may send values to named areas of output windows.
- Output window – an output window displays summary match statistics that are sent to it by the statistical window. It is also possible that a code window can include areas where output values can be displayed during data entry. Thus the code window can be a combined interface for data entry and real-time statistical output.
- Additional operators and input devices – these are shown in the top left hand corner of Figure 7.1 and include devices such as iPads with iCoda software installed, allowing subsets of a code window to be used by additional operators. The main system can be set up to allow remote devices to communicate with the analyst's computer so that events and labels recorded using the remote devices are entered directly into the timeline.
- Coach / bench live feedback facility – as well as allowing remote devices to be used for data capture, the system can send important sub-views of output windows to remote devices such as iPhones and iPads. This allows coaches and players on the bench to receive match statistics live during matches. As the match video is being recorded it is also possible to display the video on remote screens through wired links to the bench. The remote display may be a delayed feed of the match video allowing coaches and players to have another look at events that have just happened in the match (for example 10s later). An additional option that has not been shown on Figure 7.1 is to allow the coach to mark critical events in the timeline during the match. This is done by having a special event in the code window called

'coach review event' or 'critical event' and this is the only event the coach needs to enter, making this data entry task simple enough that the coach is able to perform the main functions of observing and coaching during the match.

- Movie organizer – although video sequences of events of interest can be displayed interactively through the matrix or timeline, there are occasions where a single movie of carefully chosen clips is needed so that briefing sessions can run smoothly. The matrix organizer allows clips to be included into a video along with titles, annotations and other relevant information. This video can then be saved to run as a standalone video or be played from within the package.

- External video server – this is a password protected website containing a timeline, matrix and match video allowing players to review relevant passages of play at a time and location suitable to them. Doing this video analysis activity away from training environment allows squads to make better use of training facilities during squad training sessions. The material may be provided within a wider coaching information management system that also includes training log data and other coaching related communication. Examples of such systems are Replay (Replay Analysis, London, UK) or Team Performance Exchange (Team Performance Exchange, Best, Netherlands).

Special purpose match analysis systems

Advantages and disadvantages of special purpose systems

Special purpose systems use a conceptual model of the given sport, allowing data to be stored and retrieved about relevant match events. Other requirements of such systems are that they provide commonly used quantitative outputs in formats that are familiar to practitioners in the sport. Special purpose match analysis packages are developed for particular sports and can be used in practical or academic contexts. Some special purpose packages are developed for individual use (O'Donoghue and Ingram, 2001; Williams, 2004) while others are commercially available such as Crickstat. Existing general purpose match analysis systems could be applied to the same sports as special purpose systems, taking advantage of the known benefits of general purpose systems. However, Williams (2004) listed the following disadvantages of general purpose match analysis systems:

- The user has a limited amount of capture options.
- The interface is too standardized and there is limited flexibility in the screen layout of such systems.
- The analysis of data is restricted to the general functions provided.
- The systems provide video capture and review facilities that may not always be necessary and which add to the cost of such systems and the computers on which they are used.

The advantages of special purpose systems are:

- We don't have to pay for un-needed features of general purpose packages.
- Sport specific data structures can be used.
- Sport specific output representations that are commonly understood in the given sport can be used.
- Input of events can follow match syntax restricting the selection of events to just those possible in the current game state.
- Sport specific events such as the need to cancel an event record if a tennis player makes a successful use of the challenge system can be programmed into the system.
- The system can be programmed to perform detailed sport specific analysis of data that would have had to be done in Excel or other data processing packages if a general purpose package was used.
- Data consistency checks can be programmed based on known constraints for behaviour patterns in the given sport.

Examples of these advantages will be discussed when covering different special purpose match analysis systems. Four systems are covered, with the first two being commercially available packages for soccer and cricket and the other two being highly specialist systems developed for particular research projects

There are some disadvantages to using special purpose systems that must be acknowledged. Firstly, they need to be programmed and this can require time, programming skill and be costly. Secondly, systems produced for single users are typically not as well documented as commercial systems developed for multiple users. It may be difficult to maintain special purpose systems as hardware changes. For example, O'Donoghue and Ingram's (2001) system was developed in a DOS based version of a third generation language. At one time, they needed to transfer the raw point data into a Windows based machine from the computer which had been used but this computer only had a 3.5 inch disk drive. The file was almost four times the capacity of a 3.5 inch disk and so a utility had to be written to dump the data onto disks in four sections. Once this had been done, the lap top used in O'Donoghue and Ingram's (2001) study could be consigned to the Centre of Performance Analysis (CPA) museum!

Commercial special purpose systems

There are now general purpose and special purpose systems that have been developed commercially for the coaching and teaching markets. Nicholson (1997) predicted the commercialization of notational analysis in general, identifying the needs of the coaching market. The systems used in academic research at the time were not considered suitable for the coaching market. Nicholson (1997) identified four areas where systems needed to improve in order to satisfy the requirements of the coaching market. Firstly, commercial systems need to be fast and easy to use. Secondly, they need flexibility to be able to provide ad hoc information needs. Thirdly, they need to communicate information effectively to the coaching audience. The fourth area where improvement was needed was that systems needed to be used in a practical support mechanism rather than being restricted by formal hypotheses. Nicholson's (1997) prediction of snowballing of commercial success of match analysis has been realized, with competing organizations today marketing general purpose and special purpose systems.

The Prozone company is best known for its player tracking system that has been used in soccer and rugby union. However, Prozone also provides a soccer specific match analysis system that is used to analyse typical video footage that follows the on-the-ball action. The benefits of this system are that it is affordable to teams from amateur to elite levels of soccer, does not need to be installed permanently at a single stadium and has been developed using requirements elicited from expert coach users. The system provides the data entry, interactive video analysis and statistical outputs that would be found in general purpose match analysis systems but also provides soccer specific outputs such as pass maps and the pitch location of other types of event. The system has been shown to have good reliability when operated by trained users (Bradley et al., 2007). The system does have flexibility to allow users to use different subsets of the features available and its data can also be exported for more detailed analysis in spreadsheets and statistical analysis packages. While the MatchViewer system is used to analyse a single match, Prozone also provide special purpose systems to analyse trends in data produced from multiple matches analysed in MatchViewer.

Crickstat DV is a special purpose match analysis system used in cricket. The system integrates match video with objective data relating to match events and also allows data from other systems used in cricket to be imported. For example, some versions of the product allow Hawkeye (Hawkeye Innovations, Basingstoke, UK) data to be imported. Information about match and ball settings can be entered at the beginning of match analysis together with details of the teams competing. The outputs of the system include cricket specific visual representations such as wagon wheel diagrams which can be viewed from multiple perspectives, three dimensional views of wickets displaying information about deliveries, work charts showing cumulative runs made and Manhattan charts displaying individual frequency information for overs played. Other cricket specific information relating to batting partnerships is available together with video sequence output. There are special purpose systems used to analyse matches and provide summary statistics on media channels (Kirkbride, 2013). These include the statistics provided for the official websites of Grand Slam tennis tournaments, statistics for international matches provided by the Fédération Internationale de Football Association (FIFA's) website (www.fifa.com) and the International Rugby Board's (IRB's) website (www.irb.com). Other organizations analyse soccer matches and provide data on commercial bases, for example Opta (www.optasports.com).

Single user systems

Williams (2004) developed a system for specific use in his own PhD study where there was no need for interactive video feedback. The system produced specific ball in play, possession and territory timings for rugby matches. Williams was able to develop an entity relationship model of the data required in his own study, from which a special purpose database was implemented. The system was developed in Visual Basic and produced individual game reports in the form required.

O'Donoghue and Ingram (2001) produced a special purpose computerized match analysis system for tennis. This system was specifically designed to capture timing factors and tactical data for tennis matches being observed during live television coverage. The first main benefit of the system was that it followed the syntax of service and point ending events when recording timings. This ensured that all first serves, second serves, repeated first and second serves due to lets and the instants at which points ended were recorded in the correct order. This not only recorded timing details, but also whether the point emanated from a first or second service. The user then entered the number of shots played in the point after the counting serve and followed a menu structure to enter tactical data during the 20s between points. The first piece of information entered was point type (ace, double fault, serve winner, return winner, server to net first, receiver to net first or baseline rally). The type of point entered dictated what other information was needed. For example, if the point was an ace, double fault, serve winner or return winner then no further information was needed as the point winner would be obvious from the type of point. If, however, the point was a net point or a baseline rally then further information needed to be entered in order to determine who won the point. For net points, the cause of going to the net and the outcome of going to the net were requested, with the user choosing a menu item in each case. The cause of going to the net could be following a good serve, following a good approach shot, being drawn to the net or luck if the ball struck the net before crossing the net or was played short through an unintentional miss-hit. There were outcomes of net points where the player at the net won the point at the net through a volley, smash, drop shot or opponent error. There were net points where the player at the net lost the point by making an error at the net, being lobbed or being passed. There were other net points that continued with the player at the net retreating from the net and either winning or losing with the point ending on a winner or an error. Similarly, baseline rallies were either won or lost by the serving player with the point ending with a winner or an error.

The system also made within point consistency checks, flagging possible data entry errors which would need to be corrected before the next point commenced. For example, if there were an even number of shots in the rally including the counting serve then the point was either won by the server with a winner or lost by the server with an error. Similarly, if there were an even number of shots in the rally including the counting serve, then the point was either won by the receiving player with a winner or lost by the receiving player with an error. If the data entered violated these constraints then the system could flag a data entry error.

How to program a match analysis system

The development of a special purpose system to analyse a given sport provides the opportunity for developers to provide features that are not always possible in general purpose match analysis systems. This section describes how O'Donoghue and Ingram (2001) included the ability to automatically update the score and the serving player in tennis. This was done using information about the score at the beginning of the previous point and what happened in the point. At the beginning of the observation, the user would enter who was serving and the score in sets, games and points at the start of coverage. Knowing the score at the start of a point and knowing who won the point allows the score at the end of the point to be determined. The score is displayed by the system, allowing the user to check it agrees with the score called by the umpire before confirming the data entered ready for the point. If the scores disagree, the user needs to re-enter the data correctly. The algorithm for updating the score is shown in the remainder of this section. Firstly, the variables used in the algorithm are identified.

```
{* COMMENT: Main variables *}
{* COMMENT: sets, games and points for players A and B before the
   point is played *}
SA, GA, PA, SB, GB, PA
{* COMMENT: Points are 0,1,2,3,4, rather than Love, 15, 30, 40, etc
   *}
{* COMMENT: sets, games and points for players A and B after the
   point is played *}
NewSA, NewGA, NewPA, NewSB, NewGB, NewPA {* Score after the point
   is played *}
Server {* COMMENT: Player serving for this point - 'A' or 'B' *}
NewServer {* COMMENT: Player serving for the next point - 'A' or
   'B' *}
{* COMMENT: we also need to know the player who is serving within a
   tie-break *}
TBServer {* COMMENT: Player serving for this tie-break point - 'A'
   or 'B' *}
NewTBServer {* COMMENT: Player serving for the next tie-break point
   - 'A' or 'B' *}
PointWinner {* COMMENT: Player who wins the point - 'A' or 'B' *}
Tournament {* COMMENT: 1 = Australian, 2 = French, 3 = Wimbledon, 4
   = US Open *}
Gender {* COMMENT: 1 = Female, 2 = Male *}
```

It is necessary to have two pairs of variables for serving players: one pair is for player serving in normal games (Server and NewServer) while the other pair is for the player serving in tie-breaks (TBServer and NewTBServer). When a tie-break is being played we need to use Server to represent the player who served first in the tie-break. This is because the other player will serve first in the first game of the next set, if further set(s) are to be played. Therefore, the player serving the last point in the tie-break does not determine who serves in the next point.

There are some general conditions that apply to the match that can be set up at the beginning of the match. For example, if the match is a women's singles match then we know it is the best of three sets otherwise it is the best of five sets. If the match is being played at the US Open then we know there is a tie-breaker in the final set whereas there is no tie-breaker in the final set at the other three tournaments. The code setting Boolean (TRUE or FALSE) variables is shown below.

```
{* COMMENT: There is a tie-breaker in the final set of the US Open
   *}
IF Tournament = 4 THEN
  TieBreakInFinalSet = TRUE
ELSE
  TieBreakInFinalSet = FALSE
ENDIF

{* COMMENT: Women's singles matches are best of 3 sets, men's
   singles matches are best of 5 sets *}
IF Gender = 1 THEN
  FinalSet = 3
ELSE
  FinalSet = 5
ENDIF
```

A general design principle of this score update algorithm is that we do not change the current score (SA, SB, GA, GB, PA, PB) within the algorithm in preparation for the next point. Instead, we inspect the current score and determine new variables to represent the score when the point is completed (NewSA, NewSB, NewGA, NewGB, NewPA, NewPB). Once the algorithm has computed the new score, the new point can be prepared for by assigning the values of the new score variables to the current score variables. This also applies to the variables representing the serving player for the current point (Server) and the serving player for the next point (NewServer).

Rather than writing a single procedure to update the score and serving player, the algorithm is written as a hierarchy of procedures so that the code is decomposed into manageable sections. This can be done in a top-down fashion starting with the overall control algorithm before writing the lower level detailed algorithms that it calls. Alternatively, a bottom-up approach could be used by developing procedures to deal with detailed aspects before writing the higher level procedures that invoke these. We will use a combination of top-down and bottom-up approaches to illustrate the development of the score update algorithm. Firstly, we will develop some useful functions which can be used within the hierarchy of procedures. The first function simply determines who the other player is when we need to change the server, for example. This function is defined in terms of a formal parameter (Player) which is a character representing the player ('A' or 'B'). The result of the function is evaluated to a character as shown by the type of the function and the statements assigning a character value to the function Other.

```
FUNCTION Other(Player : CHARACTER) : CHARACTER
IF Player = 'A' THEN
  Other = 'B'
ELSE
  Other = 'A'
ENDIF
END Other
```

This function can now be invoked using either Server or TBServer as an actual parameter to be represented by the formal parameter Player. For example we might have a statement:

```
NewServer = Other(Server)
Or
NewTBServer = Other(TBServer)
```

The second function is a Boolean function to determine if the current score means that a tie-break is being played or not. The function uses formal parameters to represent the score in sets and games. When checking whether we are in a tie-break or not, we may use the current set and game score. However, if checking to see if we are about to enter a tie-break the actual parameter for one of the game scores will be one greater than the game score at the beginning of the last point of the 12th game in the current set. The type CARDINAL is the set of positive whole numbers including zero. This function uses the global variables FinalSet and TieBreakInFinalSet in order to determine the truth of whether the current score means the match is in a tie-break.

```
{* COMMENT: Function to determine if we are in a tie-breaker or not
   *}
FUNCTION InTieBreak(SetsA, SetsB, GamesA, GamesB: CARDINAL) :
   BOOLEAN;
IF (GamesA = 6) AND (GamesB = 6) AND (TieBreakInFinalSet OR
   (SetsA+SetsB+1 <FinalSet))
THEN
  {* We are in a tiebreak *}
  InTieBreak = TRUE
ELSE
  {* We are not in a tiebreak *}
  InTieBreak = FALSE
ENDIF
END InTieBreak
```

Now we will consider the top-level algorithm for updating the score and serving player once the point winner is known.

```
{* COMMENT: Initialization of game state variables for this point
    *}
IF InTieBreak(SA, SB, GA, GB) THEN
  PointsRequired = 7
ELSE
  PointsRequired = 4
ENDIF

{* Main algorithm to update score *}
IF PointWinner = 'A' THEN
  IF (PA+1 >= PointsRequired) AND (PA+1-PB >= 2) THEN
    {* COMMENT: A has also won the game *}
    NewPA = 0; NewPB = 0; NewServer = Other(Server);
    {* COMMENT: if match entering tie-break, we need to set up
        server within the tie-break *}
    IF InTieBreak(SA, SB, GA+1, GB) THEN
      NewTBServer = NewServer
    END;
    {* COMMENT: A will have also won set if the current game
      was a tie-break or winning the game means A has at least 6
      games and is at least 2 games ahead of B*}
    IF InTieBreak(SA, SB, GA, GB) OR
    ((GA+1 >= 6) AND (GA+1-GB >=2))
      THEN
      {* COMMENT: A has also won the set *}
      NewGA = 0; NewGB = 0; NewSA=SA+1; NewSB=SB;
      IF SA+1 = (FinalSet+1)/2 THEN
        {* COMMENT: A has won the match *}
        Finalization
      ENDIF
    ELSE
      {* COMMENT: New Game *}
      NewGA=GA+1; NewGB=GB; NewSA=SA; NewSB=SB;
    ENDIF
  ELSE
    {* COMMENT: Game continues *}
    NewPA=PA+1; NewPB=PB;
    NewGA=GA; NewGB=GB;
    NewSA=SA; NewSB=SB;
    NewServer=Server;
    IF InTiebreak THEN
      UpdateTiebreakServer
    ENDIF
  ENDIF
```

```
ELSE {* B has won the point *}
   {* COMMENT: This is the same as before but exchange 'A' and 'B'*}
END
```

We need a Finalization procedure to perform any summary analysis or to make any outputs that we need when the match is over. If the current point and the next point are within a tie-break, we will need to change the serving player within the tie-break if an odd number of points have been played. This is done using the UpdateTiebreakServer procedure shown below.

```
PROCEDURE UpdateTiebreakServer
PointsPlayed = PA+1+PB
IF PointsPlayed MOD 2 = 1 THEN
   {* An odd number of points have been played so far in the tie-
     break *}
   NewTBServer = Other(TBServer)
ELSE
   {* An even number of points have been played so far in the tie-
     break *}
   NewTBServer = TBServer
ENDIF
END UpdateTiebreakServer
```

The automatic updating of the score line during data entry, consistency checking of data entered, syntax driven menu structure and ability to produce a single file of summary indicators from multiple match files are clear advantages of programmers being able to develop special purpose systems. The programmers have much greater control in developing such a system than if they were tailoring a general purpose system to be used with their sport.

Other special purpose systems have been used within academic settings for teaching computerized notation and for doing projects. Ponting and O'Donoghue (2004) described a suite of Windows based systems used for analysing for a number of sports including squash, soccer and rugby. These systems were not directly integrated with match videos but designed to be used by a user while observing a performance on a video and periodically pausing the video to enter events. The systems used the event variables proposed by Hughes and Franks (2004) with time, event type, player / team performing the event and location on the playing area being entered. The systems provide statistical output as well as scatter plots showing locations of events on the playing surface.

Human–computer interaction – ergonomics

Input devices

Match analysis is a user intensive task with details of match events being frequently recorded during live observation or post-match analysis. Player tracking systems have allowed automation of some aspects of match analysis, but for many tactical aspects of play it is still necessary for expert observers to observe matches and enter events. Therefore, human–computer interaction and ergonomics have always been relevant areas of computer science for match analysis systems. Developments in human–computer interaction have been exploited by computerized notational analysis systems (Hughes, 1998; Hughes and Franks, 1995). The earliest systems used keyboards to input data. For example, O'Donoghue (1998) developed the Computerized All-Purpose Time-motion Analysis Integrated (CAPTAIN) system where keyboard function keys were used to enter different movements. Sports could be defined with up to nine movements and a keyboard overlay for the sport could be printed by the system. This keyboard overlay assisted system operators in pressing the correct keys when entering time-motion data. Hughes (1997) reviewed early developments in computerized notational analysis and analysis of coach behaviour. Concept keyboards and digitization tablets have been used in academic research (Treadwell, 1987) and scouting (Dufour, 1991). With the advent of Windows interfaces, graphical user interfaces (GUIs) allowed the input areas previously shown on digitization tablets to be set up as on-screen buttons. However, while GUIs are a technological advance over keyboards, they are not as effective for live match analysis systems. This is because the operator needs to focus on three things when using a GUI: the match under observation, the mouse and the location of the mouse pointer on the screen. With keyboard input, the operator directly presses the relevant key while observing the match. There is still a need to check the screen to ensure events entered are being recorded as shown by the emerging event list displayed on the screen. Touch sensitive screens were a further input mechanism used in computerized match analysis (Claudio and Dimas, 1995). Apple's iPad has been used in match analysis with systems such as sportscode and Dartfish providing apps for iPad data entry (Brown, 2012). Sportstec provide the iCoda system that allows data entry on code windows shown on iPad devices, with the data entered sent wirelessly to the timeline on a central Apple Macintosh computer system. This involves running a Coda session on the central Mac and using a coding form on the iPad. The data will be received by the central Mac computer in XML format during the process of updating the timeline. The benefits of distributing input over several input devices had been recognized before the invention of iPads. For example, Toledano et al. (2001) described a match analysis system where several analysts operated computers that were connected to a head coach's computer. The links were wired but radio communication was possible at extra cost. The data entry apps developed for iPads by companies like Dartfish and Sportstec have provided a cost-effective distributed data entry for match analysis.

Bar code scanners have also been used for data entry within match analysis systems (Buchanan et al., 2013). Events are represented by short mnemonics which are translated into barcodes. The barcodes are printed on a coding sheet in a way that represents the workflow of analysis activity for the given sport. The action of scanning a given barcode seems similar to the actions of pressing a key on a keyboard or using a tablet. An interesting area of future research would be to compare the reliability of data entry and usability of barcode scanning with alternative input methods using the same set of match events.

Palmtop or handheld computers have improved the portability of match analysis systems. One such system is Pocket Focus that works with the Focus X2 system. The category set that represents the sport behaviour is downloaded onto a handheld computer, which can be used for data entry during a match where filming may not be permitted. The data recorded on the handheld computer can be synchronized with publicly available match footage at a later time, permitting the integrated video analysis supported by the Focus X2 system. Similarly, Dartfish can be used to enter timed match events on an iPad with the data being synchronized with match video later.

Voice-over input for match analysis was first attempted in 1988 (Taylor and Hughes, 1988). Since then, the Focus X2 system has incorporated a voice input facility (Focus Voice). This has been used in soccer match analysis with a reliability assessment revealing five or fewer errors in 12 matches when 1,146 to 1,577 events were entered using a category set of 39 different values (Cort, 2006). The errors reported by Cort (2006) were errors in the Focus Voice system recognizing spoken words. There may be additional perceptual errors or data entry errors made during verbal coding prior to Focus Voice dealing with the spoken codes. These additional errors may be due to normal observational issues or may be additional errors resulting from the need to verbally code events. Users of different input mechanisms need to consider the frequency and nature of data entry and the most ergonomic way for the user to enter the data reliably. In many cases, it could be that a combination of input mechanisms could be used to enter data.

Computerized match analysis systems are used in an environment where other audio-visual technology may be operated simultaneously by the analyst. For example, the author has analysed netball matches live using his right hand to press hotkeys set up in sportscode while using the left hand to control the camera. This can be done where the laptop is on a table at a suitable height for data entry. Where matches are filmed from a side-on view there is less of a need to zoom in and out with the camera than when an end-on viewing position is used. Viewing position and space available for equipment, chairs, tables and personnel need to be considered when planning data entry tasks using systems. The location of power supplies and battery capacities also need to be considered at match venues. It is possible to use an additional camera operator, allowing the analyst to focus on data entry. There are also ergonomically designed camera handles and remote control devices to make camera control, zooming and panning much smoother during live match analysis. The available technology and the wider analysis environment need to be considered when developing match analysis systems.

Ubiquitous computing is an area of computer science with great potential in match analysis. Ubiquitous computing is where computerized systems are integrated into everyday life activities in a non-invasive way. In sports performance, innovative diagnostic systems have been developed in rowing, table tennis and biathlon rifle shooting (Baca, 2006). The table tennis system is a good example of how computers can be used to capture detailed information without interfering with the athlete or any equipment being used by the athlete. Accelerometers beneath the table measure vibrations caused by ball impacts. The vibration signal is processed by an algorithm that estimates a ball landing position with a reliability of 0.020 ± 0.011m. Another facility used in table tennis records ball impacts and then computes the time intervals between these. Further advances in ubiquitous computing were reviewed by Baca et al. (2009) and many of these are relevant to match analysis. They classified the developments into two categories. Firstly, there is miniaturization of devices and the ability to communicate data wirelessly over longer distances. The second category of development in ubiquitous computing relevant to match analysis is data processing algorithms and increasing their intelligence. Emerging technologies that are relevant to match analysis are the various types of sensors for monitoring players and playing equipment, communication technologies and sport specific algorithms to analyse tactical aspects (Gréhaigne and Godbout, 2013; Lames and Siegle, 2011; Lemmink and Frencken, 2013; O'Donoghue, 2011).

Output devices

Early systems output information on printers and visual display units (computer screens). The main commercial general purpose match analysis systems (Dartfish, sportscode, Nacsports and Focus) can all provide split screen views where performances have been filmed from different positions. This could allow a wide angle view of play as well as a closer-up traditional view of play. Alternatively, we could have one view focusing on a single player's activity on and off the ball while the second view covers general play. Indeed some systems can provide more than two views within split screen output with the flexibility for users to see all views simultaneously during some parts of briefings and to view a specific view during other parts.

Another recent development is output of video onto iPod and other portable devices. In the 2009 Carling Cup Final, Manchester United beat Tottenham Hotspur 4–1 on penalties after the match ended 0–0 after extra time. Manchester United's goal keeping coach, Eric Steele, used an iPod to help the goalkeeper, Ben Foster, prepare for the penalty shootout (http://www.guardian.co.uk/sport/blog/2009/mar/02/manchester-united-carlingcup, accessed 2 July 2013). Ben Foster watched videos of his opponents taking penalty kicks in previous matches on the iPod during the short break between extra time and the penalty shoot-out. Wireless communication also allows live display of sections of Apple Macintosh screens on remote iPods and iPads. This allows output statistics to be viewed by coaches during matches. Match briefings and debriefings can be done using large screens or data projectors.

A further technological development that could be exploited by match analysis systems is 3D virtual environments (Liebermann et al., 2002) and 3D TV (Ponting, 2006). This is viewed using liquid crystal shutter glasses that are synchronized with stereoscopic images being displayed on the screen. The images to be viewed by the left and right eye are displayed alternately with the shutter glasses ensuring that each eye only sees the images intended. This gives the sensation of viewing images in three dimensions which may be beneficial for short but critical video passages to be considered during briefing sessions. Ponting's (2006) review of potential technologies for sports performance analysis also described virtual reality TV which could provide smell and feel sensations to viewers. This is not expected to be a commercial broadcast product before 2020 and so its use within match analysis is not feasible in the near future.

One of the first mentions of the possibility of virtual reality output in match analysis systems was when the Amisco system was presented at the World Congress of Science and Football III (Billi et al., 1995). The Amisco system is a player tracking system that records the locations of all players throughout the match. This information about the location of players on the playing surface allows the possibility of images of match play being shown from virtual camera angles of interest. These virtual viewing positions could be from an individual player's location or the referee's location. The basic location data stored does not give an indication of individual limb location or posture. Technology has been developed since to produce three-dimensional models of play from multiple camera data (Venatrack's Real View product, http://Vimeo.com/40826079, accessed 29 March 2013). The Venatrack Company has since been liquidated but the technology it developed is worth considering in a review of outputs from match analysis systems. The system used up to 30 cameras at a game which were connected to a computer at the match venue that produced the three-dimensional model from the different camera data. This was communicated back to the headquarters studio allowing critical incidents to be viewed from any virtual angle and distance.

Video and multimedia technology

The importance of video feedback was recognized before the existence of commercial video analysis systems. Athletics books show series of frames of video of technique (Arnold, 1985, 1986; Jones, 1985, 1987; Johnson, 1969; Payne, 1985). Prior to multimedia computers, video cassette recorder (VCR) machines played match videos but had the disadvantage that video tape rewinding and forward winding could disrupt match briefings. The Capture and Analysis of Behavioural Events in Real-time (CABER) system integrated match video with a database of timed events where the computer controlled the rewinding and forward winding of the video tape through an RS-232 interface lead (Patrick, 1985; Patrick and McKenna, 1986, 1987). Despite the improvements on using video without computer control, there was still a need for video tape rewinding and forward winding during match briefings. The development of affordable multimedia personal computers has solved this problem. Video can now be stored on random access computer disk allowing standard software such as Microsoft Media Player to interactively access video sequences. This ability for random access combined with the timed match databases used in systems like CABER has been used in multimedia video feedback systems that avoid the need for tape winding. The Match Analysis Video Integrated System (MAVIS) was an early prototype and used a match event database so that criteria for events of interest could be used to directly access video sequences of interest (O'Donoghue et al., 1995, 1996a, 1996b). The Norwegian Football Association, particularly their head coach Egil Olsen, was among the earliest pioneers of computerized match analysis in soccer (Olsen and Larsen, 1997). In the 1990s, they progressed through three stages of developing their match analysis support. Firstly, a computerized match and player analysis system was developed. The second stage was to use a database and provide interactive video feedback. The third stage of their development plan was to provide more detailed information within valid and reliable player profiles. Commercial systems available today use the basic architecture of a list of timed match events and an integrated video (tagged), but with much greater analysis functionality than the MAVIS prototype. Dartfish, for example, includes the stromotion™ feature which can be used in two ways. Firstly, it constructs a single image from multiple video frames showing athlete or object movement on a background constructed from the background images shown in individual frames. The second way in which it can be used is to leave 'ghost images' on video frames showing the path travelled by an athlete or object. Both of these uses of stromotion have potential benefit for the analysis of tactical movement in game sports.

There are video cameras that record video onto disk for later download onto computer disk. Live data entry and video tagging requires video frames to be captured by the computer during the match. Before digital video cameras were available, it was necessary to use analogue to digital converters for match videos to be recorded onto computer disk (Ponting and O'Donoghue, 2004). Digital video cameras can be connected directly to multimedia computers using firewire cables. More recently, Intel's Thunderbolt interface has been used to communicate high definition video footage between video cameras and computers running match analysis systems.

Future areas of development that may be relevant to match analysis are the use of video hotspots. A video hotspot is an area of a video frame that can be accessed by the user in order to obtain other data. For example, we might wish to click on a particular player within the frame to access structured information about the player from a database. This type of analysis of video frames is available and has been used in 'V-commerce' (www.videoclix.tv, accessed 17 September 2013). Marketing organizations can produce videos. Objects and people in the videos are tracked and associated with other information about those objects.

Data management and analysis

Early keynote addresses at academic conferences covered the early advances in data storage that were exploited by match analysis systems (Hughes and Franks, 1995). The experience of using early technology presented many challenges for match analysis. The CPA at Cardiff Metropolitan University has custody of some artefacts of the early days of match analysis research and practice. The Commodore Pet was restricted to external tape storage for data and programs alike. The BBC Microcomputer used an external hard disk but this was limited to 100kb. The limited storage capacity of the available hardware meant that system developers had to devise means of processing data in segments or in multiple steps, swapping data in and out of main memory. The advances in storage technology have been so rapid that the external hard disks used by many analysts today (2013) have comparable capacity to video servers used in university performance analysis laboratories 10 years ago (Ponting and O'Donoghue, 2004). These advances in storage have facilitated multimedia applications, particularly the development of general purpose video tagging systems.

The sports performance analysis community has been quick to develop applications to exploit technological advances. These applications are data analysis applications that require the developers to create suitable databases for the applications to be applied to. Player tracking data have been analysed extensively in the investigation of work rate (see Leser and Roemer, Chapter 5 'Motion tracking and analysis systems'). This type of data can also be analysed with respect to strategy and tactics (Gréhaigne and Godbout, 2013; Lames and Siegle, 2011; Lemmink and Frencken, 2013). Spatial aspects of team games that are established in coaching literature include depth and width (Daniel, 2003), concentration of players and delay (Worthington, 1980) and balance of defence (Olsen, 1981). Algorithms have been developed to process player tracking data to determine sectors of coverage (Gréhaigne et al., 1997), balance of the defence (O'Donoghue, 2011) and other spatial variables relating to tactics (Duarte et al., 2012; Robles et al., 2011). Spatial metrics have been explored in an attempt to identify measurable properties of collective behaviour in team games associated with success or different tactical styles. The smallest polygonal shape that can be formed including all outfield players on a team is one such example (Seabra and Dantas, 2006). Space defence occupancy (SDO) zones within these areas have been found to discriminate between teams of known different tactical styles. Lames et al. (2013) compared the space between soccer players whose team was in possession and their opponents. This was a single match case study but did find that players had significantly less space from their opponents in those possessions leading to a scoring opportunity than the possessions that didn't. Timmermann and Dellnitz (2013) trained self-organizing maps (SOMs) to identify clusters of similar basketball plays using player tracking data. Lopes et al. (2013) proposed the use of Voronoi diagrams to define areas of the playing surface that game players were closer to than any other player at any instant in time in the match. Fonseca et al. (2013) developed these further to produce separate sets of Voronoi diagrams for each team at any instant in the match. Analysis of overlapping Voronoi diagrams allows variables representing the spatial interaction between the two teams.

Frequency distribution data are of limited use in sports where dynamic behaviour of states and transitions to new states is relevant to tactical analysis. For example, in martial arts, there are situations where athletes have options which are associated with opportunities and risks (Brown, 2012). Temporal analysis algorithms have been developed applied to match data (Borrie et al., 2002). Specifically, T-patterns have been detected in soccer performance using the THÈME 5.0 software (Sarmento et al., 2013). T-patterns are repeated temporal patterns of events that occur in the same order and with similar time intervals between events within the T-pattern.

While artificial neural networks have been used to analyse technique (Lamb and Bartlett, 2013) within sports performance, their use in match analysis is at an early stage. Player tracking data recorded at frequent intervals (25Hz) provides a large volume of data that may be better analysed as a pattern than using statistical techniques. Perl et al. (2013) have reviewed the use of SOMs to the analysis of tactical patterns in soccer and basketball as well as action sequences in handball. Data mining is an area where multiple match data could be analysed to discover patterns of play that may be associated with success. However, there has been no automatic mining of tactical match data to date, with data mining algorithms testing pre-set hypotheses (O'Donoghue, 2006, 2007) rather than mining the data to discover potential hypotheses.

Other areas of analysing multiple match data include sports performance profiling (O'Donoghue, 2013). This is an area where multimedia technology has been proposed to provide a more synergetic profile composed of quantitative data, related video sequences and other relevant performance data (Butterworth et al., 2013). Prozone provide various packages for multiple match data analysis including trend analysis within or across seasons.

Software engineering issues in match analysis

Requirements analysis

Much match analysis activity is done using commercially available software packages with well understood sets of functions. Match analysis using these packages is a single computer application area that has matured in recent years. However, there is still a need to apply software engineering principles during the development of match analysis systems when using these packages. The 'software crisis' is a term used for delivery delays, high maintenance costs and other related problems of software projects (Sommerville, 1992: 3). Requirements analysis is a critically important phase because misunderstandings about system requirements between developers and users can lead to costly delays in system delivery. It is possible that a great deal of design and implementation work could be done before users and developers realize there has been a misunderstanding as to what was required. There are different types of requirements that need to be agreed between developers and system users. Functional requirements of match analysis systems include input data, output information, system functions, data stores and data flows between functions and data stores. The output information to be produced by match analysis systems takes a variety of forms including match statistics, video clips and diagrammatic presentation of information (Carling et al., 2005: 34–44). The usability of a system is influenced by its interface which needs to be laid out in the best way to support efficient data entry. As well as functional requirements, non-functional qualities need to be specified. These are qualities such as hardware dependability, power consumption of equipment and response time of system functions. Requirements should be elicited from stakeholders who represent multiple viewpoints of the system. These viewpoints include the coaching context, development issues, performance factors in the sport and high performance management. After some initial requirements are discussed, a prototype system can be developed and used as a vehicle to elicit further requirements. This iterative process of requirements elicitation and prototype development involves system developers and users. Pilot work helps assess the feasibility of system functions and the ability of operators to perform data entry tasks in real time. There are occasions where the final system is a compromise between what the users desire, technological constraints of match analysis packages and the limits to what developers can deliver within set deadlines.

Script programming

The statistical window of sportscode can be programmed to compute information using data in the timeline of recorded events. Developers of systems have the option to use a statistical window or not. The decision about whether to use a statistical window depends on how often the system is to be used and how easy or hard it is for users to calculate the required information without a statistical window. If the system is going to be used for a single tournament of three matches, it is not worth developing a statistical window just to calculate percentages that users could easily calculate using other means. For example, if a matrix provides the frequencies of different types of possession and the frequencies of those types of possession that resulted in scores, then the matrix can be copied and pasted into a spreadsheet which calculates the percentage of each possession type that resulted in a score. If, on the other hand, the system is to be used over several seasons with 30 to 40 matches being analysed per season, then the effort of programming a statistical window is justified.

Like any software system, developers should design a statistical window before commencing programming. They should consider the information that needs to be produced, the data from the timeline that is going to be used and the best way of laying the statistical window out. Even if the information produced by the statistical window is to be sent to an output window and the users will not look at the statistical window, it is still important that the analyst is able to check information produced by the statistical window.

A statistical window can be laid out in a similar way to an Excel spreadsheet. Strategies for accessing data sources and making repeated use of the same scripts will be familiar to analysts who use functions in Excel. Once a column is completed, the entire column including the scripts can be copied to other columns by holding down ALT-CMD and dragging the column to the new columns it is being copied to. This saves a lot of time during the development of statistical windows. A further software engineering issue is maintenance. If we wish to change some variables (rows in the statistical window), we need to paste the amended script into each cell in the relevant rows. In future, it may be possible that systems such as sportscode use an object oriented approach where a class can be defined and then multiple objects in a statistical window can be defined to be of that class. This means that any changes to the class, whether to local variables or to the scripts applied to the variables, need only to be made once within the class.

Interpreted code

The scripts within statistical windows are interpreted rather than compiled. This means that as scripts are run, each instruction in turn within the script has to be translated into machine executable form and then executed. The translation process takes time that makes the execution of scripts slower than if equivalent complied code was used. A compiled program would have been translated once into a machine executable form which would have been stored for repeated execution without need for further translation. There are advantages and disadvantages to using interpreted code over complied code. An advantage is that during system development, we do not have to compile the whole system every time a change is made. The main disadvantage of interpreted code, when developing the system, is that it does not support structured programming. The scripts need to be implemented as sequences of instructions rather than a hierarchy of statements. So we cannot use selection (IF) statements that invoke sequences of assignment statements within the 'THEN' and 'ELSE' parts. This means that we need to approach the development of data processing algorithms by avoiding the use of large sections of code requiring iteration or selection. The main disadvantage of interpreted code, when the system is being used, is that it can slow the system down. Very large statistical windows, such as the 21 player example the author developed for netball, can take several minutes to execute. Script interpretation in sportscode cannot be expected to be as efficient as the execution of spreadsheets in widely used and finely tuned packages such as Excel. This means that some developers only do the processing that needs to be done in statistical windows before copying and pasting the cell values into Excel for further processing, tabular and graphical output.

Object oriented approach

The algorithm to automatically update the tennis score, shown earlier in the chapter, followed a data oriented approach. In other words, the data structures holding the score before and after a tennis point are separated from the algorithm that updates the data. The algorithm involved four levels of nested IF statements, which is not possible in an interpreted script language. This means that we need to approach the development of the score line algorithm in a different way to the algorithm developed by O'Donoghue and Ingram (2001). Instead of having a single data structure containing the different variables that we need, we can use an object oriented approach with different cells of the statistical window containing different values within the score and the script needed to process these during the update.

When developing any statistical window, we need to consider a number of questions. What can be used in sportscode? How does sportscode work? What do we wish to do? Exactly what do we wish to do? How can we do this in sportscode? There are some global variables that can be stored in chosen cells of the statistical window. These include the number of sets required to win the match and whether a tie-break is used in the final set or not. There are also questions we need to ask about the specific algorithm being developed. Is it good enough to know that the score is deuce or advantage or do we need to know number of deuces played? Is the score to be displayed as a live output of the system during data entry? Do we wish to store the score at the start of each point as a label within the timeline instance for the point? Another possible consideration is that the user needs an over-ride to the automatic update facility in case of a penalty point, a point needing to be replayed because of a let or the video coverage being forwarded to later in the match. As Figure 7.2 shows, the system is made up of a code window, a statistical window, an output window and a timeline of events.

The basic system has a code window with two exclusively linked events. One event is called 'Serve' but the instance stored in the timeline actually represents the whole point that commences with the serve. The other event is called 'End Pt [Point]' but the instance stored in the timeline represents the full inter-point period that commences when the point ends. There are two value labels that can be entered by the user and 20 other labels that are entered automatically by the statistical window. The two activated data labels are: Player A win[s the point] and Player B win[s the point].

There are two value labels for Player A Serve and Player B Serve. These are activated by the statistical window but, in the event of a manual over-ride, the user could set the player serving the next point. Similarly there are 18 within game point score labels (0–0 through to deuce as well as advantage server and advantage receiver) that are activated automatically by the statistical window but can be entered by the user if we need to over-ride the algorithm. The statistical window has cells to store the score at the beginning of the current point and the score after the current point has been completed. There are six steps in the algorithm which are outlined as follows:

1   When the user presses the Serve button to start a new point, the statistical window copies the score at end of previous point into the score at the start of the current point. The Serve event deactivates any inter-point break event that

Code window

Output window

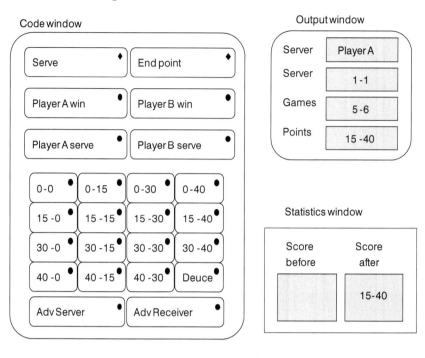

Figure 7.2 Architectural design of the tennis system to be implemented in sportscode (the black circles denote value labels while the black diamonds denote event buttons)

had been active before the current point commenced. The script pushes the correct server and game score labels so that they are included in the current Serve (point) event in the timeline.

2   The user indicates whether Player A or Player B won the point using the appropriate label.

3   Having entered the point winner, the user presses End Pt to complete the Serve (point) event. This starts off a series of tasks that the statistical window performs automatically in steps 4 and 5.

4   The statistical window determines the score at the end of the point using detail of the player who won the point and the score at the beginning of the point. The Serving player for the next point is also determined.

5   The statistical window sends the updated score to the output window.

6   Now we are back to Stage 1 waiting for the user to press the Serve (point) button to start the next point.

Figure 7.3 shows the order in which cells of the statistical window are evaluated. This is determined by cells containing scripts which refer to other cells. For example, to determine the new score in sets, we firstly need to have updated the game score. Similarly to determine the new score in games, we need to have determined the points score. The approach used here is like long addition in arithmetic. When a game (or set) is completed, the game score (or set score) is changed to 0–0 but it is necessary to carry one game (or set) to be added to the next level of the score. There is no need for iteration within the code because the score line update scripts are invoked every time the timeline changes. Note that the statistical window uses 0, 1, 2, 3, ... to represent points within games but these can be output as Love, 15, 30, 40, ... in the output window. A further feature of this statistical window is that Player A's score is shown to the left of Player B's score both before and after the point irrespective of who is serving. The statistical window is, however, programmed to send the score with respect to the serving player to the output window.

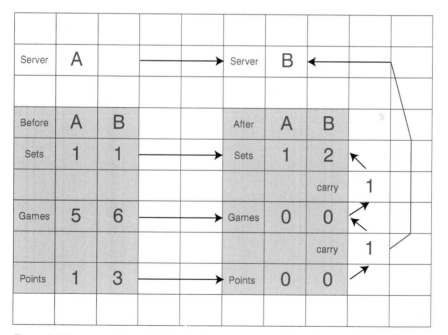

Figure 7.3 Layout of the statistical window to automatically update tennis score line (the arrows show temporal orders of cell evaluation)

System maintenance

Once a system has been developed and tested, it is put into operation. Users need to be trained in order to operate the system reliably. During the lifetime of a system, it may need to be upgraded for various reasons:

1   Changing coach information requirements.
2   Rule changes in the sport.
3   Taking advantage of more powerful software or hardware facilities.

To enhance software maintenance, good programming practice should be used with meaningful variables names, effective use of commenting within scripts and documentation of the system specification and design.

Conclusions

Match analysis is a relatively mature application of computing with successful commercial packages available for specific sports as well as general purpose systems that can be used with multiple sports. There is still a need to use the discipline of software engineering in developing such systems. Other areas of computer science that are relevant to match analysis are human–computer interaction, image processing, multimedia technology, artificial intelligence and distributed systems.

Study tasks

1   Outline the differences between match analysis and other purposes of sports performance analysis. Read 'Introduction'.
2   Discuss the components provided by general purpose match analysis packages and how they work together. Read 'General purpose match analysis systems'.
3   Discuss the advantages and disadvantages of developing a special purpose match analysis system for a game sport of your choice. Read 'Special purpose match analysis systems'.
4   Think of the important events to be recorded within a sport of your choice. Which of these are instantaneous events and which have a non-zero duration? What lead time and lag time (pre-roll and post-roll) would you use for each event type and why? Read 'General purpose match analysis systems'.
5   Consider the data to be entered into a match analysis system in a game sport of your choice. Consider the user's task during live data entry. Discuss the advantages and disadvantages of alternative peripheral devices that could be used to enter events. Read 'Human–computer interaction – ergonomics', subsection 'Input devices'.
6   Discuss an area of tactical performance in a team game that could be analysed using player tracking data. How can it potentially be operationalized? Read 'Human–computer interaction – ergonomics', subsection 'Input devices'.

7   Imagine you have a sportscode system which has recorded scores in rugby union. The main events are tries (worth 5 point each), conversions (worth 2 points each), penalties (worth 3 points each) and drop goals (worth 3 points each). There are value labels for teams 'A' and 'B'. The '+' and '*' symbols are used to represent the addition and multiply operators respectively. Write a script to determine the points score for Team 'A'. Read the section on Software engineering - script programming.'

8   Consider the event records to be stored in a match database in a sport of your choice. What type of analyses of these events could automatic data mining algorithms perform on such data? What type of sports performance information might such algorithms find? Read 'Data management and analysis'.

Recommended further reading

Baca, A., Dabnichki, P., Heller, M. and Kornfeind, P. (2009) 'Ubiquitous computing in sports: A review and analysis', *Journal of Sports Sciences*, 27: 133546.

Liebermann, D.G. and Franks, I.M. (2008) 'Video-feedback and information technologies', in M. Hughes and I.M. Franks (eds) *Essentials of Performance Analysis: an introduction* (pp.40–51), London: Routledge.

References

Arnold, M. (1985) *Hurdling*, London: British Amateur Athletics Board.

Arnold, M. (1986) *The Triple Jump*, London: British Amateur Athletics Board.

Baca, A. (2006) 'Innovative diagnostic methods in elite sport', in H. Dancs, M. Hughes and P.G. O'Donoghue (eds) *Performance Analysis of Sport 7* (pp.411–18). Cardiff, UK: UWIC CPA Press.

Baca, A., Dabnichki, P., Heller, M. and Kornfeind, P. (2009) 'Ubiquitous computing in sports: A review and analysis', *Journal of Sports Sciences*, 27: 1335–46.

Billi, E., Garbarino, J.M., Eposito, M. and Giogi, J.M. (1995) 'Towards the realisation of a computer system for analysing the tactics of collective sports', 3rd World Congress of Science and Football, Cardiff, UK, 9–13 April 1995.

Borrie, A., Jonsson, G.K. and Magnusson, M.S. (2002) 'Temporal pattern analysis and its applicability in sport', *Journal of Sports Sciences*, 20: 845–52.

Bradley, P., O'Donoghue, P.G., Wooster, B. and Tordoff, P. (2007) 'The reliability of ProZoneMatchViewer: A video-based technical performance analysis system', *International Journal of Performance Analysis in Sport*, 7(3): 117–29.

Brown, E. (2012) 'Design and review of a mobile analysis system for judo competition', presentation at the World Congress of Performance Analysis IX, Worcester, UK, 25–28 July 2012.

Buchanan, D., Cook, D. and Seeley, J. (2013) 'Use of barcode scanning for notational analysis', in D. Peters and P.G. O'Donoghue (eds) *Performance Analysis of Sport IX* (pp.251–7), London: Routledge.

Butterworth, A., O'Donoghue, P.G. and Cropley, B. (2013) 'Performance profiling in coaching: a review', *International Journal of Performance Analysis in Sport*, 13: 572–93.

Carling, C., Williams, A.M. and Reilly, T. (2005) *Handbook of Soccer Match Analysis: a systematic approach to improving performance*, London: Routledge.

Claudio, R. and Dimas, P. (1995) 'Pen based computing: breakthrough in match observation and analysis', 3rd World Congress of Science and Football, Cardiff, UK, 9–13 April 1995.

Cort, M. (2006) 'Voice activated data entry and performance analysis: Going back to the future', in H. Dancs, M. Hughes and P.G. O'Donoghue (eds) *Performance Analysis of Sport 7* (pp.87–8), Cardiff, UK: UWIC CPA Press.

Daniel, J. (2003) *The Complete Guide to Soccer Systems and Tactics*, Spring City, PA: Reedswain Publishing.

Duarte, R., Travassos, B., Araújo, D., Marques, P. and Taki, T. (2012) 'Identifying individual tactical profiles according to playing position in association football', *World Congress of Performance Analysis of Sport IX, Book of Abstracts* (p.26), Worcester, UK, 25–28 July 2012. http://www.sportsci.org/2012/WCPAS_IX_Abstracts.pdf (accessed 25 August 2014)

Dufour, W. (1991) 'Computer assisted scouting in soccer', in J. Clarys, T. Reilly and A. Stibbe (eds) *Science and Football II* (pp.160–6), London: E and FN Spon.

Fonseca, S., Milho, J., Travassos, B., Araújo, D. and Lopes, A. (2013) 'Measuring spatial interaction behavior in team sports using superimposed Voronoi diagrams', *International Journal of Performance Analysis in Sport*, 13(1): 179–89.

Gréhaigne, J.-F., Bouthier, D. and David, B. (1997) 'A method to analyse attacking moves in soccer', in T. Reilly, J. Bangsbo and M. Hughes (eds) *Science and Football III* (pp.258–64), London: E and FN Spon.

Gréhaigne, J.-F. and Godbout, P. (2013) 'Collective variables for analysing performance in team sports', in T. McGarry, P.G. O'Donoghue and J. Sampaio (eds) *Routledge Handbook of Sports Performance Analysis* (pp.101–14), London: Routledge.

Hughes, M. (1997) 'Computerized notation of sport', in M. Hughes (ed.) *Notational Analysis of Sport I and II* (pp.27–41), Cardiff, UK: UWIC CPA Press.

Hughes, M. (1998) 'The application of notational analysis to racket sports', in A. Lees, I. Maynard, M. Hughes and T. Reilly (eds) *Science and Racket Sports II* (pp.211–20), London: E and FN Spon, London.

Hughes, M. and Franks, I.M. (1995) 'History of Notational Analysis of Soccer', Keynote address, 3rd World Congress of Science and Football, Cardiff, UK, 9–13 April 1995.

Hughes, M. and Franks, I.M. (2004) 'Sports analysis', in M. Hughes and I.M. Franks (eds) *Notational Analysis of Sport: systems for better coaching and sports performance*, 2nd ed. (pp.107–17), London: Routledge.

Johnson, C. (1969) *Hammer Throwing*, London: British Amateur Athletics Board.

Jones, M. (1985) *Discuss Throwing*, London: British Amateur Athletics Board.

Jones, M. (1987) *Shot Putting*, London: British Amateur Athletics Board.

Kirkbride, A.N. (2013) 'Media applications of performance analysis', in T. McGarry, P.G. O'Donoghue and J. Sampaio (eds) *The Routledge Handbook of Sports Performance Analysis* (pp.187–209), London: Routledge.

Lamb, P. and Bartlett, R. (2013) 'Neural networks for analysing sports techniques', in T. McGarry, P.G. O'Donoghue and J. Sampaio (eds) *Routledge Handbook of Sports Performance Analysis* (pp.225–36), London: Routledge.

Lames, M. and Siegle, M. (2011) 'Positional Data in Game Sports – Validation and Practical Impact', Keynote address, 8th International Symposium of Computer Science in Sport, Shanghai, China, 21–24 September 2011.

Lames, M., Siegle, M. and O'Donoghue, P.G. (2013) 'An exploratory evaluation of measures of space creation and restriction in soccer', in D. Peters and P.G. O'Donoghue (eds) *Performance Analysis of Sport IX* (pp.275–81), London: Routledge.

Liebermann, D.G., Katz, L., Hughes, M.D., Bartlett, R. M., McClements, J. and Franks, I.M. (2002) 'Advances in the application of information technology to sport performance', *Journal of Sports Sciences,* 20(10): 755–69.

Lemmink, K. and Frencken, W. (2013) 'Tactical performance analysis in invasion games', in T. McGarry, P.G. O'Donoghue and J. Sampaio (eds) *Routledge Handbook of Sports Performance Analysis* (pp.89–100), London: Routledge.

Lopes, A., Fonseca, S., Leser, R., Baca, A. and Paulo, A. (2013) 'Using spatial metrics to characterize behaviour in small-sided games', in D. Peters and P.G. O'Donoghue (eds) *Performance Analysis of Sport IX* (pp.258–66), London: Routledge.

Nicholson, A. (1997) 'Commercialisation and the future success of sports notation', in M. Hughes (ed.) *Notational Analysis of Sport I and II* (pp.255–6), Cardiff, UK: UWIC CPA Press.

O'Donoghue, P.G. (1998) 'The CAPTAIN System', in M. Hughes and F. Tavares (eds) *Notational Analysis of Sport IV* (pp.213–9), Porto, Portugal: University of Porto.

O'Donoghue, P.G. (2006) 'Elite tennis strategy during tie-breaks', in H. Dancs, M. Hughes and P.G. O'Donoghue (eds) *Performance Analysis of Sport 7* (pp.654–60), Cardiff: CPA UWIC Press.

O'Donoghue, P.G. (2007) 'Data mining and knowledge discovery in performance analysis: an example of elite tennis strategy', Proceedings of the 6th International Symposium of Computer Science in Sport, Calgary, 3–6 June 2007.

O'Donoghue, P.G. (2011) 'Automatic recognition of balance and in soccer defences using player displacement data', Keynote address, 8th International Symposium of Computer Science in Sport, Shanghai, China, 21–24 September 2011.

O'Donoghue, P.G. (2013) 'Match analysis for coaches', in R.L. Jones and K. Kingston (eds) *An Introduction to Sports Coaching: connecting theory to practice,* 2nd ed. (pp.161–75), London: Routledge.

O'Donoghue, P.G. and Ingram, B. (2001) 'A notational analysis of elite tennis strategy', *Journal of Sports Sciences,* 19: 107–15.

O'Donoghue, P.G., Robinson, J. and Murphy, M.H. (1995) 'An object oriented intelligent notational analysis multimedia database system', in J. Murphy and B. Stone (eds) *Object Oriented Information Systems '95* (pp.169–72), London: Springer-Verlag.

O'Donoghue, P.G., Robinson J. and Murphy, M.H. (1996a) 'A database system to support immediate video feedback for coaching', Proceedings of the 14th IASTED International Conference of Applied Informatics, Innsbruck, Austria, 20–22 February 1995, pp.258–61. Anaheim, CA: Acta

O'Donoghue, P.G., Robinson, J. and Murphy, M.H. (1996b) 'MAVIS: A multimedia match analysis system to support immediate video feedback for coaching', in M. Hughes (ed.) *Notational Analysis of Sport III* (pp.276–85), Cardiff, UK: UWIC CPA Press.

Olsen, E. (1981) *Fotballtaktikk,* Oslo, Norway: Norwegian School of Sport Sciences.

Olsen, E. and Larsen, O. (1997) 'Use of math analysis by coaches', in T. Reilly, J. Bangsbo and M. Hughes (eds) *Science and Football III* (pp.209–20), London: E and FN Spon.

Payne, H. (1985) *Athletes in Action: the official International Amateur Athletic Federation book on track and field techniques,* London, UK: Pelham Books.

Patrick, J.D. (1985) 'The CABER project: The capture and analysis of behavioural events in real-time', *Proceedings of the 1985 ACM Conference,* pp.92–98. New York: ACM.

Patrick, J.D. and McKenna, M.J. (1986) 'A generalized system for sports analysis', *Australian Journal of Science and Medicine in Sport,* September: 19–23.

Patrick, J.D. and McKenna, M.J. (1987) 'The CABER computer system: a review of its application to Australian rules football', in J. Clarys, T. Reilly and A. Stibbe (eds) *Science and Football II* (pp.267–73), London: E and FN Spon.

Perl, J., Tilp, M., Baca, A. and Memmert, D. (2013) 'Neural networks for analysing sports games', in T. McGarry, P.G. O'Donoghue and J. Sampaio (eds) *Routledge Handbook of Sports Performance Analysis* (pp.237–47), London: Routledge.

Ponting, R. (2006) 'Technological advances and performance analysis', in H. Dancs, M. Hughes and P.G. O'Donoghue (eds) *Performance Analysis of Sport 7* (pp.227–38), Cardiff, UK: UWIC CPA Press.

Ponting, R. and O'Donoghue, P.G. (2004) 'A user group's evaluation of commercial performance analysis software', in P.G. O'Donoghue and M. Hughes (eds) *Performance Analysis of Sport VI* (pp.262–6), Cardiff: UWIC CPA Press.

Robles, F., Castellano, J., Perea, A., Martinez-Santos, R. and Casamichana, D. (2011) 'Spatial strategy used by the World Champion in South Africa'10', *World Congress of Science and Football VII, Book of Abstracts* (p.75), Nagoya, Japan. London: Routledge.

Sarmento, H., Barbosa, A., Anguera, M.T., Campaniço, J. and Leitão, J. (2013) 'Regular patterns of play in the counter-attack of the FC Barcelona and Manchester United football teams', in D. Peters and P.G. O'Donoghue (eds) *Performance Analysis of Sport IX* (pp.57–64), London: Routledge.

Seabra, F. and Dantas, L.E.P.B.T. (2006) 'Space definition for match analysis in soccer', in H. Dancs, M. Hughes and P.G. O'Donoghue (eds) *Performance Analysis of Sport 7* (pp.43–58), Cardiff, UK: UWIC CPA Press.

Sommerville, I. (1992) *Software Engineering*, Wokingham, UK: Addison-Wesley.

Taylor, S. and Hughes, M. (1988) 'Computerized notational analysis: A voice interactive system', *Journal of Sports Sciences*, 6: 255.

Timmermann, R. and Dellnitz, M. (2013) 'Analysis of team and player performance using recorded trajectory data', in D. Peters and P.G. O'Donoghue (eds) *Performance Analysis of Sport IX* (pp.282–8), London: Routledge.

Toledano, M.A.P., de las Mercedes Macias Garcia, M. and Ibanez, S.J. (2001) 'Software for the analysis and the quantitative and qualitative evaluation in sports of team', in M. Hughes and I.M. Franks (eds) *Performance Analysis, Sports Science and Computers* (pp.17–27), Cardiff: UWIC CPA Press.

Treadwell, P. (1987) 'Computer aided match analysis of selected ball games (soccer and rugby)', in T. Reilly, A. Lees, K. Davids and W. J. Murphy (eds) *Science and Football* (pp.282–7), London: E and FN Spon.

Williams, J.J. (2004) 'The development of a real-time data capture application for rugby union', in P.G. O'Donoghue, and M. Hughes (eds) *Performance Analysis of Sport VI* (pp. 253–61), Cardiff: UWIC CPA Press.

Worthington, E. (1980) *Teaching Soccer Skills*, London: Henry Kimpton Publishers Ltd.

8 Information and communication technology-enhanced learning and training

Josef Wiemeyer and Florian 'Floyd' Mueller

Introduction

Information and communication technology (ICT) has since its beginnings played a role in supporting the process of learning and training. In this chapter we focus on the learning and training of cognitive and motor competences in sport. We call it sports learning and training. We note that these ICTs have not always lived up to their associated high expectations. In particular, the appearance of new technologies often polarizes experts on learning and training. Some, such as enthusiastic early adopters, overestimate the opportunities of the new technology, while others deplore the end of traditional learning. Often, neither parties' visions materialize, but after a short period of hype (and a long period of follow-up research) the new technology takes its place in the arsenal of ICT tools for the enhancement of learning and training.

Every technology has its strengths and weaknesses. In consequence, the purpose of this chapter is to first discuss the requirements of the sport field to support and enhance learning and training. After this, we ask to what extent technology can offer additional value such as facilitating enhanced effectiveness, efficiency and motivational support, summarizing what has been achieved so far in the field.

Therefore, this chapter has three main parts:

- First, we discuss what is required by and expected from ICT-enhanced learning and training (ICT-ELT) in sport.
- Second, we articulate what has been achieved so far in terms of existing ICT-ELT.
- Finally, we look into the future by articulating our opinion about what upcoming research and development projects should aim for.

What is required by ICT-ELT in sport?

To answer this question, we begin by articulating what we mean by 'enhancement' (see for example Kirkwood and Price, 2014). The Oxford online dictionary defines enhancement as 'an increase or improvement in quality, value, or extent'. We focus on quality in our context of ICT-ELT and therefore name our objective to be 'improved quality'. 'Quality' for us means 'a distinctive attribute or characteristic possessed by someone or something' (Oxford online dictionary), which can pertain to different aspects of ICT-ELT, for example learning outcomes, training processes and learning and training conditions.

We propose that the requirements of ICT-ELT may be specified as follows: ICT-ELT should be at least as effective and efficient as 'traditional' learning and training processes, while offering additional value that justifies the technical effort often associated with deploying technology. However, to identify what makes ICT-ELT more effective and efficient or offers additional value, the mechanisms of learning and training have to be discussed as well as the complex interactions between learners or trainees, teachers or coaches, learning and training settings and the technology.

In consequence, we start by defining the concepts of learning and training as well as the concept of ICT. Based on this, we articulate the requirements, taking into account the complex interactions of learners or trainee, teachers or coaches, learning and training settings and the information and communication technology.

Learning and training

'Learning' denotes a more or less permanent change of behaviour and experience (such as knowledge and skills) achieved by means of exercise and practice. Learning can pertain both to the ability to retain knowledge and skills as well as transfer knowledge and skills to new situations.

Humans can learn in different ways and according to various mechanisms. Three key streams of learning theories can be identified:

- *Behaviourism* claims that learning is a process of establishing and modifying associations of stimuli (S) and responses (R). Important learning mechanisms modifying the S–R connections are temporal contiguity, repetitions and the application of positive or negative reinforcement. This approach can be termed 'stimulus-centred'.
- *Cognitivism* claims that the learning process is a more or less complex process of information processing: learners take up information, process information (e.g. selection, abstraction or integration) and present information (e.g. by verbal or sensory-motor behaviour). Important learning mechanisms are the establishment and maintenance of internal representations in memory. In this regard quality and quantity of learning information (e.g. multimodality and multicodality of instruction or feedback) as well as the information processing capabilities of the learners (e.g. working memory capacity, learning style) play important roles. This approach can be termed 'information-centred'.
- *Constructivism* claims that the individual learner is involved in an active process of constructing knowledge and skills. Important conditions for effective learning and training are authentic learning contexts and social interaction. This approach can be termed 'learner-centred'.

Numerous approaches have been proposed based on these three main streams (for a review see Wiemeyer, 2008). Furthermore, concerning ICT-ELT, the approaches of self-regulated learning (SRL) are important. Several SRL mechanisms have been proposed comprising cognitive and meta-cognitive strategies as well as the use of internal and external resources (e.g. Schmitz and Wiese, 2006). However, numerous prerequisites have to be fulfilled first to fully exploit the benefits of SRL (e.g. Bjork, Dunlosky and Kornell, 2013). Furthermore, other basic psychological models are also relevant, for example specific theories of motivation, emotion and volition, as well as general theories of human behaviour, beyond the approaches mentioned above directly concerned with learning and training.

Taken together, existing approaches to learning and training and to the regulation of human behaviour claim that learning happens on different levels, e.g. on cognitive, perceptual, emotional, motivational, volitional and behavioural levels. In practice, numerous processes located across these levels interact in dynamic ways.

'Training' denotes all interventions intended to systematically and sustainably enhance and stabilize sport performance or minimize regress of this performance. Learning and training in sport has many facets ranging from learning new motor skills to improving physical fitness. Whereas training can pertain to all factors of sport performance including coordination (i.e. sensory-motor skills and abilities), conditioning (i.e. strength, endurance, speed and flexibility), tactics, psychological and social factors, learning is more or less constrained to the psycho-motor factors and mechanisms.

ICT

The term 'information and communication technology' denotes all digital or electronic artefacts serving the purpose of information presentation, exchange and communication. Examples are: ubiquitous and mobile computing technologies, multimedia devices, augmented and virtual reality, and digital games

ICT-ELT in sport – framework and recommendations

When applying ICT to learning and training in sport, the complex interactions of ICT, learners or trainees, teachers or coaches and learning context have to be taken into consideration (see Figure 8.1).

Figure 8.1 shows that the application of ICT to learning and training in sport requires an appropriate fit of four components:

- *Learners and trainees*. The characteristics of learners and trainees, e.g. knowledge, skills, experience with ICT, attitudes and interests, motivation and volition as well as social interactions, influence how the learning context is arranged, which ICT can be applied and how the teacher acts.
- *Teachers and coaches*. The characteristics of teachers and coaches, e.g. roll, function, knowledge, media competence, didactic competence and attitude,

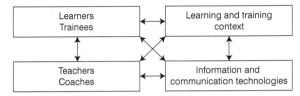

Figure 8.1 ICT-supported learning and training as a complex interaction of learners, teachers, learning context and ICT (source: adapted from Wiemeyer 2008, p. 299)

also influence how the learners are treated and which ICT can be successfully applied.

- *Learning and training context.* The learning and training context, e.g. learning and training (L&T) goals and objectives, type and complexity of content and L&T methods, is also an important factor determining the success of ICT-ELT. Different learning matter and learning goals require different teaching methods including use of ICT.
- *Information and communication technologies.* Finally and maybe most importantly (e.g. Parsazadeh et al., 2013), the ICT itself, including aspects of usability, interactivity, adaptability and adaptivity, quality of presentation and communication, can open and constrain options for learners and thus can be a key success factor of ICT-ELT.

Therefore, there is no easy answer to the question, 'what is required by the application of ICT in learning and training?' Rather an appropriate and specific fit of all factors has to be established and dynamically adjusted to enhance learning and training. Furthermore, there are many options for ICT-ELT: for example, ICT can replicate, complement or substitute teachers' actions as well as offer new modes of interaction with the learning and training content (e.g. Kirkwood and Price, 2014).

The following list of requirements has been compiled based on the relevant literature, particularly from reviews and meta-analyses (e.g. Clark and Mayer, 2008; Bernard et al., 2009; Zawacki-Richter, Baecker and Vogt, 2009; Cook, Levinson and Garside, 2010; Tamim et al., 2011; Parsazadeh et al., 2013) and our own experiences with ICT-ELT.

1 General principles: ICT-ELT should
   - Be easy to use.
   - Establish an appropriate fit of all relevant components of the L&T process, as outlined above.
   - Be systematically based on theoretical concepts and empirical evidence to establish effective, efficient and motivating learning and training processes.
   - Include appropriate formative and summative evaluations addressing the relevant procedural characteristics and the results (e.g. attitude, learning gains, motivation, emotions) as well as the numerous mediators and moderators of L&T (see also Wiemeyer, 2008; Zawacki-Richter, Baecker and Vogt, 2009; Wiemeyer and Hardy, 2013).

2 Presentation of information should
- Include multimodality and multicodality, i.e. information should be presented to multiple sensory modalities to support the formation and integration of multiple internal representations (codes) in a contiguous, coherent and non-redundant way.
- Elicit the appropriate cognitive load to enhance learning and training,[1] i.e. avoid underachievement by individually tailored quality and quantity of the presented information.

3 Instructions, as one of the most important prerequisites of learning and training, should
- Be comprehensive and clear.
- Deliver information concerning the task to be solved, the goals, the means necessary to solve the task and/or the solution to the task.
- Be delivered verbally, visually or audio-visually.
- Be fit to the teaching goals, learning matter and learners' characteristics concerning quality and quantity.

4 Interactivity, e.g. feedback,[2] interactive animations, simulations and games (e.g. Lee, 1999; Vogel et al., 2006; Bernard et al., 2009), should
- Enhance the personal involvement of the learners.
- Support both informational and motivational aspects of learning and training.
- Consider the fact that interactive engagement usually takes time and adds to the total learning time.

5 Adaptation and individualization should
- Be employed concerning knowledge, skill and ability level of the learners (e.g. IHEP, 1999). For example, complexity of the learning matter, arrangement of learning steps, navigation mode (control by learner versus system) etc. should be tailored to the learners' characteristics.
- Comprise more global offline modifications ('macro adaptation') as well as local online modifications ('micro adaptation'; see Kickmeier-Rust and Albert, 2012).

6 Personalization should be realized, for example, by the use of humanoid pedagogical agents (e.g. Clark and Mayer, 2008; Yilmaz and Kiliç-Çakmak 2012),

7 Collaboration and communication should be implemented as
- Learner–learner or learner–teacher interactions (e.g. Bernard et al., 2009).
- Many forms of synchronous or asynchronous communication for collaborative and cooperative learning as it is usually superior to individual learning (e.g. Susman, 1998; Means et al., 2009).

8 Navigation and guidance should
- Support easy and fast orientation within the learning and training environment.
- Interact with the learners' characteristics.

9   Mobility and ubiquity should be ensured by
   •   Ubiquitous availability – independent of space and time.
   •   The use of portable ICT devices, if possible (e.g. Wu et al., 2012).
10   The adequate use of self-regulatory activities should be supported.
11   Self-reflection should be supported.

What has been achieved by existing technologies? – technology, theory and evidence

Various ICTs have been developed for and applied to learning and training in sport and other fields. Due to extensive research and development activities in the field of ICT-ELT, 'more than 60 meta-analyses have appeared in the literature since 1980, each focusing on a specific question addressing different aspects such as subject matter, grade level and type of technology' (Tamim et al., 2011: 5). In these meta-analyses, effect sizes of ICT-ELT (versus conventional interventions) in all application fields range from 0.3 to 0.7, i.e. groups using learning and training with ICT perform about one half of a standard deviation better than groups with traditional (non-ICT) learning and training. However, effect sizes are heterogeneous in almost all studies indicating that moderating factors have to be considered.

The following list is not meant to be complete, but rather shows the big variety of ICT in the area of learning and training in sport:

•   video technologies
•   stationary and mobile measurement systems (including ubiquitous computing technologies)
•   animations and simulations
•   multimedia learning systems (MLS)
•   augmented reality (AR)
•   virtual reality (VR)
•   tools for communication and collaboration
•   tools for self-reflection
•   game technologies including their use in Serious Games.

In the following text, the different tools and technologies are discussed in more detail according to the demands discussed in the previous section.[3]

Video technologies

Video technologies offer many options for instruction and feedback. Sport movements can be easily recorded or rendered and presented in different ways, e.g. in slow motion, with repetitions etc. Video has various degrees of freedom, e.g. camera perspective, focus, zoom, level of abstraction etc. Therefore it is difficult to assess the general impact of video technologies on learning and training. Furthermore, application aspects like schedule or frequency of feedback and instruction play an important role. In this regard, the 'guidance hypothesis' (e.g. Marschall, Bund and Wiemeyer, 2007; Sigrist et al., 2013) claims that too much information may lead to an information dependency causing distraction from intrinsic information sources and unrealistic expectations of success. Overall, the application of video technologies in sport has been proven effective, particularly in perceptual or motor skill learning for novices and beginners. Furthermore, additional interventions like self-estimation, attentional cues, annotations by teachers, moderate level of abstraction etc. have been experimentally confirmed to enhance video training (e.g. Swinnen, 1988; Daugs et al., 1989; Pang, 2010).

In conclusion, concerning the above-mentioned, requirements for video technologies are:

- easy to use;
- based on sound theoretical and empirical evidence;
- offering flexible bimodal information for feedback and instruction;
- offering some basic options for interactivity and adaptability;
- indifferent concerning personalization;
- offering moderate options for collaboration and communication;
- easy to navigate;
- applicable to self-regulation and self-reflection (via self-confrontation).

Training with measurement systems

All over the world, numerous stationary or mobile sport devices equipped with various sensors to monitor the training process have emerged. Measurement systems have been developed, for example, for rowing, diving, track and field disciplines, swimming, alpine skiing and boxing. In modern systems, ubiquitous and wearable computing technologies are widely applied (e.g. Baca et al., 2009; Nusser and Senner, 2010). These systems are designed to provide precise biomechanical and physiological real-time feedback about movement characteristics and strain. This extrinsic feedback goes beyond mere visual video feedback and is able to convey information about movement characteristics. Feedback can be presented acoustically or visually or can be haptic (see Figure 8.2). Therefore, training with measurement systems offers powerful options to enrich the learners' processing of intrinsic feedback.

In many research and development projects, however, as Daugs (2000) complained, scientific foundation as well as empirical validation is limited. Generally, augmented feedback theories (e.g. Farfel, 1983) or generic theoretical frameworks (e.g. Schmidt, 1991) have been proposed to explain the enhancement of learning and training by measurement systems.

In conclusion, measurement systems for training are:

- often difficult to use;
- often lack theoretical and empirical substantiation and validation;
- offering restricted collaboration and communication;

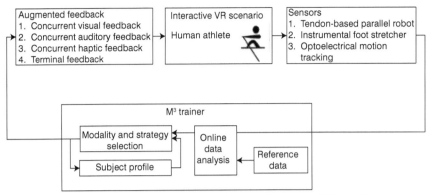

Figure 8.2 Example of a measurement system (source: Rauter et., 2011, p. 3)

- interactive, but non-adaptive and not personalized;
- delivering instruction and feedback in real-time or with short delays;
- establishing navigation and guidance by a specific GUI, normally operated by experts;
- normally employing multimodal displays.

Animations and simulations

Animations and simulations offer interesting options for interaction (e.g. Wiemeyer, 2000; Chang, Wu and Lin, 2012). The most important advantage of animations is the dynamic visual illustration of time-dependent processes. Taking the example of a complex gymnastic skill illustrated in Figure 8.3, compared to complicated serial verbal descriptions, animations can preserve the spatiotemporal relations of the movement components. Furthermore, animations can be controlled, for example they may be displayed picture by picture or in slow motion.

Another application area of animation is the illustration of computational simulations. To be effective, learning with simulations requires appropriate instructions (Lee, 1999) and should be focused on learners' control (Vogel et al., 2006).

In conclusion, interactive animations and simulations are:

- more or less easy to use – depending on the complexity of the represented system, the structure of the animation or simulation system and the quality of instructions;
- based on sound theory and empirical evidence[4] confirming their effectiveness;
- often supporting multimodal displays;
- an appropriate means for interactive instructions;
- usually neither adaptive nor personalized;
- not specifically supportive of collaboration or communication;[5]
- dependent on the quality of the GUI concerning navigation and guidance;

Figure 8.3 Screenshot of interactive three-dimensional animations

- mobile and ubiquitous by online and offline availability – depending on computational demands;
- not specifically addressing self-regulation and self-reflection.

Multimedia learning systems

MLS are complex aggregations of static and dynamic media. MLS show a variety of different types. In general, they can be divided into (system-controlled) learning programmes and (learner-controlled) learning environments (e.g. Wiemeyer, 2008). MLS can be offered offline and online, as 'pure' MLS or as a combination of physical presence and virtual learning ('blended' or 'hybrid learning'). Internet-based MLS usually offer additional functions for synchronous and asynchronous communication and collaboration, e.g. email, forum, chat and wiki functions.

MLS have been applied to cognitive and motor learning in sport. MLS for cognitive learning have been developed for university and school education. MLS often focus on learning the basics of sport practice, rules, physical education (PE) teaching and sport theory, such as motor control and learning and biomechanics.

Concerning cognitive learning in sport, evidence confirming the superiority of MLS is equivocal (e.g. Kibele, 2011; Roznawski and Wiemeyer, 2010; Papastergiou and Gerodimos, 2013). A general pattern in the results is that learners' attitudes can be improved, while any knowledge gain is consistent with traditional learning.

Applications of MLS to learning in sport are rare. The working group of Vernadakis has published several studies on multimedia learning in basketball (Vernadakis et al., 2008), volleyball (Vernadakis et al., 2006b) and long jump (Vernadakis et al., 2006a). A further study has been published by Leser, Baca and Uhlig (2011) for soccer. The common result of these studies is that MLS did not show any benefit compared to traditional learning.

Huang et al. (2011) presented an Internet platform for PE education including videos, two dimensional (2D) animations and three-dimensional (3D) virtual reality. Qualitative feedback by teachers and students was positive, but the system was used just as a complement.

Huynh and Bedford (2011) examined a specific visual badminton system for perceptual training. They could show that three groups (beginners, intermediate level, advanced level) improved their anticipation significantly over a 10-week training period. However, due to a missing no-treatment control group the results may have been caused by repeated testing.

Papastergiou et al. (2013) applied a web-based learning environment (WBLE) to the acquisition of a serial gymnastics routine consisting of eight motor skills (e.g. ball bouncing or ball swinging). The WBLE was used as an add-on to face-to-face instruction (blended learning). One blended-learning group was compared to a pure face-to-face group. The instruction phase lasted four weeks. Whereas knowledge improved significantly only in the WBLE group, skill performance and compliance to rhythm improved equally in both groups. WBLE usage time increased from 54.3 minutes (16 of 38 students) in the first week to 70.5 minutes (29 of 38 students) in the fourth week. Therefore, treatment control was poor.

Taken together, the existing studies rarely confirm the superiority of multimedia learning regarding learning and training cognitive, perceptual and motor skills. Learning with MLS is different, but not generally more effective or efficient than traditional learning. Furthermore, many studies suffer from methodological problems, such as treatment control, a missing control group or the confounding of technology and instructional conditions.

Concerning the specified requirements, MLS in sport are:

- more or less easy to use;
- based on sound theory, but only with limited (positive) evidence, often of low quality;
- often presenting information via multiple modalities;
- often delivering information in many different ways using static and dynamic media;
- supporting adaptation and personalization dependent on the particular system;
- offering numerous options for synchronous and asynchronous collaboration and communication;
- often engaging comprehensive navigation and guidance;
- mobile and ubiquitous dependent on the MLS technology;
- sometimes requiring self-regulation, however, this is rarely explicitly addressed;
- usually not explicitly supporting self-reflection.

Augmented reality

Augmented or mixed reality denotes ICT that superimposes computer-generated information on the perception of the 'real' world, for instance by a head-mounted display. In sport, only a few applications have been developed, for example for basketball (Kahrs et al., 2006; Figure 8.4) and karate (Tanaka et al., 2010).

Figure 8.4 shows the basketball system developed by Kahrs et al. (2006). A first test of the system with pupils yielded scoring rates of above 50 per cent.

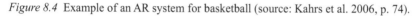

Figure 8.4 Example of an AR system for basketball (source: Kahrs et al. 2006, p. 74).

Tanaka et al. (2010) have developed a mixed-reality system for karate training, using reaction time as an outcome measure. The system records the position and posture of the trainee and uses this data to superimpose the trainee and a virtual opponent on the screen. A small-number, cross-sectional study with five experts and six novices revealed that the reaction times of the novices were significantly slower compared to the experts and that the novices strongly depended on the visualization of their own position.

Virtual reality

VR denotes ICT that was developed to establish complete immersion. Compared to the extensive use of AR systems in sensory-motor rehabilitation, VR systems are not as widespread in the field of sport, but the number of systems is continuously growing (for a recent review see Fluet and Deutsch, 2013). Possible reasons for this development are the further advances of powerful computers and the availability of inexpensive sensors (such as inertial sensors and 3D cameras).

VR systems have been developed for bobsled, hockey, speed-skating, golf (Katz et al., 2008), table tennis (Todorov et al., 1997; Brunnett, Rusdorf and Lorenz, 2006), rowing (Zitzewitz et al., 2008; Rauter et al., 2013 – see Figure 8.5), dance

Figure 8.5 Example of a VR system in rowing (source: Rauter et al., 2013, p. 3)

(Chan et al., 2011), Tai Chi (Chua et al., 2003), swimming (Fels et al., 2005), martial arts (Tanaka, 2009), handball, rugby (Bideau et al., 2010) and soccer (SMS Lab, ETH Zurich; Bandow, Witte and Masik, 2012). However, scientific validation is not often available.

The systems typically include a 3D projection system (computer-assisted virtual environment (CAVE) or screen), a head-mounted display and a camera and/or motion sensor system (see Figure 8.5). Sometimes actuators are also used to establish authentic (reaction) forces. Many systems are just prototypes that have not (yet) been subjected to experimental validation.

In conclusion, AR and VR are:

- often expensive and difficult to set up and use;
- often lacking theoretical foundation and empirical evidence;[6]
- multimodal, but bear the risk of sensory mismatch and simulator sickness;
- authentic concerning real-time interactions and feedback;
- often adaptive, but not personalized;
- mostly offering only limited options for collaboration and communication;
- restricted concerning navigation and guidance;
- offering extremely limited mobility and ubiquity;
- offering options for self-regulation and self-reflection.

Tools for communication and collaboration

Based on the idea of web 2.0 and user-generated content, modern web-based learning and training systems offer a great variety of options for communication and collaboration. Examples for synchronous communication are chat, video conferencing and audience response systems, whereas email, forum, blog and wiki enable asynchronous communication.

General findings

Overall, as has been mentioned above, enhanced student–student and student–teacher communication can have a positive impact on ICT-ELT (Bernard et al., 2009), but many issues are still to be addressed, for example the impact of the learners' characteristics, technology, problem presentation, scaffolding etc. (e.g. Resta and Laferrière, 2007).

Hrastinski (2008) discusses the benefits and disadvantages of synchronous versus asynchronous e-learning. In asynchronous e-learning learners tend to work more task-oriented, exchange more information and the quality of their ideas is higher. In synchronous e-learning, personal and social participation is more pronounced, leading to more enjoyable, but less deep interactions.

Forum discussion, blogs and wikis

Furthermore, particular communication tools have been separately analysed.

- Singhal and Kalra (2012) discuss the significance of forum discussions. They conclude that forum discussions are ambivalent. On the one hand, forum discussions foster the active contributions of the learners; on the other hand, the more learners engage in posting comments and commenting on comments the more cognitive load increases to maintain orientation, assess quality and retrieve information. Therefore, a (human or automatic) moderator is often needed.
- Sim and Hew (2010) review the use of blogs as 'space where discourse can occur between learners, between learners and instructors as well as between learners and the larger Internet community' (Sim and Hew, 2010: 151). Sim and Hew (2010) show that blogs can be used for several educational purposes, e.g. learning journal, knowledge log, personal diary, communication, assessment and task management. Evaluations, mainly based on self-reports, reveal that blogs can enhance learning by improved self-reflection, intellectual exchange, organization of knowledge, accessing additional information, quality and depth of thinking etc. However, quality of working with blogs depends on numerous factors and poses additional challenges like tutorial guidance, privacy issues, resources (time, technology) and quality assurance.
- Parker and Chao (2007) claim that applying wikis to academic education yields many options, e.g. lab book, collaborative writing, or knowledge base

and benefits are, for example, enhanced peer interaction, facilitated sharing and distribution of knowledge, higher levels of thought and reflection and improved retention. Of course, there are also numerous challenges, like quality management, balancing autonomy and guidance and establishing a 'community of practice' ensuring true and engaged collaboration of all learners (see also Pardue, Landry and Sweeney, 2013). Despite the widespread use of wikis, no review or meta-analysis is available.

Audience response systems

Electronic or audience response systems (ERS, ARS) denote systems that enable students to respond to questions, tasks etc. posed by the teacher during the lecture. Modern systems allow teachers to arrange comparatively simple tasks or questions, which can be individually answered by the audience using a remote interface (e.g. keypad, laptop or cell phone). The answers can be aggregated to descriptive statistics that can be displayed by a projector (see Figure 8.6). ARS have several advantages (Kay and LeSage, 2009; Boscardin and Penuel, 2012). They:

- enhance learner engagement by offering a safe, anonymous way to participate in classroom learning;
- provide instant, comprehensive and collective feedback to both learners and teachers. this way, teachers can check the understanding of the students and students can compare their knowledge with their peers;
- facilitate increased class attendance as well as enhanced peer and class discussions.

Figure 8.6 Audience response system used at Darmstadt (left side: question display on the screen; right side: keypad)

Estimation

Concerning the specified criteria, tools for communication and collaboration are:

- nowadays easy to use;
- based on sound theoretical frameworks, but heterogeneous experimental evidence,[7] at least for some systems;
- multimodal, depending on the particular tool;
- an appropriate means to enhance instruction and feedback;
- not adaptive and personalized;
- stimulating collaboration and communication;
- simple to navigate and provide guidance;
- mobile and ubiquitously available;
- not appropriate for self-regulation, but support self-reflection.

Tools for self-reflection

In the previous section, the use of blogs as a means for self-reflection was mentioned. In particular fields of education, electronic portfolios play an increasing role, e.g. in medical education (Buckley et al., 2009) and teacher education (Butler, 2006). A portfolio can be defined as a 'collection of evidence that is gathered together to show a person's learning journey over time and to demonstrate their abilities' (Butler, 2006: 2). In educational settings, two particular components are often included: documents that are the result of students' learning (e.g. short summaries, papers or presentations) and documents that include students' reflection on their own learning process (e.g. learning journal or diaries).

(E-)portfolios are used to 'increase students' self-awareness, to foster students' ability to learn independently and to encourage students to reflect on their own performance' (Buckley et al., 2009: 283). However, the existing studies are extremely heterogeneous and most studies just focus on students' attitude. The results of a meta-analysis published by Buckley et al. (2009) reveals that portfolios can have positive effects, particularly on the following aspects of learning:

- reflection/ self-awareness;
- achievement of course objectives;
- independent learning.

However, most of the dependent measures are self-reports. High-quality experimental studies are mostly missing so far. Combined with the critical review published by Bjork, Dunlosky and Kornell (2013), the conclusion may be drawn that self-reflection and self-regulation will only enhance learning when learners are able and willing to apply these techniques (for a list of 11 'success criteria' see Butler, 2006).

In summary, (E)-portfolios as tools for self-reflection are:

- easy to use (after an appropriate introduction);
- supported by sound theory and ample evidence;[8]
- optionally multimodal;
- instructive and interactive;
- adaptable and can be personalized;
- enabling of collaboration and communication;
- more or less simple to navigate, with low guidance;
- highly mobile and ubiquitously available;
- an appropriate means to support and enhance self-regulation and particularly self-reflection.

Game technologies including their use in Serious Games

Recently, there has been a rise in approaches that draw on play and, in particular, game thinking in order to facilitate learning outcomes (Djaouti, Alvarez, Jessel and Rampnoux, 2011). These approaches are often summarized under the term 'Serious Games'; these are games that aim to foster outcomes beyond entertainment (Djaouti et al., 2011). Games have previously been used to support learning; however, with advancements in ICT, new opportunities emerged that support the implementation of game elements that were either difficult to achieve previously or allow new game experiences. For example, ICT allows the easy measurement of achieved performance outcomes and the sharing of this data online, which can then be used to facilitate the emergence of a competition between players. A commercial example is the Apple Nike+ system (Apple, n.d.), a mobile phone app that measures joggers' speed and distance and supports them with training plans in order to provide advice on how to improve their performance. Moreover, the system also allows the opportunity to engage in online jogging competitions with other joggers who can be far away and run at different times.

Approaches such as these that take an existing activity and turn it into a competition have recently been dubbed 'Gamification' (Deterding et al., 2011) and subsequently criticized as being a too simplistic view on how to facilitate play, as play is much more than competition (Deterding, 2012).

We note that a game is not necessarily immediately 'fun', but rather it is important to know that playfulness can emerge from engaging with a game that is well designed (Salen and Zimmerman, 2004). As such, we can see research on Serious Games as approaches to understand what aspects of a game can facilitate attitudes in players that make learning activities more enjoyable. For a list of 22 approaches that aim to facilitate the emergence of playfulness, see the work on the 'PLEX card', design cards to remind designers of the many ways that playful approaches can be facilitated (Lucero and Arrasvuori, 2010).

Serious Games have an affinity with many of the previous ICT-ELT sections above as they also often deploy video, virtual and augmented reality, ubiquitous technologies, animation and simulation, multimedia and tools for communication and collaboration. As such, these learning facilitators can be seen as underlying enablers for Serious Games, where they can benefit from each other.

There are two aspects to Serious Games when it comes to learning and sports that we would like to highlight here. First, sport can be seen as a form of play, because the athletes voluntarily choose to overcome unnecessary obstacles (Suits, 2005). In particular, sport has structured rules and goals and as such can be seen as bodily games (Salen and Zimmerman, 2004; Kretchmar, 2005). Therefore, sports are already games and therefore Serious Games do not 'introduce' play into a non-play activity, but rather offer unique opportunities and challenges when it comes to sport. In particular, we propose that Serious Games have the opportunity to remind sports participants of the playful character of their activity, which in return could facilitate engagement, resulting in positive learning outcomes.

On the other hand, we see a challenge for designers when it comes to Serious Games and learning in sports: self-determination theory suggests that 'autonomy' is a key enabler for engaging in digital games (Rigby and Ryan, 2011). Autonomy means that the player has meaningful choices in the game and an ability to make these choices. In sports games, this can mean that players should have many choices of how to perform the required bodily actions within the game. However, when it comes to teaching in sports, it often requires very specific movements, sometimes repeated many times over in order to facilitate specific learning outcomes. Moreover, alternative movements are often discouraged, for example in rehabilitation exercises. We can see a conflict here between the need to facilitate specific movements to foster specific learning outcomes and the autonomy's ability to support engaging game experiences. This conflict could be a key challenge when designing Serious Games for learning in sports.

On the other hand, with the increased interest in Serious Games (Djaouti et al., 2011), guidelines have started to emerge that can aid designers when creating these games (Gee, 2003; Isbister, Flanagan and Hash, 2010). Unfortunately, these guidelines often focus on cognitive learning aspects and there is therefore little knowledge when it comes to designing Serious Games for learning in sports (for one exception see Wiemeyer and Hardy, 2013). Another exception is the guidelines for the design of 'exertion games', i.e. digital games where the outcome of the game is determined by physical effort (Mueller et al., 2011). Guidelines for these exertion games exist (Mueller et al., 2011); however, they often focus on facilitating engaging experiences rather than learning outcomes. For example, Dance Dance Revolution (Wikipedia, 2014) can be regarded as a dance training tool. Studies confirm that these games can be fun (Behrenshausen, 2007); however, research on how effective these games are in teaching specific movement skills is rare (Charbonneau, Miller and LaViola, 2011). If studies exist, they most often focus on energy expenditure, arguing that games can motivate people to engage in physical activities, which can result in welcomed personal energy investment (Berkovsky, Coombe, Freyne, Bhandari and Baghaei, 2010). Besides a focus on energy expenditure, the second most popular focus in terms of evaluating the use of commercial games seems to be balance training (e.g. Vernadakis et al., 2012).

However, we note that these exertion games might not need to be as efficient as traditional learning methods, but rather complement existing teaching approaches, drawing on their strength to engage people rather than facilitate specific learning outcomes.

Therefore, we note that applications of Serious Games towards the sport domain:

- draw on ICT in order to implement game elements that aim to facilitate playfulness in players;
- are aimed to facilitate increased engagement through these game elements;
- often focus on this enhanced engagement with the assumption that this will ultimately be beneficial to further learning outcomes;
- represent a young field with only limited theoretical and empirical evidence so far on efficacy and effectiveness;
- promise unique opportunities with emerging advances in technology to draw on and rejuvenate the play aspect in sport, engaging people with it further.

Concerning the above-mentioned criteria, we note that Serious Games are:

- usually easy to use;
- based on limited theory and empirical evidence, with some exceptions;
- multimodal;
- often employing implicit instructional methods;
- highly interactive and adaptive;
- partly personalized, collaborative and communicative, depending on the game and the game genre;
- easy to navigate;
- partly mobile and ubiquitously available;
- open to self-regulation and not supportive of self-reflection.

Table 8.1 provides an overview of the different ICT-ELT systems and components.

What has not been achieved yet? – visions, recommendations and future directions of research and development

Despite more than 40 years of ICT-ELT and substantial research and development activities, there is unfortunately still no comprehensive and well-structured picture available. Of course, this unsatisfying situation is due to the extraordinary number of factors influencing the complex interaction between learners or trainees, teachers or coaches and learning context as well as the large number of different ICT-ELT systems (see Figure 8.1). We note though that ICT is constantly further developing, while learning and training can hardly keep pace with this development.

For the future, we identify the following challenges:

Table 8.1 Overview of ICT for learning and training in sport (+ fully applies; o partly applies; – does not apply; +/– heterogeneous)

Aspect	Video	Measurement systems	Animations and simulations	MLS	AR & VR	Digital games	Communication and collaboration	Self-reflection
Ease of use	+	o	o	o	–	+	+	+
Theory/Evidence	+	–	+	o	o	o	+	+
Evaluation methods	+	–	+	o	o	+	+/–	o
Multimodality/-codality	o	o	o	+	+	+	+/–	+
Instruction	+	+	+	+	+	o	+	+
Interaction	o	+	+	+	+	+	+	+
Adaptation/Individualization	o	–	–	+/–	+	+	o	+
Personalization	o	–	–	o	–	o	o	+
Collaboration/Communication	o	–	o	+	+/–	o	+	+
Navigation/Guidance	+	o	o	+	o	+	+	o
Mobility/Ubiquity	+	o	+	+	–	o	+	+
Self-regulation	o	–	–	o	–	+	o	+
Self-reflection	+	–	–	–	–	–	o	+

- Scientific substantiation of ICT-ELT must be improved, particularly concerning high-quality experimental studies like randomized controlled trials (RCT). Eventually, quality standards for research and development of ICT-ELT systems should be developed. The evidence-based approach in medicine is an interesting model for classifying the quality of evidence concerning particular medical treatments (e.g. Schulz, Altman and Moher, 2010; for a critical discussion see Steen and Dager, 2013).
- Whereas studies examining single ICT-ELT systems do exist, there is a need for studies integrating multiple ICT-ELT systems to examine the best of the single systems. In this regard, we consider the integration of games and 'more serious' ICT-ELT as a promising direction for research and development, for example the coupling of digital games and tools for communication, cooperation and self-reflection.
- Furthermore, an important issue is to develop specific theories and models integrating the different levels of learning and teaching, such as cognitive, emotional, motivational, volitional, sensorimotor and social levels.
- Personalization and adaptation of the ICT-ELT systems often need to be improved, particularly in systems that are employed in self-regulated learning and training.
- Dynamic and unobtrusive methods for assessment and control of learning progresses, learning difficulties and current psychophysical state could be improved.
- More research should be dedicated to finding and examining appropriate settings for successful applications of ICT-ELT. For example, Life-Long Learning (L^3) can be performed in various contexts like home or vocational settings. In this regard, self-regulated ICT-ELT will likely gain influence in the future.

As an exciting vision, tailored, individually adaptive and adaptable ICT-ELT systems may emerge, combining effective and efficient informational and motivational techniques. These systems will boost learning and teaching by an optimal and context-sensitive combination of multimodal information presented in a comprehensive and motivating way, interactivity that is continuously adapted or adapting to the requirements of the particular context, facilitating an appropriate switch between individual and collaborative and cooperative learning and teaching as well as self-reflection, self-regulation and control by the system.

Conclusions

In conclusion, we have presented an overview of the field of ICT for sports learning and teaching, highlighting the opportunities and pitfalls that exist, illustrated through several examples from our own and other people's work in research and industry. Our work is aimed at being an initial attempt at summarizing current advancements in the field, highlighting what has been achieved so far and where we see prospects for future developments. Our major contribution is a table that categorizes the key approaches of ICT-enhanced learning and teaching in sports and describes the major achievements and shortcomings. We hope with our work we are able to guide researchers and practitioners who want to foray into the field by providing them with a structured approach to begin their investigations, as well as offer people with expertise on the topic with an initial understanding of how this field could be systematically described and understood. The existing results suggest that it is worthwhile continuing work on ICT-ELT in sport. However, ICT-ELT is not a panacea to all the unsolved issues of learning and teaching, but rather offers new opportunities that have to be meticulously examined. To sum it up, we believe there is no reason for extreme attitudes towards ICT-ELT in sport, neither one of extreme enthusiasm nor extreme pessimism. In contrast, a nuanced balanced attitude is the best way forward for the field. This is in line with our personal goal to gradually advance the field of ICT-ELT in sports. We believe this will ultimately lead to the best outcomes, as even a long way always requires a first step.

Study tasks

1   Develop *concrete criteria* for evaluating the quality of an ICT-ELT system. Ask: 'What makes a good ICT-ELT application?'
- ease of use
- theoretical basics
- evaluation
- instruction
- interaction
- adaptation/ individualization
- personalization
- collaboration/ communication
- navigation/ guidance
- mobility/ ubiquity
- self-regulation
- self-reflection
2   Apply the criteria for evaluating ICT-ELTs from Table 8.1 to an existing ICT system available to you, for example a Serious Game, an animation or a simulation, or an augmented or virtual reality system.
3   Read a paper presenting an ICT-ELT application or an ICT-ELT study and examine its quality. Consider the criteria specified in this chapter.

Recommended further reading

There are numerous publications giving an overview of ICT-ELT. Here are some examples.

Dabnichki, P. and Baca, A. (eds) (2008) *Computers in Sport*, Southampton: WIT Press. (In this book selected ICT-ELT systems are presented as well as experts in the field address multimedia learning.)

Ritterfeld, U., Cody, M. and Vorderer, P. (eds) (2009) *Serious Games. Mechanisms and effects*, New York: Routledge. (This book gives a comprehensive overview of Serious Games. Conceptual aspects are addressed as well as methods and examples.)

Steinmetz, R. and Nahrstedt, K. (2004) *Multimedia Applications*, Berlin, Heidelberg: Springer. (In this book an interdisciplinary approach to multimedia is proposed. The book provides a broad understanding of multimedia systems and applications.)

Furthermore, relevant papers have been published in the *Journal of Computer Science in Sport* as well as journals and conference proceedings of computer science, e.g. IEEE, AACE and ACM journals.

Notes

1   Note, that (1) cognitive load must not be reduced to a minimum, but rather to an optimum to provoke adequate cognitive effort (e.g. Rendell, 2010) and (2) sometimes overload is deliberately provoked to motivate learners to initiate learning activities to bridge the gap between low state of competences and high task demands.
2   Note, that the significance of extrinsic feedback for ICT-ELT is a matter of controversy (e.g. Cook, Levinson and Garside, 2010; Means et al., 2009).
3   Because the criteria of appropriate fit and cognitive load are difficult to estimate they have been omitted.
4   However, some evaluation studies show a big variety, ranging from qualitative to experimental.
5   It is important to note that animations and simulations can be used to collaborate and communicate, for example via the Internet.
6   Evaluation methods are often limited to a small sample or case studies.
7   Evaluation methods show a wide range, with self-reports dominating and only few experimental studies.
8   However, evaluation methods predominantly comprise self-reports.

References

Apple (n.d.) 'Nike + ipod'. Retrieved from <https://www.apple.com/ipod/nike/run.html> (accessed 11 June 2014).

Baca, A., Dabnichki, P., Heller, M. and Kornfeind, P. (2009) 'Ubiquitous computing in sports: A review and analysis', *Journal of Sports Sciences*, 27(12): 1335–1346.

Bandow, N., Witte, K. and Masik, S. (2012) 'Development and evaluation of a virtual test environment for performing reaction tasks', *International Journal of Computer Science in Sport*, 11: 4–15.

Behrenshausen, B.G. (2007) 'Toward a (kin) aesthetic of video gaming: the case of dance dance revolution', *Games and Culture*, 2(4): 335.

Berkovsky, S., Coombe, M., Freyne, J., Bhandari, D. and Baghaei, N. (2010) 'Physical activity motivating games: Virtual rewards for real activity', *Proceedings of the SIGCHI Conference on Human Factors in Computing Systems* (pp. 243–252), ACM, April 2010. New York: ACM

Bernard, R.M., Abrami, P.C., Borokhovski, E., Wade, C.A., Tamim, R.M., Surkes, M.A. and Bethel, E.C. (2009) 'A meta-analysis of three types of interaction treatments in distance education', *Review of Educational Research*, 79(3): 1243–1289.

Bideau, B., Kulpa, R., Vignais, N., Brault, S. and Multon, F. (2010) 'Using virtual reality to analyze sports performance', *IEEE Computer Graphics and Applications*, 30(2): 14–21.

Bjork, R.A., Dunlosky, J. and Kornell, N. (2013) 'Self-regulated learning: Beliefs, techniques and illusions', *Annual Review of Psychology*, 64: 417–444.

Boscardin, C. and Penuel, W. (2012) 'Exploring benefits of audience-response systems on learning: A review of the literature', *Academic Psychiatry*, 36(5): 401–407.

Brunnett, G., Rusdorf, S. and Lorenz, M. (2006) 'V-Pong: An immersive table tennis simulation', *IEEE Computer Graphics and Applications*, 26 (4): 10–13.

Buckley, S., Coleman, J., Davison, I., Khan, K.S., Zamora, J., Malick, S., Morley, D., Pollard, D., Ashcroft, T., Popovic, C. and Sayers, J. (2009) 'The educational effects of portfolios on undergraduate student learning: A Best Evidence Medical Education (BEME) systematic review. BEME Guide No. 11', *Medical Teacher*, 31(4): 282–298.

Butler, P. (2006) 'A review of the literature on portfolios and electronic portfolios'.Retrieved from <http://www.eportfoliopractice.qut.edu.au/> (accessed 9 April 2013).

Chan, J.C., Leung, H., Tang, J.K. and Komura, T. (2011) 'A virtual reality dance training system using motion capture technology', *IEEE Transactions on Learning Technologies*, 4(2): 187–195.

Chang, C.W., Wu, Y.P. and Lin, H.W. (2012) 'An animation assisted training system for the baseball cover, relay and cutoff play', *International Journal Computer Science Sport*, 11(2): 41–51.

Charbonneau, E., Miller, A. and LaViola Jr, J.J. (2011) 'Teach me to dance: Exploring player experience and performance in full body dance games', *Proceedings of the 8th International Conference on Advances in Computer Entertainment Technology*, ACM, Lisbon, Portugal, p. 43. New York: ACM.

Chua, P.T., Crivella, R., Daly, B., Hu, N., Schaaf, R., Ventura, D., Camill, T., Hodgins, J. and Pausch, R. (2003) 'Training for physical tasks in virtual environments: Tai Chi', *Virtual Reality Proceedings*, IEEE, ACM, 22–26 March 2003, pp. 87–94. New York: ACM.

Clark, R.C. and Mayer, R.E. (2008) *E-Learning and the Science of Instruction: Proven Guidelines for Consumers and Designers of Multimedia Learning*, San Francisco, CA: Pfeiffer.

Cook, D., Levinson, A. and Garside, S. (2010) 'Time and learning efficiency in Internet-based learning: A systematic review and meta-analysis', *Advances in Health Sciences Education*, 15(5): 755–770.

Daugs, R. (2000) *Evaluation sportmotorischen Messplatztrainings im Spitzensport [Evaluation of Training with Measurement Systems in Elite Sports]*, Köln: Strauß.

Daugs, R., Blischke, K., Olivier, N. and Marschall, F. (1989) *Beiträge zum visuomotor-ischen Informationsumsatz im Sport [Contributions to Visuo-motor Information Transformation in Sport]*, Schorndorf: Hofmann.

Deterding, S. (2012) 'Paideia as paidia: From game-based learning to a life well-played'. Retrieved from <http://gamification.de/2012/08/14/sebastian-deterding-paideia-as-paidia-from-game-based-learning-to-a-life-well-played/> (accessed 11 June 2014).

Deterding, S., Dixon, D., Nacke, L., O'Hara, K. and Sicart, M. (2011) 'Gamification: Using game-design elements in non-gaming contexts', *Proceedings of the 2011 Annual Conference Extended Abstracts on Human Factors in Computing Systems* (pp. 2425–2428), ACM, Vancouver, BC, Canada, 7–12 May 2011. New York: ACM.

Djaouti, D., Alvarez, J., Jessel, J.P. and Rampnoux, O. (2011) 'Origins of Serious Games', in M. Minhua, A. Oikonomou and L. C. Jain (eds) *Serious Games and Edutainment Applications* (pp. 25–43), London: Springer.

Farfel, W.S. (1983) *Bewegungssteuerung im Sport [Control of Movements in Sport]*, Berlin (Ost): Sportverlag.

Fels, S., Kinoshita, Y., Chen, T., Takama, Y., Yohanan, S., Gadd, A., Takahashi, S. and Funahashi, K. (2005) 'Swimming across the Pacific: A VR swimming interface', *IEEE Computer Graphics and Applications*, 25(1): 24–31.

Fluet, G.G. and Deutsch, J.E. (2013) 'Virtual reality for sensorimotor rehabilitation post-stroke: The promise and current state of the field', *Current Physical Medicine and Rehabilitation Reports*, 1(1): 9–20.

Gee, J.P. (2003) 'What video games have to teach us about learning and literacy', *Computers in Entertainment*, 1(1): 1–4.

Hrastinski, S. (2008) 'The potential of synchronous communication to enhance participation in online discussions: A case study of two e-learning courses', *Information & Management*, 45(7): 499–506.

Huang, C.H., Chin, S.L., Hsin, L.H., Hung, J.C. and Yu, Y.P. (2011) 'A web-based e-learning platform for physical education', *Journal of Networks*, 6(5): 721–727.

Huynh, M. and Bedford, A. (2011) 'An analysis of the skills acquisition trainer for badminton program: Exploring the effectiveness of visual based training in sport', *International Journal of Computer Science in Sport*, 10(2): 5–17.

IHEP (Institute for Higher Education Policy) (1999) 'What's the Difference'. Retrieved from <http://www.ihep.org/%5Cassets%5Cfiles%5C/publications/S-Z/WhatDifference.pdf> (accessed 11 June 2014).'

Isbister, K., Flanagan, M. and Hash, C. (2010) 'Designing games for learning: Insights from conversations with designers', *Proceedings of the 28th International Conference on Human Factors in Computing Systems* (pp. 2041–2044), Atlanta, Georgia, USA, 10–15 April 2010. New York: ACM.

Kahrs, L., Raczkowsky, J., Manner, J., Fischer, A. and Wörn, H. (2006) 'Supporting free throw situations of basketball players with augmented reality', *International Journal of Computer Science in Sport*, 5(2): 72–75.

Katz, L., Parker, J., Tyreman, H. and Levy, R. (2008) 'Virtual reality', in A. Baca and Dabnichi, P. (eds) *Computers in Sport* (pp. 3–41), Southampton: WIT.

Kay, R.H. and LeSage, A. (2009) 'Examining the benefits and challenges of using audience response systems: A review of the literature', *Computers & Education*, 53(3): 819–827.

Kibele, A. (2011) 'An elearning module for the biomechanical analysis of motor performance in sports–a learning tool for academic teaching', *International Journal of Computer Science in Sport*, 10(1): 68–73.

Kickmeier-Rust, M. and Albert, D. (2012) 'Educationally adaptive: Balancing Serious Games', *International Journal of Computer Science in Sport*, 11(1): 15–28.

Kirkwood, A. and Price, L. (2014) 'Technology-enhanced learning and teaching in higher education: What is 'enhanced' and how do we know? A critical literature review', *Learning, Media and Technology*, 39(1): 6–36.

Kretchmar, R. (2005) *Practical Philosophy of Sport and Physical Activity*, Champaign, IL: Human Kinetics.

Lee, J. (1999) 'Effectiveness of computer-based instructional simulation: A meta analysis', *International Journal of Instructional Media*, 26(1): 71–85.

Leser, R., Baca, A. and Uhlig, J. (2011) 'Effectiveness of multimedia-supported education in practical sports courses', *Journal of Sports Science and Medicine*, 10(1): 184–192.

Lucero, A. and Arrasvuori, J. (2010) 'PLEX cards: A source of inspiration when designing for playfulness', Proceedings of the 3rd International Conference on Fun and Games, ACM, Leuven Belgium, 15–17 September 2010, pp. 18–37. New York: ACM.

Marschall, F., Bund, A. and Wiemeyer, J. (2007) 'Does frequent augmented feedback really degrade learning? A meta-analysis', *Bewegung und Training*, 1: 74–85.

Means, B., Toyama, Y., Murphy, R., Bakia, M. and Jones, K. (2009) *Evaluation of Evidence-based Practices in Online Learning: A Meta-analysis and Review of Online Learning Studies*, Washington, DC: U.S. Dept. of Education.

Mueller, F., Edge, D., Vetere, F., Gibbs, M.R., Agamanolis, S., Bongers, B. and Sheridan, J.G. (2011) 'Designing sports: A framework for exertion games', CHI '11: *Proceedings of the Sigchi Conference on Human Factors in Computing Systems*, ACM, Vancouver, BC, Canada, 7–12 May 2011. New York: ACM.

Nusser, M. and Senner, V. (2010) 'High-tech-textiles in competition sports', *Procedia Engineering*, 2(2): 2845–2850.

Pang, Y. (2010) 'Improving hybrid learning of physical education by video review', *Advances in Web-based Learning–ICWL 2010* (pp. 230–239), Berlin and Heidelberg: Springer.

Papastergiou, M. and Gerodimos, V. (2013) 'Can learning of basketball be enhanced through a web-based multimedia course? An experimental study', *Education and Information Technologies*, 18: 459–478.

Papastergiou, M., Pollatou, E., Theofylaktou, I. and Karadimou, K. (2013) 'Examining the potential of web-based multimedia to support complex fine motor skill learning: An empirical study', *Education and Information Technologies*, March: 1–23.

Pardue, J., Landry, J. and Sweeney, R. (2013) 'Wiki mass authoring for experiential learning: A case study', *Information Systems Education Journal*, 11(6): 59–70

Parker, K. and Chao, J. (2007) 'Wiki as a teaching tool', *Interdisciplinary Journal of E-learning and Learning Objects*, 3(1): 57–72.

Parsazadeh, N., Zainuddin, N.M.M., Ali, R. and Hematian, A. (2013) 'A review on the success factors of e-learning', The Second International Conference on e-Technologies and Networks for Development (ICeND2013), The Society of Digital Information and Wireless Communication, Malaysia, pp. 42–49, Retrieved from http://sdiwc.net.

Rauter, G., Sigrist, R., Baur, K., Baumgartner, L., Riener, R. and Wolf, P. (2011) 'A virtual trainer concept for robot-assisted human motor learning in rowing', *BIO Web of Conferences*, 1: 1–4.

Rauter, G., Sigrist, R., Koch, C., Crivelli, F., van Raai, M., Riener, R. and Wolf, P. (2013) 'Transfer of complex skill learning from virtual to real rowing', *PloS One*, 8(12): e82145.

Rendell, M.A. (2010) 'Cognitive effort in contextual interference and implicit motor learning', Doctoral dissertation, Victoria University, Australia.

Resta, P. and Laferrière, T. (2007) 'Technology in support of collaborative learning', *Educational Psychology Review*, 19(1): 65–83.

Rigby, S. and Ryan, R. (2011) *Glued to Games: How Video Games Draw Us in and Hold Us Spellbound*, Santa Barbara, CA: ABC-Clio.

Roznawski, N. and Wiemeyer, J. (2010) 'Interactivity and e-learning–an experimental study', *International Journal of Computer Science in Sport*, 9(1): 61–75.

Salen, K. and Zimmerman, E. (2004) *Rules of Play: Game Design Fundamentals*, Boston, MA: The MIT Press.

Schmidt, R.A. (1991) *Motor Learning and Performance: From Principles to Practice*, Champaign, IL: Human Kinetics.

Schmitz, B. and Wiese, B.S. (2006) 'New perspectives for the evaluation of training sessions in self-regulated learning: Time-series analyses of diary data', *Contemporary Educational Psychology*, 31(1): 64–96.

Schulz, K.F., Altman, D.G. and Moher, D. (2010) 'CONSORT 2010 statement: Updated guidelines for reporting parallel group randomised trials', *BMC Medicine*, 8(1): 18.

Sigrist, R., Rauter, G., Riener, R. and Wolf, P. (2013) 'Augmented visual, auditory, haptic and multimodal feedback in motor learning: A review', *Psychonomic Bulletin & Review*, 20(1): 21–53.

Sim, J.W.S. and Hew, K.F. (2010) 'The use of weblogs in higher education settings: A review of empirical research', *Educational Research Review*, 5(2): 151–163.

Singhal, A. and Kalra, B.M. (2012) 'A literature review of online discussion forum in e-learning scenario', *International Journal of Advanced Research in Computer Engineering & Technology (IJARCET)*, 1(4): 704–708.

Steen, R.G. and Dager, S.R. (2013) 'Evaluating the evidence for evidence-based medicine: Are randomized clinical trials less flawed than other forms of peer-reviewed medical research?', *FASEB Journal: Official Publication of the Federation of American Societies for Experimental Biology*, 27(9): 3430–3436.

Suits, B. (2005) *The Grasshopper: Games, Life nd Utopia*, Peterborough, ON: Broadview Press.

Susman, E.B. (1998) 'Cooperative learning: A review of factors that increase the effectiveness of cooperative computer-based instruction', *Journal of Educational Computing Research*, 18(4): 303–322.

Swinnen, S. (1988) 'Post-performance activities and skill learning', in O.G. Meijer and K. Roth (eds) *Complex Movement Behaviour: 'The' Motor-action Controversy* (pp. 315–338), Amsterdam: Elsevier.

Tamim, R.M., Bernard, R.M., Borokhovski, E., Abrami, P.C. and Schmid, R.F. (2011) 'What forty years of research says about the impact of technology on learning a second-order meta-analysis and validation study', *Review of Educational Research*, 81(1): 4–28.

Tanaka, K. (2009) 'Virtual training system using feedback for sport skill learning', *International Journal of Computer Science in Sport*, 8(2): 1–7.

Tanaka, K., Hasegawa, M., Kataoka, T. and Katz, L. (2010) 'The effect of self-position and posture information on reaction time', *International Journal of Computer Science in Sport*, 9(3): 4–14.

Todorov, E., Shadmehr, R. and Bizzi, E. (1997) 'Augmented feedback presented in a virtual environment accelerates learning of a difficult motor task.', *Journal of Motor Behavior*, 29(2): 147–158.

Vernadakis, N., Avgerinos, A., Zetou, E., Giannousi, M. and Kioumourtzoglou, E. (2006a) 'Comparison of multimedia computer assisted instruction, traditional instruction and combined instruction on learning the skills of long jump', *International Journal of Computer Science in Sport*, 5(2): 17–32.

Vernadakis, N., Zetou, E., Avgerinos, A., Giannousi, M. and Kioumourtzoglou, E. (2006b) 'The effects of multimedia computer-assisted instruction on middle school students' volleyball performance', in E.F. Moritz and S. Haake (eds) *The Engineering of Sport 6, Volume 3: Developments for Innovation* (pp. 221–226), New York: Springer.

Vernadakis, N., Zetou, E., Tsitskari, E., Giannousi, M. and Kioumourtzoglou, E. (2008) 'Student attitude and learning outcomes of multimedia computer-assisted versus traditional instruction in basketball', *Education and Information Technology*, 13: 167–183.

Vernadakis, N., Gioftsidou, A., Antoniou, P., Ioannidis, D. and Giannousi, M. (2012) 'The impact of Nintendo Wii to physical education students' balance compared to the traditional approaches', *Computers & Education*, 59(2): 196–205.

Vogel, J.J., Vogel, D.S., Cannon-Bowers, J., Bowers, J.C., Muse, K. and Wright, M. (2006) 'Computer gaming and interactive simulations for learning: A meta-analysis', *Journal of Educational Computing Research*, 34 (3): 229–243.

Wiemeyer, J. (2000) 'Animation and simulation in sport science education – examples and evaluation', in A. Baca (ed.) *Computer Science in Sport* (pp. 308–314), Wien: öbv & hpt.

Wiemeyer, J. (2008) 'Multimedia – between illusion and realism', in A. Baca and P. Dabnichi (eds) *Computers in Sport* (pp. 291–318), Southampton: WIT.

Wiemeyer, J. and Hardy, S. (2013) 'Serious Games and motor learning – concepts, evidence, technology', in K. Bredl and W. Bösche (eds) *Serious Games and Virtual Worlds in Education, Professional Development and Healthcare* (pp. 197–220), Heshey, PA: IGI Global.

Wikipedia (2014) 'Dance Dance Revolution', Retrieved from <http://en.wikipedia.org/wiki/Dance_Dance_Revolution> (accessed 11 June 2014).

Wu, W.H., Jim Wu, Y.C., Chen, C.Y., Kao, H.Y., Lin, C.H. and Huang, S.H. (2012) 'Review of trends from mobile learning studies: A meta-analysis', *Computers & Education*, 59 (2): 817–827.

Yilmaz, R. and Kiliç-Çakmak, E. (2012) 'Educational interface agents as social models to influence learner achievement, attitude and retention of learning', *Computers & Education*, 59(2): 828–838.

Zawacki-Richter, O., Bäcker, E. M. and Vogt, S. (2009) 'Review of distance education research (2000 to 2008) - Analysis of research areas, methods, and authorship patterns', *International Review of Research in Open and Distance Learning*, 10(6): 21–50.

Zitzewitz, J. von, Wolf, P., Novaković, V., Wellner, M., Rauter, G., Brunschweiler, A. and Riener, R. (2008) 'A real-time rowing simulator with multi-modal feedback', *Sports Technology*, 1(6): 257–266.

Index